FROZEN WOMEN
flowing thoughts

UNMASKING WOMANHOOD--
A SYMPHONY OF MONOLOGUES

An Anthology

FROZEN WOMEN
flowing thoughts

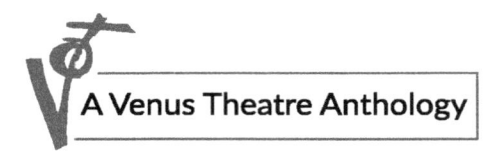

A Venus Theatre Anthology

PALMETTO
PUBLISHING
Charleston, SC
www.PalmettoPublishing.com

© 2024

NOTICE TO ALL READERS:
All the works in *Frozen Women/Flowing Thoughts* remain the copyright of the individual author. Purchase of this book does not grant any right to perform the work, permission should be sought from authors or their agents. The authors assert their moral right to have the work performed as written.

Hardcover ISBN: 979-8-8229-4814-3
Paperback ISBN: 979-8-8229-4815-0
eBook ISBN: 979-8-8229-4816-7

VENUS THEATRE PRESENTS:

FROZEN WOMEN
flowing thoughts

UNMASKING WOMANHOOD--
A SYMPHONY OF MONOLOGUES

An Anthology

CONTENTS

CHAPTER ONE: VENUS VETERANS   1

Doc Andersen-Bloomfield; *Where Mama Left Off*   2

Claudia Barnett; *Destiny (*A Monologue From *Feather)*   6

Maureen Chadwick; *The Commandant*   8

Cindy Cooper; *Swimmingly Yours*   18

Cecilia Copeland; *Ending Monologue From Light Of Night*   23

Migdalia Cruz; *Miriam's Flowers*   25

Fengar Gael; *Bat Scat Fever*   27

Carolyn Gage *The Last Reading Of Charlotte Cushman*   29

Paula Kamen; *Micki From Jane: Abortion And The Underground*   32

Jayme Kilburn; *Ding. Or, Bye Bye Dad | Hamiere (Speed Dating)*   36

Daria Miyeko Marinelli; *Coming Home*   43

Robin Rice; *Off the Edge without a Ruler*   45

Alana Valentine; *Suffocation Bay*   51

Kathleen Warnock; *How To Get Married In Five Steps And 17 Years*   63

Christ Wind; *Portia*   67

CHAPTER TWO: AGE OF THE MOTHER   71

Christine Benvenuto; *Remember Me, Mr. Smith?*   72

Allison Fradkin; *Holy Inappropriate*   77

Melinda Gros; *This Is My First Pandemic A Monologue From The Play Another Homecoming*   79

Fran Handman; *The Sticking Point*   82

Allston James; *Negative Is, Negative Does*   89

Moriah Joy; *Tearing Out My Hair: And Other Ways To Deal With Life*	92
M. Kamara; *Black Joy* By	96
JM Lahr; *Big Bold And Beautiful*	100
Helen Cheng Mao; *I Hate Depression Screenings From Waiting For The Gyn*	103
Karissa Murrell Meyers; *On The Greenbelt*	105
Elena Naskova; *The Love Of My Previous Life*	107
Dorian Palumbo; *She Got The Movie*	109
Jass Richards; *The Annual Staff Retreat*	112
Chloe Selavka; *Cat Lady*	115
Samara Siskind; *Carhenge*	119
Kanika Asavari Vaish; *Eight Ways To Plead With A God*	123
Chloë Whitehorn; *How To Not Die Horribly In A Fire*	128
CHAPTER THREE: AGE OF THE CRONE	**133**
Ben Beck; *The Loopin' Ladies Of Loredo*	134
Liz Coley; *The Good Wife*	138
Kristen Lowman; *It's Big And Red*	142
Sherry Macdonald; *Hot Milk*	148
Jennifer O'grady; *Nest*	154
Marj O'neill-Butler; *Don't Look At Me Like That*	160
Kathryn Rossetter; *Please Marry My Dad*	162
Joyce Newman Scott; *The Happy Place*	166
Germaine Shames; *If Only I Had Married Aiden Fuller*	168
Julia Weinberg; *Carla Keeps Talking*	172
CHAPTER FOUR: AGELESS AND ARCHETYPAL	**175**
Allie Costa; *Power Pose*	176
Vivienne Glance; *Modern Gods*	178

Judy Klass; *Salt*	193
Judith Pratt; *The Fat Lady Speaks*	197
Nora Louise Syran; *Madame Medusa Would Prefer A Chardonnay*	201
CHAPTER FIVE: BIOGRAPICAL	**207**
Renée Baillargeon; *Kim's Story, The Story Of Kim Sang Mai*	208
Molly Breen; *Mimi Alford*	212
Grace Cavalieri; *Anna Nicole Smith In Court*	217
Paddy Gillard-Bently; *It Was Isadora*	219
Dana Leslie Goldstein; *Anzia, A Fiction*	222
Paula Hendrickson; *The Dance: A Monologue Based On Real Events*	226
Judit Hollos; *The Stone Ship*	230
Melissa Milich; *I Ain't Tired Yet: A Play And Prayer About Sojourner Truth*	232
D. Lee Miller; *Ball And Chain*	238
Martha Patterson; *The Beauty Of The Dado. A Monologue For Edith Wharton*	240
Faye Sholiton; *The Family Zoom*	243
Nina Solomita; *Fania*	248
CHAPTER SIX: REPRODUCTIVE	**254**
Victoria Z. Daly; *Figure Out How To Live*	255
Alli Hartley-Kong; *Synchronized Swimming*	259
Caytha Jentis; *Sugar And Spice*	262
Rebecca Kane; *Orbit*	264
Stacey Lane; *Uterus-Less*	267
Ali Maclean; *The Girl Who Survived The Highway Hunter*	271
Aleks Merilo; *The Nearest Far Away Place*	276

Amy Judith Reuben; *A Trick Baby's Tale*	281
Bara Swain; *Regrettable*	285
Octavia Washington; *Babybreath*	290
CHAPTER SEVEN: SENSATIONS	**299**
Ella Baldwin; *Crinoidea*	300
Ana Sorina Corneanu; *Dopamine Deficiency*	306
Layli Rohani; *Things My Mother Told Me While Standing In Front Of A Mirror, Getting Dressed*	308
Madison Sedlor; *Excerpt From Shadows And Regrets - Jozi*	311
CHAPTER EIGHT: TRANSGENDER	**314**
William Robert Carey; *Danielle*	315
Carol Lee Campbell; *Let The Winds Of Mystery Take Us*	318
Joan Lipkin; *Dinner*	321
Fwft Bio's And Contact Info	324

CHAPTER ONE

VENUS VETERANS

An Anthology

Where Mama Left Off
by Doc Andersen-Bloomfield

Setting: An old tree house in rural countryside, Brownsville, Texas
Character: **TINDA MAE:** *30's-40's (in accordance with casting) Texan*
Time: present

A staircase or a high platform or a stool representing an ancient tree house. Tinda Mae is struggling get up it. She makes it.

TINDA MAE: (*panting*) Whoooeee! (*sitting down on the edge, dangling her feet*) Wadn' quite sure I could make it up here again. Lordy. Must be a good twenty years. (*gesturing*) My brother's tree house . . . (*sing songy*) *or-so-he thought*. Daddy tol' me once, 'Girls don' climb trees, much less have their own tree house. Them's for boys.' So, bein' who I am, stubborn an' all, I promptly claimed my brother's tree house for ma own. Climbed it proudly ever' day.

(*smiling*) Mama named me Tinda, Kickapoo for 'fire'. She's part . . . (*sighs*) or she was. Tol' me females need strong names, if thayze gonna make it in this life. Turns out, she was right. (*beat*) A-gain.

Brought a lotta books up here and enjoyed (*fingers making speech marks*) "family life (*double take*) from afar". Seemed ta work better that a way. Leastways, for our family.

Frozen Women Flowing Thoughts

Ain't much ta see from up here. Brownsville, Texas, was not known for a lot back then and it seems thayze kept up the proud tradition. Nuthin' but dry land, brown grass, scrub brush, and the good ole Rio Grand-ee River. An' a whooooole lotta brown folks (*gesturing in front of her*) tryin' ta get across (*beat*) trying to get to (*sighing*) freedom, a life without hunger or fear, I s'pose. Most of 'em didn't know how to swim back then, but that never stopped 'em. Hell, it ain't stoppin' 'em taday, even though it's a thousand times worse. No siree. Now, they take your babies off ya, put 'em on a plane to nowhere . . . plunk 'em in cages. (*softly*) Not even a name tag on some of 'em.

I hear thayze writin' numbers on their arms now. (*pause, softly to herself*) Numbers . . . on their arms.

(*staring out at the river*) Sometimes we found 'em drowned. Once, I was 'bout twelve, an' I seen this pregnant woman with a youngin' on a homemade raft of sorts? An' they was sinkin'. The woman saw me lookin' from up here and cried out in Spanish ta help her. I shinnied down my tree house as fast as I could, and went runnin' to Daddy ta tell 'im. He looked exasperated 'cos I'd stopped his work and he said, (*Daddy's stern voice*) "Tinda Mae, you're not to mind them wetbacks, ya hear? Look the other way. It's none a our business." An' then, he started his tractor back up. I watched him drive past the field of our artichoke crop and saw all them migrants a workin' there and wondered if they was lookin' the other way like Daddy.

That was the time I learned right quick, then and there, don't—tell--Daddy. Go--fin'--Mama.

'*Wetbacks*' was what most folks useta call'em then. They had a load a unkind names: 'greasers, beaners . . .pepper bellies" . . . all sortsa nasty names. Hell, my brother, who I hadn't seen in years, leastways 'til the funeral last week, he still has quite a vocabulary on 'im. He, too, subscribes to the Daddy philosophy of (*in brother's voice*) "you're not to mind—look the other way and it's none a our business". Translation, "Ain't it great to be better than them brown people?"

So, anyway, I run ta Mama in the house and tell her the wetbacks is sinkin' in the Rio and one of 'em's pregnant. Mama puts down the wash an' moves fast like, down the yard and over the field ta where ma tree house stands on the bank a the river. She looks, sees what's happenin', answers the woman in Spanish, takes off her shoes, *aaaaan' her skirt!!* An' she jumps inta the river. She's out there a ways when she looks back at me, she's dog paddlin' away.
(*calling*) "Tinda Mae?"
"Yeah, Mama?"
"You forgotten how ta swim?"
"No."
"Well then, get your sweet ass out here, girl."
"Yes, Ma'm".
We saved 'em that day. I took the child an' mama put her arm around the neck a that pregnant woman and began swimmin' slowly back to the bank. An' it wadn't easy. I'm here ta tell ya, that woman was heavy. So it took a bit a doin' ta get her up on the bank. Mama made sure she was alright an' the child an' then, finally, when she caught her breath, she looked di-rectly inta my eyes.

"Tinda Mae," she said quietly. "Don' ever let me hear ya call them wetbacks again. Thayze *humans*, ya hear?'
"Yes, Ma'm." An' after that, I had a whole new perspective on Mama.
(*staring out, sadly*) Oh, Mama, I am *surely* gonna miss you. You never looked the otha way. After that day, you was a giant in my head an' heart.
Ma brother's right pleased the thayze gonna build a big wall at the bottom of our property . . . (*sing songy*) *he th-inks!* Border patrol men, thayze ever'where now. Copters up in the air buzzin' all day and night. Can't fine no privacy on your own land no more, leastways, the pickers we hire. Never seen so much as a policeman 'roun' here, durin' ma growin' up years. If there was, he'd probably been down at the WhatABurger in town, where burgers an' shakes is free if you was the right color, and wore a badge.
(*smiling slightly*) Ma brother's furious with me right now. After Daddy died a few years back an' left the farm to Mama, she took over. It was like she was just *waitin'* to *be in charge*. She had new housin' built for the migrant pickers, with real plumbin' an' runnin' water.

She even raised their pay. Then, a whole lotta folks came lookin' to work here. Then she started turnin' a real good profit . . . she was right proud a herself. I was proud a her, too.

Las' week we had the readin' a her will. She left the *whole* damn farm . . . (*happily disbelieving*) *ta me!?!* Now, that was a surprise right there. An' I was fixin' to share it with that fool I call a brother, but then, (*beat*) I started listenin' to 'im. (*beat*) An' listenin', (*beat*) *an' listenin'* . . .

I've refused to allow the Border Police on my property now. I've even signed a petition . . . a couple of 'em. Goin' to a meetin' tomorra with the like-minded . . . not that there's that many 'roun' these parts.

(*proudly*) I'm *takin' over* where Mama left off.

(*thinking; softly*) You was a Goliath to my David, Mama, and I will carry on for ya. From now on, I'm lookin' di-rectly at what matters, 'cos **it-is-my-business**. **

   ** *Where Mama Left Off* is now in full length form (a four hander: 3f & 1m).

Destiny (a monologue from *Feather*)
by Claudia Barnett

Setting: The bedroom. When the play begins, a framed print of Monet's Water Lilies hangs above the bed. It is soon replaced by a growing series of original paintings. These paintings are primitive in style and bright in color, but they are interesting to look at and not badly done.

Character: NATALIE, 27-37.

(Synopsis of Feather: Stalked by a dream demon who looks exactly like her husband, Natalie follows the advice of her friend Paulette, "a self-taught expert in self-help," who tells her to paint the nightmare images. Natalie dedicates herself to the project, transforming herself into an artist, her bedroom into a gallery, and her demon into a muse.)

My twin sister was Destiny, but my parents were always so mysterious when they mentioned her, I never realized that was her name. I thought it was a euphemism for her condition, which was dead.
My first act in this lifetime was murder, my twin sister strangled by my umbilical cord.
My parents named her just in time for the funeral, two days after her death, our birth. They chose the name to comfort themselves, to relieve the burden of responsibility that had descended upon them. Her middle name was Faith.
Because I never knew her, I imagined her, and at first she was exactly like me: She looked like me, dressed like me, and she hated her hair—like me. I called her by my own name, Natalie.

Later, she was clumsy and ineffectual, scrawny, with stringy hair, and she wore the ugly old clothes from the back of my closet, the ones I couldn't stand. I blamed her for the things I broke and thought of her as Gnat, spelled with a *G*.

But finally she became a fairy tale princess: the prettiest and the best loved. And I was the ugly stepsister.

When my mother looked at me, she saw Destiny. She saw the void where my sister should have been, and she always looked so sad. I wondered if she blamed me, and I knew I was never enough.

I felt guilty for not loving my sister, so I would try to appease her. I'd never wear my prettiest dress because I considered it hers. I saved her the cupcake with the thickest frosting, on a china plate, till it got stale.

Then in high school, I stopped thinking about Destiny all the time. I stopped believing in fairy tales.

Until recently. Until around the time I got married.

Fairy tales are okay if you're the ugly duckling but not if you're the ugly stepsister. Then you don't turn into a swan. You just end up trying to squeeze your foot into a shoe that doesn't fit.

THE COMMANDANT
by Maureen Chadwick

A featureless backdrop with mood-adjustable lighting.

An old woman - MARY - sits bent over in an armchair, wearing a candlewick dressing gown and gumboots, an array of self-made medals on her chest, a military-style peaked cap with silver braid on her head, and a monocle on a cord around her neck.

She's in one of her cloudy, agitated moods - clenched fists drumming the arms of her chair - struggling to remember her purpose.

MARY: *(old-fashioned upper-class English accent)* Focus-on-the-task-in-hand…Focus-focus-hocus-pocus-buggering-bollocking – *(perks up)* Ah!

New girl's coming for interview today. One last chance to stay in the game…
But fear not, I shall rally. Always up for a new challenge. Even at the age of – what am I now…?
(calculates, smirks) Even at the age of one hundred and forty-six!
(checks herself) Shush! Don't tell.

(looking aside) And lo! Hither she comes! Escorted by my trusty companion, Alice.
Who, as I recall, needs a sharp reminder that I'm still the acting Commandant here…

Frozen Women Flowing Thoughts

She observes the two unseen characters enter.

(fixing her monocle to appraise the new girl) Hm... So you're Feliciana stroke "Call-me-Filly" from the agency, Alice tells me?

(aside) First impression not unfavourable. Unlike the last frizzy-haired goblin she tried to foist on me!

(to Filly, all charm) Hm? Less of a mouthful you say? Methinks it a perfectly delightful mouthful, my dear. And as a former equestrian I'm sure I've had many a fine filly in my time. 'Though I fear Alice has failed to tell you my staff normally call me 'Sir'...

(tips her cap with saluting hand, gratified) Correct! At ease. Meaning pull up a chair, m' dear.

No, not you, Alice. You can despatch yourself to the kitchen and prepare the tea and cake.
If you would be so kind?

Emits low growl at uncooperative response.

That was an order, Alice.
(aside) Huffety-huff, stompety-stomp. Just wants us to nab her, let her settle, then 'break her in gently'! But as an experienced interrogator, I'm not obliged to explain my methods...

(back to Filly, covering, all charm) Poor Alice. She's had a difficult time lately, trying to manage by herself. Hence very keen to employ you and readily impressed by your credentials.
But in the forces we do 'Trial by Scotch'. Any objections?
If so, overruled.
Respect for ceremony's an essential requirement in my line of service. As is deference to the chain of command. So – let us raise a toast anew – to 'Deeds, not words!'

Suspends arm, waiting for brain to catch up.

An Anthology

Ah! Medals! 'Course you may ask me about my medals. Or why else would I be wearing 'em? Hm?
(upward glance) Cautionary note to passing magpies, however - these are merely cheap dress copies. I keep the originals under lock and key...
(to Filly) Anyway - representing my proudest...

(selects silver medal attached to green, white and purple ribbon) WSPU Medal of Valour.
As bestowed on me by Mrs Pankhurst herself. For being the first militant Suffragette to be force-fed in Holloway Prison.

She's somewhat perplexed by Filly's response.

Meryl Streep? Don't remember her. There was a Muriel Struthers...?

(ploughing on) Anyway, agonising though it was to have thick rubber tubes shoved down one's nostril, vomiting and choking, fortunately for you that didn't diminish our resolve.
Quite the contrary. But then suddenly - boom! - had to abandon our own cause to help the bloody Government fight the Boche! Which I most certainly declined to do by joining the Needlework Guild.

Thence my next gong...

(selecting a silver cross with purple ribbon) Order of the British Empire. As invested by His Majesty King George the Fifth. In honour of my subsequent war work as Commandant and Co-Founder of the original Women's Police Force.

Makes modest bow in receipt of awed response.

Yup! From law-breaker to law-enforcer in less than a decade! And thus pretty much to-and-fro thereafter in defence of my sex and my country... Lost causes both, I've oft been told. Yet here I still am, battling on. Cigar in hand! *(mimes smoking)* So... What d'you make of all that, then?

(adjusts monocle) Hm... I was prepared for you to feel somewhat more incredulous as to my timeline. But I conclude Modern European History isn't one of your own accomplishments?

(aside) Can't decide if she's sly or stupid...

(to Filly) Well be that as it may - I'll come back to that - *(struggling to retrace her thread)* Consequently - as I was saying - still battling on - if you'll allow me to finish?
Thank you. Consequently - as I was saying - be whatever as it may da-di-da-di-da - things are as they blah-di-blah... Ah!

(Sharp swerve to 'Cockney' accent) An' I'll tell yer this fer nuffink, young lady, fings bloomin' well ain't wot they use' t' be fer an ol' soldier like me.
(picking up steam) All this bloomin' whatchamacallit compu'er malarkey? Ain't got a bloomin' clue, 'ave I? Can't even type me own bloomin' name, cos I never bloomin' well 'ad to, did I! But I'm buggered if I'm lettin' it be tarred, fevvered 'n' spat on...

(back on imperious track) Anyway, consequently - if I've got your attention?
Consequently, therefore - in order to preserve one's legacy and promote one's cause in this ignorant day and age - what one needs to recruit is a trusty aide-de-camp equipped with modern-day communications know-how. Proficiency in which - having studied your curriculum vitae in detail, unbeknownst to Alice - I note you include in your list of 'Supplementary Skills'. Hm?

Good. Now you understand <u>my</u> professional requirements extend beyond your assisting dear Alice to maintain the house and garden.

Acknowledges satisfactory response.

Excellent.

(calls out) Bring out the tea and cake, Alice!

(aside) Hm… Have to agree – thus far - poor kid does seem usefully needy and biddable…
And rather taken with me, I'd say…
A few more tests to pass yet. Plus the vital question as to stamina…

Brightens up.

And here we all sit in dreamy cake-land out in the garden…
Late Summer sun on the lawn, blue skies above, birdsong in the trees, bees-a-buzz in the flowerbeds. Blissful Filly having a 'heavenly moment', saying she just wants to close her eyes and never wake up! Alice on maximum alert to steer me to surrender…

(back to business) Talking of 'heavenly moments', Filly - I was suddenly transported back into the cockpit of my old de Havilland Moth - flying over the Black Country during the General Strike of '26…

Hm? Oh - did I fail to mention I trained as a pilot?
(indicating another bit of regalia) Hence my 'wings'.

Absolutely imperative the Women's Reserve form our own air arm. As I finally persuaded Mr Churchill, given the enemy peril we both foresaw looming nigh on the horizon…

(to Alice, sharp) Wouldn't have won the bloody war without women in uniform, would he?

Well if I can make my own point, bugger Churchill! What I'm trying to share with Filly - if I'm allowed to finish - is that heavenly moment I myself experienced –

(gazing upwards) And I can almost feel myself back there right now, Filly…
High up in the skies, joy stick in hand, flying over the hitherto aptly named 'Black Country'… when for once its great chimney stacks were struck idle - their foul black breath blown away on the four winds…

Frozen Women Flowing Thoughts

And - as I looked down - it was as if the edge of a curtain had been lifted on a strange and beautiful vision spread out below me...

A clean new England such as I'd never before seen nor imagined possible - where Jerusalem might indeed be builded and sheep safely graze...

Whereupon I too closed my eyes and wished that it could last forever...

But alas, the dark pall of industry swept down over it again - and the engines of war cranked back up - and consequently blah-di-blah...

Slumps, out of steam, confused as to where she now is.

Slurpety-slurp, scoffety-scoff, chattety-mindless-chattety-chat... Not a spark of resistance – not a notion - just eat their gruel, take their medicine, and meekly go into that dark night...
No, I don't need changing! - Patronising little skivvy! - Well just you wait – all of you - I shall rally - I'll show the whole bloody lot of you gutless ninnies!
And don't think I haven't still got my trusty old pistol...

Jolts back up.

You don't have to keep prodding me, Alice! I was just taking a 'power nap'. And of course I've been following the conversation – and delighted you reference rugby in your list of 'Hobbies and Interests', Filly. But have to say - for attack and style - and being the oldest surviving of 'em all - only club for me's the Barbarians. And as Alice may recall, it was my privilege to be in the VIP stand at Cardiff Arms Park when they first smashed the Wallabies back in '48. Officially in my capacity as Chief of Staff, Women's Section, of the British Union of Fascists...

(aside, with triumphant glint) Filly totally flummoxed. Alice glaring daggers. Then flounces off to drown herself in gin...

(back to Filly) Yup. Another forbidden word for you, Filly. The very worst of the 'F' words.
But at the time it seemed a natural progression for many of us former Suffragettes.
Only bloody party that took us seriously, whatever Alice may prefer to forget…

(jolts aside) What? No I do not want to play bloody Bingo! I'm trying to conduct an interview, if you don't mind!

And everybody stop saying 'No worries'! 'Course I've got worries! Same bloody worries anyone with a conscience would've had centuries ago! Young girls being sold into the sex trade - poor bloody animals tortured in the name of Science - men vilifying us for even challenging their God-given dominion…
And now - in this beyond Orwellian day and age? Far from atoning for the sins of their forefathers, the bearded youth of today apparently claim the right to colonise our entire sex and invade our lavatories! And who's to stop 'em if we just sit around eating cake, trying to be 'kind'?

Well good luck to you all if you think any of our hard-won rights are set in stone.
But I'm not being force-fed again by anyone!

Deep breath. Man-spreads legs and leans forward.

Okay… History lesson, children. Since the dawn of time men have done everything in their power to big themselves up by putting us down. And of course women of my vintage made mistakes trying to liberate ourselves! Damned if we did, damned if we didn't…
But I didn't join the Blackshirts to send anyone to the gas chambers! Just seized m' only chance to carry on recruiting and training women to defend the peace!
(upwards) Which by rights I should've been put in charge of by appointment to Scotland Yard!

Frozen Women Flowing Thoughts

(back to Filly) Anyway, point is - resolved though I remain to clear my name and preserve my legacy - you won't be any help 'less you're committed to staying the distance...

Good. Then let me put my final question to you as it was once put to me, whilst on official business in Berlin...

(extracting something from her pocket) I believe the modern term for this is a 'mind game' - but in my day it was called ein Gedankenexperiment...

Either way, point is to listen very carefully and consider it very seriously as a true test of character, hm?

So - I'm about to open this little silver box and offer you a miraculous pill - developed in secret by the world's most advanced medical scientists - which, if you choose to take it, will immediately suspend your biological ageing process both physically and mentally - and extend your potential lifespan by a good hundred years...

However... take it or not - you may still be run over by a bus or murdered in your bed - or likewise decide to throw yourself off a cliff or shoot yourself in the head...
In other words, all I'm offering you is an enhanced life-extension opportunity - with all your faculties intact - plus optional get-out clause if required - take it or leave it. Understood?

Good. And you're obliged to decide on your answer - yes or no - without asking any more questions. And on a count of three, starting from - One... Two... Three -

Are you sure?

A 'no-brainer', you say? You'd be surprised how many people would run a mile! But all these don't-wanna-knows and nay-sayers haven't got the guts to face the future. Just want to see themselves safely off into their own graves and leave the next generation to deal with their mess.

So, here – *(extends her hand)* Yours to take…

Then recoils - staring at her empty hand.

Fucking fuckers! Stolen my pill! Bloody enemy agents everywhere!

(draws herself up, defiantly) But I shall not be silenced…

Heaves herself to her feet, cursing.

Ach! Scheisse! Bloody leg…

Hauls herself painfully around the back of her chair – to reaffix her monocle and stand poised behind her podium.

(to audience) 'Deeds Not Words'… Our proud Suffragette motto… And Mrs Pankhurst's defining principle to separate us from the rest of the law-abiding Suffrage movement and face the most virulent forms of opposition: howling derision, physical assault, police violence, and brutal imprisonment…

Imagine, then, our profound disillusionment on finally winning the right to vote, only to find it was little more than an empty vessel… Not a single ex-suffragette - myself included - succeeded in her bid to be elected to parliament. And the prospect of achieving the full social and political emancipation of our sex remained a distant dream…

Then hope finally sprang anew - as a fresh generation of militant feminists rose up to carry our baton forth…
Drops monocle and raises 'Women's Lib' clenched fist.

Equal pay for equal work! Equal educational and job opportunities! Free contraception and abortion on demand! State-subsidised childcare! Freedom from male violence and sexual oppression!…
(lowers fist) Anyway, blah - you name it, it was bloody hard fought-for…

Lighting state begins to dim.

But now - if the clock is to be turned back to the Dark Ages - and the very concept of 'Womanhood' dismissed as heresy by crusading zealots...?
Well, in the whole history of our struggle, none of us would have seen that coming.
(voice breaking) And I could scream and shout till I drop - but who's listening...?

Faces up to her final admission.

Can't be a sainted Suffragette if you end up in thrall to Hitler and Mussolini! No matter how well-intentioned your motives - however sincere your beliefs - your righteous anger...
Anyway, blah. All m' own fault, Filly. Guilty as charged. Finito.
Just let me be a lesson to open the eyes of your own generation to their delusions…
Because fascism comes in many forms - but it always wields an iron fist...
(hauling herself back round to her seat, resigned) So best I leave you to look after Alice - whose constancy I have not deserved - but whom I trust, in her heart, to know that she is - always was - the true love of my life...

And I pray thee help her garden grow - and keep her safe from alcoholic temptation…
And grant me one final wish - to plant a good English apple tree on my grave...
A Worcester Pearmain. That would suit.
She raises two-fingered 'pistol' to head.
BANG!
Then droops - staring into her own abyss.

An Anthology

Swimmingly Yours
by Cindy Cooper

Setting: The locker room of a swimming pool. The year is 1969.
*Character: **GERTRUDE "TRUDY" EDERLE***
*Further Description: **GERTRUDE "TRUDY" EDERLE** (1905-2003) is the first woman to swim the English Channel, breaking the records of the five men before her. After her highly publicized Channel swim in 1926, Ederle seems to disappear from the public spotlight. We see her many years after the famous swim when much of her life has evolved in a different direction.*

>   GERTRUDE EDERLE *is the first woman to swim the English Channel in 1926. It is 1969 now.*
>   *Everything about her seems straight-forward, reflecting perhaps her parents' New York-German heritage. She is extremely hard-of-hearing and wearing an outfit that reflects swimming -- goggles, nose plugs, a robe.* SHE *carries a scrapbook, taken from a locker.*
>   SHE *looks up as if seeing someone. When* SHE *first starts speaking,* SHE *shouts.*

HEY! I REMEMBERED THE SCRAPBOOK FOR THE CHILDREN.

WHAT?

Frozen Women Flowing Thoughts

> As if someone has pointed to her ear, SHE quickly puts in a hearing aid.

I don't mean to blast you out. I take off this silly hearing aid before the swimming class with the deaf children.

> Finishes adjusting hearing aid.

I'm always afraid of scaring folks off when they find out I'm practically deaf. I told my fiancée back -- oh, 40 years ago -- back in 1929 -- I said, "Now that all this channel swimming's made me deaf, sweetheart, I bet you don't want to marry me." 'Course I was just joking. And he looked at me and moved his lips very slowly, so I could read what he was saying. "I do believe that's the case, Trudy," he said. And you know, I never saw the man again.

> SHE laughs at this.

Now, then. Here's the photographs. My Olympic medals. Letters.

> A letter falls out.

Oh, yes, I remember this one.

> SHE reads and half recites the letter.

"What a bully accomplishment to be the first woman to swim the English Channel!

And to beat the records of the five men before you by over two hours! Gertrude Ederle, believe me, I write with my best wishes for your speedy recovery and hope you will not have any regrets."

Ach! Regrets? Can you imagine?

> SHE laughs.

Do I have regrets?

TRUDY pulls off her hearing aid, puts on a red swimming cap as she steps into a completely different world.

I wore a red bathing cap. And a black swimsuit, with a silk flag of the United States right on it. It's the same suit I wore at the Olympics in 1924.

It is the day of the Channel swim. EDERLE talks to William Burgess – unseen -- who is her trainer.

"Before I start off, I want to thank you for serving as my trainer on the Channel swim, Mr. Burgess. Having somebody who's made the swim gives me courage."

SHE starts rubbing on jellies.

"Olive oil, first. Lanolin second. Then, the special blend of petrolatum and lard."

"But I got something to say, Mr. Burgess. You know, I tried last year and the people in the boat pulled me out before I got across."

"Yes, sir, I know it's bad weather conditions and there's powerful currents ... and jellyfish ... and that the water temperature is only 57 degrees."

"I <u>know</u> it took you nineteen tries before you made it yourself. But Mr. Burgess ... my father's a fruit merchant. I couldn't afford coming over on the steamer, or training, or paying for the escort boat. I had to take on a commercial sponsor. You know, that means I won't be able to go to the Olympics again. That's a lot to give up, Mr. Burgess. That's how much I want to swim the Channel."

"I know the people in the boat think they're looking out for the swimmer. But, Mr. Burgess, you're not a member of the Women's Swimming Association we have in New York City. You saw the Victrola they installed in the boat? With my favorites – '*Yes, We Have No*

Frozen Women Flowing Thoughts

Bananas' -- and *'Let Me Call You Sweetheart?'* They want me to make it!"

"There. I think I'm all greased up."

Starts shaking out limbs, making final adjustments.

"The point is, Mr. Burgess, you're going to be in the boat with the reporters and photographers and I want you to know I am not coming out until I walk on the beach in England. Don't try to pull me out. The Women's Swimming Association is counting on me."

Once you're in the ocean everything else disappears. All of a sudden, there's nothing but what's inside yourself. The water washes over you. The waves crash from the right and the left and from the front and the back. Some of them are eighteen feet high, seem like they're going to swallow you. And all you can hear is the roar of the water, in every direction, until it feels like it's in you and not that you're in it. You know then that you're all alone with the ocean ... just you and it.

Three miles to go. I hear a call over the rush of the water from the boat. Mr. Burgess.

"You've got to give up."

I can hardly believe what he is saying. I let his words roll off me like the waves and I throw myself into the water for more of it.

At 9:40 p.m., on August 6, 1926, I walk out of the ocean in Kingsdown, England with the English Channel swim record.

SHE laughs.

They were so sure I wouldn't make it that they had already printed an editorial. "In contests on physical skill, speed, and endurance, women must forever remain the weaker sex." Ach!

> EDERLE laughs, shakes her head, steps back out, puts on her hearing aid. SHE picks up the scrapbook again.

Oh, there were hard times afterwards. The nervous breakdown. The slip ... my back was in a cast for four and a half years. And I suppose it's true, Gertrude Ederle is not exactly a household name.

> Looks at letter.

But do I regret it?

Have you ever heard that song ... *Let Me Call You Sweetheart*?

> SHE hums and sings a bit of it.

You see, I came back home, and I was the sweetheart of all of New York City. They had the biggest ticker tape parade ever for me ... Gertrude Ederle, the daughter of a common German immigrant. Two million people fill the streets, flooding it until it looks like the ocean, and cheering for me until it sounds like the roar of the waves. They throw confetti from the buildings, and I ride down the street in a brand new car and hold my arms out to them. Oh, I suppose it's true, they have forgotten me now ... all those people. But, you see ... I shall never forget them.

Ach. I have to go and start the lessons. You see, once I teach the deaf children how to swim like champions in the ocean ... they shall not forget me.

> SHE folds the letter in half, snaps the book shut, takes off her hearing aid, humming and singing slightly.

'*Let Me Call You Sweetheart* ...'

Ending Monologue from Light of Night
by Cecilia Copeland

Setting: A basement in the suburbs

Stephanie:
Blue-Grey, Plumb, and Silver
A reflection in sync with the sky
Undulating and rolling
In a landscape of motion
I am on top of it
Climbing each living mountain higher than the last
And then I am beneath the surface
Going deeper and deeper
Reaching through the dark eternity
For a firm place to stop
My hands grope
My legs kick
My lungs burn
My eyes are blind
But I am alive…

(From the darkness.)
A veces no tengo palabras,

Sometimes I don't have the words,

                                                           (From the darkness.)

pero si espero en silencio,

but if I wait in the silence,

                                                           (From the darkness)

Buscando en la oscuridad un hilo de araña...

groping in the darkness for the thread of a spider...

                                                         (From the darkness.)

ellos regresan a mí.

they come back to me.

MIRIAM'S FLOWERS
by Migdalia Cruz

Setting: At a church altar with a white plaster "Pieta" in the South Bronx, 1975.
Character: MIRIAM NIEVES— A Puerto Rican girl of 16.

Further Description: **Miriam's Flowers**, *written in 1990, is about Miriam, whose little brother, Puli, was run over by a train while chasing a baseball. She then begins to mutilate herself and give herself to any man who would have her. Their mother Delfina, also, sinks deeper and deeper into despair. This play solidified my preoccupation with mourning the dead.*
In this scene, Miriam goes to the church to talk to the Virgin Mary about the cuts on her arms.

SCENE 20

MIRIAM talking to the statue of the Virgin holding the crucified Christ in a church.

MIRIAM

I'm the invisible girl, Mary... always searching for a hole in the wall to pull myself through to get to the other side. The other side is only for me, I could see myself then. I could feel my fingertips then and the pointy pieces of skin being torn down the sides of my fingers. I could see the scars then, on the bottom of my thumbs from the Wilkinson Swords — I write on myself with them. I carve myself into my hands. And for Lent, Mary, I'll cover them with purple cloth. I keep my gloves on in the church, until everybody leaves and then I come to you. To show you.

(SHE takes off her gloves.)
See? I show you mine and then I can touch yours...

(SHE places her hands on the carved wounds of Jesus.)
They feel so fresh Jesus. Like mine. I can smell the blood on them. Smells like violets and sweet coffee with five sugars — Like Ma takes it...

(Pause)
I'm never gonna die— not from my wounds anyway. I never go in deep and I don't make them long. I make little points that add up to a picture, a flower picture.
And sometimes they so pretty they make me cry, and I like that, because when I get those tears on my hands and on my arms, they sting, and then I know I'm alive cause it hurts so bad. Does that happen to you too?

Bat Scat Fever
by Fengar Gael

(a monologue for a shy, unkempt, uncombed, young woman with horn-rimmed glasses)

I know who you are: you're the people mother hired to be my companions. If you do decide to stay, she'll insist you call me Theodora and not Thea or Teddy, and I'm sure she warned you that I suffer from asthma and consider myself vulnerable, so my Covid standards are extreme which is why I'm using Zoom to keep you at a safe social distance. I've imprisoned myself here and see no one but mother and the backs of delivery men. I'm so anxious that after mother's gone shopping, I treat her like a leper since who knows how many customers were breathing on the bagels? I hoard boxes of sanitary wipes, sterilize every surface, and wear plastic gloves over my disinfected hands. Mother says I see everyone as a silent shedder and spreader which is true, so please try not be offended if ask impertinent questions about your social life and continue to keep my social distance through Zoom. You should also know that another reason mother wants me to have companions is that I suffer from insomnia exacerbated by our security alarm, but with you living here we can deactivate the system. Anyway, she thinks I'll be a test of your capacity for tolerance, so I'll hope you'll make an effort to get along even though I already have a companion, my secret pet, Coracorona, though I just call her Cora.
    (Theodora pulls a little bat from her pocket.)

She's the little bat I found sleeping in an apartment on the top floor. I don't know what possessed me. I mean, I'm terrified of bat-born plagues and yet I picked her up with my bare hands and dropped her in a birdcage left by a tenant. Bats aren't ideal pets since they have sharp teeth and minds of their own, but Cora seems to like it here -- probably because I feed her and let her loose at night, but since she keeps coming back, I assume she's happy. Look at her: imagine being the only flying mammal with limbs connected by membranes that wrap like a blanket to keep you warm. There's no need to be afraid. In fact, if you were here, I'd let you pet her, though she sometimes bites. In fact, when I first picked her up, she bit my hand. I was terrified, expecting to die of Covid or rabies, so I took a cab to the nearest emergency room. The doctor was afraid that Cora had injected her saliva into me which means I might have contracted rabies, so he gave me some shots, and said that even coming in contact with microscopic bits of bat scat is dangerous. When it dries, it looks like black beans that release airborne particles containing viruses and parasites that burrow beneath the skin, causing heart arrhythmias and creepy neurological diseases that can lead to death. But the strange thing is since Cora's bite, I'm not as depressed and can breathe deeply for a change. I feed her berries and a daily ounce of blood that comes from my fingers and toes. I know that sounds dangerous but I've never felt better, plus now I can fly, hang upside down, and produce echoing sound waves. If you're wondering how I do that it's because when I'm with Cora, I can make my soul leave my body and suddenly I'm beside her, soaring through the clouds. That's when I look down and feel a kinship with all the animals I see: the owls, pigeons, squirrels, raccoons, dogs on leashes, even the scurrying rats and mice. Before Cora, I didn't realize what I was missing, that I was suffering from species loneliness, from wild animal alienation. When I'm with Cora, I see colors I've never seen before, I hear the wind as music, and I know she'll stay with me to the ends of the Earth. Tonight we're flying over Central Park to visit the bears in the zoo, so you see, I haven't really imprisoned myself at all and if you're still inclined to stay, I might even teach you how to fly. Well, good bye for now, and sweet dreams!

  (THEODORA'S waves, then lets her body fall to the floor as her soulful self departs.)

The Last Reading of Charlotte Cushman
by Carolyn Gage

Setting: A stage set for a public reading, 1875.

Character: Charlotte Cushman: The greatest American actress of the 19th century, a fat, butch lesbian and a survivor of one of the first mastectomies. Late 50s.

Charlotte tells of her first encounter with a death—in bed with a prostitute.

CHARLOTTE: The first time I encountered death, I was twenty-three years old and in bed with a prostitute. That got your attention, didn't it…?

Well, I was twenty-three years old and living in New York. I was what they called a "walking lady," which is the actor who takes the roles too large for the chorus and too small for the leads. This was at the Park Theatre. And it was excellent training, too. Everything was repertory in those days, and during my three years as a "walking lady," I performed over a hundred and twenty different roles. But what does this have to do with a prostitute?

I'm getting to it. The Park Theatre was managed by one Stephen Price, and it is an understatement to say that Mr. Price and I did not get along. You see, Mr. Price resented any actor who was more handsome than himself. He saw it as his personal mission in life to drive me out of the company, and in February of 1839, it looked as if he just might succeed.

The Park Theatre was going to produce *Oliver Twist*, and there is a part of a prostitute in the play, Nancy Sykes. Well, in my day, no actress with any kind of reputation would touch a role like that, and Stephen Price knew it. So, naturally, he assigned it to me. If I took the part, I would be professionally ruined, and if I refused, I would be fired. Yes, Mr. Price finally had me where he wanted me.

And to tell you the truth, I considered quitting. It was quite an insult to be cast as a prostitute, and of course, he had done it in front of the whole company. But I had seen too many talented women lose out to temperament in this game, and I was determined not to be out-maneuvered. If there was a way to play Nancy Sykes without damaging my reputation, I was going to find it. And I was equally determined to see Stephen Price hoist on his own... *tiny* petard. So I accepted the part—graciously. And then I took myself down to Five Points. That was the area just east of Broadway—the worst slum in New York. And I rented myself a room at Mother Hennessey's, which was the cheapest and dirtiest rooming house I could find. That was where the streetwalkers and the drunks stayed, when they could afford a roof for the night. And it was there, at Mother Hennessey's, that I began to study the role of Nancy Sykes.

During the day, I went out on the street and watched the old women pick through the garbage, and then I watched the young women pick through the old men. I watched their hands, their hips, their elbows, their mouths, their teeth, their eyebrows. I watched them flirt, I watched them joke, I watched them steal—I watched the things that no one else was watching.

And at night, I went to the saloons, and I studied the women there. And sometimes the women studied me. On the third night, a young prostitute came into the bar. She was very sick, shaking all over, and she asked for water. They gave her a glass of whiskey, and she got sick all over the floor. The men thought this was funny. I went to help her, and it turned out she didn't have any place to stay for the night, so I took her up to my room at Mother Hennessey's, I undressed her, I helped her to bed… And then she died. That's it. That's the story. No last words, no touching prayers, no anxious faces hovering over the bed, no final embrace. A convulsion and she died. That was it.

> *"… Out, out, brief candle!*
> *Life's but a walking shadow, a poor player*
> *That struts and frets his hour upon the stage,*
> *And then is heard no more; it is a tale*
> *Told by an idiot, full of sound and fury,*
> *Signifying nothing."*

What did I do? I took her clothes. Of course, I took her clothes. I had a show to open, and they fit me… And then I went back to the Park Theatre, and I gave them Nancy Sykes. Oh, yes, I gave them Nancy Sykes. Not the whore with the heart of gold, not the feisty little spitfire from the wrong side of town—oh, no—I gave them a prostitute the likes of which they had never seen on a New York stage, even though they passed a dozen girls just like her on the way to the theatre—even though half the men would go home with one of these girls on their arm.

But I gave them a prostitute they could see, not just look at—but really see! I gave them a prostitute that made them weep the tears that no one shed that night at Mother Hennessey's. And weep they did. You see, real life is too painful for most people. That's why they come to the theatre.

An Anthology

Micki From Jane: Abortion and the Underground
by Paula Kamen

Setting: Early 1970s, Chicago. A recruitment meeting to meet new volunteers for Jane, the feminist underground abortion service on Chicago's North Side. And then a scene soon after about the logistics of performing abortions in friends' apartments and houses.
Description: In the play, Micki, born December 14, 1941, is about 30. She is very much into the excitement and extremes of the counterculture and revolutionary scene of the period but is always acting in the background. She is one of the few members of The Service (Jane) who is Black and/or working class. From the South Side of Chicago, and a pre-law student at Loyola University. Not knowing if she'll survive these turbulent years, she lives in the moment, allowing the use of her apartment for the abortions. Grew up Catholic.

Paula Kamen interviewed Marie Leaner (aka Micki) in Chicago in 1999. The following two monologues are compiled from the verbatim transcript of that interview.

First monologue:

MICKI:
I'd been involved in the Chicago Conspiracy Trial, of "The Chicago Seven," they were called. It was a trial of the "Yippies" – like Abbie Hoffman and his friends who had very colorfully tried to disrupt the 1968 Democratic convention. I was on the legal defense team. In news footage,

Frozen Women Flowing Thoughts

I'm the Black female sitting next to Bobby Seal, the Black guy, holding his hand when he's being gagged and stuff, and I'm holding the notebooks so he can write notes. So, you know, I demonstrated against the war in Vietnam and all that kind of stuff.

And then I was somewhere on the North Side a couple years after the trial was over and somebody handed me a leaflet, and it was about the Chicago Women's Liberation Union.

(An aside) My opinion about (Jane founder) Heather (Booth) and the people that she associated with was that they were a bunch of liberals, even though they thought of themselves as radicals or revolutionaries. I didn't think highly of them at the time. So, I didn't associate with them, and that's kind of how you did it in those days…
But I went up to the office of the Women's Union and kind of looked around, and the first thing that attracted me was the posters because the Graphics Collective was active then. And I was like really intrigued by the art -- the iconic, bold, colorful pictures of women from all races which really spoke to me.

> (We see projected images of art from Chicago Women's Liberation Union Graphics Collective in background)

And, you know, I had years of Catholic education on holy cards that they give you. They're like about that long, actually…you know, it's a Rubens painting or a Michelangelo reproduction, but usually it was of a mother and child and, I mean, you know, it was totally un-feminist. Even if it was a picture of Mary, it was the *Virgin Mary*. And then there was this stuff, (looking to images) which was just really revolutionary for me. It was just like, it was more of a 'yeah!' kind of thing for me where I just…I wanted to be connected to this…

How did I know you were going to ask that question? For a long time, yes, I was the only Black woman in the Women's Union and the only working-class woman. I think there were a couple of other Black volunteers in Jane....

I got my sense of injustice from just being Black in this society, and I got my sense of politics from my dad. He was very involved in his union, and he worked at the steel mills at a time when Blacks had the more undesirable jobs. And so he was always, you know, he was always in both the union's face and management's face about that, and he gained a great deal of respect from black and white steelworkers alike. When organizing, I always looked to see what kind of white people they were. Were they white people with class consciousness because they came out of a white working class background? Or were they people who were faking it, people with long hair and dirty clothes who talked about how they were down with the people? Excuse me, but I take a bath every day. Don't insult me like that. So I guess from that point on I looked at people based on their practice and their background.

Yeah, it was pretty lonely but, you know, I ignored that stuff because of the bigger picture, the bigger social issues that needed to be addressed. And as long as there was one Black voice in there, then I felt like I was making a contribution. ...I'm sure when I opened the door for people who were coming in, and several of them were Black, they were like 'OK, good. I'm all right. I've had enough of this all-white thing.' There were women who were dying, there were Black women who were dying because of back-alley abortions. So the issue of whether I was the only Black woman or the only whatever – I didn't care what organization was doing it or what color they were. They were somebody who was doing something about the problem. And I wanted to be a person who did something about the problem.

Second monologue:
(Discussing letting Jane use her apartment for performing abortions.)

MICKI

Even with the risk, it all just made sense. We had plenty of room. It was a big apartment. And so they could perform the procedure in one room. People could rest in another room until it was time to go back. And, you know, it was like it was perfect, and then we could be in the dining room or the kitchen or the back ... out of the way.

And, yeah, I remember thinking, 'Well, I could go to jail for that,' but I had done a lot of things that I could have gone to jail for. I mean you could get arrested and go to jail for demonstrating against the war. But I did those things because I believed that what I was doing was right and necessary.

And there was part of me that wanted to be in on the action, and to make sure my actions and beliefs aligned. Because it's pretty safe just to be a front house. It's another thing altogether to actually have abortions taking place in your apartment. I knew every time we had it there - and it was only like twice a month that it was in our house -- that any day the bell could ring, and it was the cops busting us. ... But when they called, I never said no. Never said no.

You have to understand. People were getting killed. You didn't trust anybody or anything. You knew people who had been in the Black Panther party who had been killed. You knew people in SDS or any number of other organizations that had just been offed or killed or just disappeared. It was like what do you have to lose? You didn't expect to live that long. I didn't expect to live past age 33.

An Anthology

Ding. Or, Bye Bye Dad | Hamiere (Speed Dating)
by Jayme Kilburn

Setting: *Speed Dating*
Character: *Hamiere. A woman.*

Hamiere interrogates her relationship with men in this speed-dating confessional.

Ding.

HAMIERE

Sometimes I have to think about women to get off. I don't think I'm gay. The thought of going downtown on a lady totally grosses me out. I know what happens down there. I'm not going to elaborate… but let's just say…it is filthy. I'm sure wieners are filthy too, but I don't deal with wieners on a daily basis. I don't have one attached to my body, getting sweaty and pee filled. There is a certain mystery to the wiener. The vagina is no mystery to me. It's just like a whole mess down there. I went to a massage place once and they told me I could keep my underwear on but said it was easier for them to do all the touching and stuff if my underwear was off so when I got undercressed I took my underwear off and this huge wave of vagina smell just filled the room. I don't know if that means I have a rotten vagina or something but I put my underwear on right quick. Anyway, putting my tongue in a vagina…no thank you.

Frozen Women Flowing Thoughts

But boobs are pretty nice. Sometimes if I can't get off I think of my boobs and another ladies' boobs rubbing up against each other. That's it. Just boobs flip flopping around. You watch tv and it's all about boobs. That's what makes a woman sexy, her big jiggly knockers. Could I go for a vagina? Maybe. But I would only want some super hot chick with a really well coiffed vagina. And since I'm not super hot myself, I feel like my chances of landing some super hot chick are pretty slim. I mean, I guess that's not totally true. Lesbian norms are different than hetero norms. At the end of the day, I just don't really feel like trying something new.

Ding.

Do you ever think about someone dying and then think about all the pity you would get if they did? I think…what if my dad died. It would be horrible and tragic. But I would be allowed to be a crumbly mess for a long time. I would be encouraged to cry and take time off from work. And "heal." People would send me food and flowers and whisper about me behind my back about how sad it is and how strong I'm being. And to my face they would be overly nice and considerate. I could stay in my pajamas all day and eat ice cream. I could reevaluate my life and go on a vacation by myself to do some "soul searching." I could talk to my ex-boyfriend and mention that my dad died in the conversation and he would feel really bad that he wasn't there for me. And I'd be like, "Yeah, it was really tough." But in my mind, I'd be like, yeah, I hope you do feel like a piece of shit you fucking asshole. I hope you call me all the time now and come over and see me cry and be touched by how vulnerable I am, you piece of crap. And tell me to cry in your arms and hug me for hours and then I'll look up at you through my tears and you will know that I am the one you're supposed to be with. And we'll kiss. And it will be magical, like in the movies. Fucker. Sometimes I just think my life would be so much better if someone died. But then I think, I would hate for someone close to me to *really* die. And what if I wished for someone to die and the wrong person died? Or one of my dogs died? Then I would just be sad all the time. But, you know, it's fun to think about.

An Anthology

Ding.

I saw this 20/20 episode about heaven and it really scared me. What do you think happens when you die? All these people said they had been to heaven but they all had different versions of it. Most mentioned a white light, but some said they went down a hallway and some said they walked through a field and one lady said that she was walking up a huge staircase and there were all these cats and dogs coming down the stairs and they were really happy. And she said she would pull their tails and it would make them even happier. What kind of person goes around pulling the tails of cats? And if you are walking up to the gates of heaven, why are you fucking with a bunch of cats? I don't think that's the kind of stuff that gets you into heaven. Some people say that what these people are experiencing is their brain dying. I'm scared to die. I haven't been the best person either. And do you think that these angels watch you when you masturbate? Sometimes I think about that as I am masturbating. I guess they don't care, but still. And what if God is just like a bad boss? You know, you have to sort of do whatever he wants and laugh at his dumb jokes, and you know that when there is a big meeting coming up he is going to get hyper critical and start micromanaging you. And you know you could do the job better than him, but you can't say anything because he's super sensitive. Man, I hope it's a good place. Better than here at least.

Ding.

I love my dogs so much. Not in a weird way. I just wish I had given birth to them. A little dog body coming out of me. It licks me and I hold it and say "I'm your mom now." Then I wrap it in a blanket and give it a little bottle. And boop its little nose. I love dogs so much. But I don't want kids. Oh my god I hate kids so much. What do you think that means?

Ding.

My sister only dates gay men now. I was always the one who was totally anti gender binaries so it's kind of funny that she has taken this like radical stance. But really, I just don't think she wants to have sex anymore. Too painful. Not like she has a small vagina too painful. Or really, I don't know. Maybe. But more like emotionally. Our dad. Maybe. I mean, we don't know anything. Just snippets of memories that add up to a bad feeling. And she kind of had a propensity to date assholes. Abusive, etc. So yeah, she doesn't like sex. She was a huge slut in high school. I mean major trash bag. Hmm. That sounds mean. I am very sex positive. I positively love sex. Well, I do and I don't. I don't like to be vulnerable but I do like to be close to someone. So basically, I do my own cock blocking. I don't outsource that shit! *(laughs awkwardly)* I didn't have sex until I was 20. Even then…not sure if it counted. He was kinda drunk and his penis was soft for most of it. I had to really shove it in. The condom broke and he freaked out and started yelling at me "do you have an STD!" "DO YOU HAVE AN STD??!!!!" And I'm sitting there like, how do I tell this guy this is my first time? But then he saw the blood and got it. But I think he also realized that he had been my first and I guess that was too much pressure for him because he said he "didn't want anything serious" and just kind of left. No goodbye or anything. So yeah. I didn't like sex very much. But eventually I did it again and it wasn't so bad.

Ding.

Soo….do you do this a lot? Seems like an odd thing to do a lot. You probably have a job or something? Can't sneak off every afternoon to get hammered at the local Motel 6 meeting stranger after stranger. I don't have a job. Well, I do but I hate it. I guess that isn't the same thing? Or is it? I don't know. But I basically lie to them a lot, say I'm sick, hit by a car, etc. Today my dog is at the vet. Not really. But that is the lie du jour. I don't know what they must think of me. Having tragedy after tragedy after tragedy. They're probably like…whaaaat is her problem? Right? *(Laughs awkwardly leading into awkward silence).* I'd quit my job for reals if I could, but I can't. I have a TON of credit card debt. I'm in credit counseling right now but it will still take YEARS to pay it off. No biggie. Just got to meet a rich man, huh? Just kidding. But not really. How much money do you make?

Ding.

You think I'm fat don't you? You think I'm too fat to be talking to someone like you? Because you're so handsome. I get it. If you must know I have a thyroid problem. And my mom died. The thyroid is one cause and the sadness is the other. If I did not have either of those problems I would be super skinny, like my sister over there. Don't look at her. Holy crap, you'll have your chance to talk to her in like 20 minutes. Excuse me. You are on a date with me now. And what I want to talk about is my thyroid problem. So, look interested.

Ding.

(Crying) I just feel so empty inside and I want to fill up the emptiness. You know? Just fill it up with something that tastes good. But the hole is never full. Never ever. And then I feel bad and I eat more and I just want to be skinny and find a good man and settle down and be happy. But I also want to like advocate for myself because fatness is not just about calories in and calories out and I am really sick of people telling me that my body is my fault or even talking about my fucking body. Like, do people come up to you and just give you health advice? Because they do with me…all the time. Strangers, loved ones, colleagues, every fucking one. How am I supposed to love myself when society tells me I'm gross but also that I should embrace my grossness and that it's really society's problem??? That's like a total mind fuck!!! *(Pause)* You are so handsome. Do you want to get out of here?

Ding.

My first love's name was Shmivis. That's his god given name. Or, the name is parents gave him. You know what I mean. We dated for two years in college but stayed friends for fifteen years after that. Then he got married and I just couldn't do it anymore. I thought he would figure it out. That we were perfect for each other. I mean, he called me all the time. I was his person, you know? I knew everything about him and he knew everything about me. I thought he would realize that that's what love is. Someone you can stand to be around for your whole life. It doesn't have to be perfect. It doesn't have to be beautiful. It just needs to be honest and comfortable. I wanted that forever. Us, cracking jokes at each other as we grew old, as our bodies fell apart. Other couples looking at us enviously…like, wow, those people are really lucky. Because who finds that? Every couple I know is so sad. It looks like so much work. I don't meet anyone who just clicks. Who have some sort of effortless sense of belonging to each other. That was the only time I really believed that love might be for me. After that, I just didn't believe anymore.

Ding.

Sometimes I pretend like I'm married. I'll get take out and pretend to call my husband and ask what he wants for dinner. Then I'll say something like "you know you can't eat onions after 7pm." Or, "I think you like the one with bacon." Then I'll laugh and say, "I love you too honey." But of course no one is on the other line. And I am really just ordering all the food for myself. Sometimes I stare at the young families in the restaurant. Some of them don't speak to each other and kind of bark at their kids, but some of them are really sweet and everything that their child does is an "awwww" or an "oooooo" and then they take a picture. Just really sweet. And then the husband looks at his wife and you can see how much he loves her for bringing this little person into the world with his DNA. They are a little family, you know? And they are so happy. And I want that. I guess everyone wants it. When I really think about it, it isn't the family so much. It's all that love. I want to be part of something that is real and happy and fulfilling. I've never felt that. And I don't even know if I'm pretending to do it right.

Ding.

My mom's dead. But before that we had a pretty good relationship. I mean, she was a drunk but she was pretty nice most of the time. There are a lot of questions I wish I could ask her. Or, that she could answer. I guess I could ask her whatever I want. Like, why didn't you fight for custody of us? If you didn't want to be around dad why did you think we would? What was your childhood like? I wish I knew more about her family. Or who my cousins were.

Every Sunday, these huge groups of families gather in the park. They have to get there really early to stake out a picnic table. So, one person will be there at like 9am, sitting there with a table decorated with balloons. Maybe they'll be setting up the condiments for the upcoming barbecue. Sometimes they just look really tired. Smoking a cigarette. Maybe enjoying the peace and quiet until everyone else gets there. Because in a few hours the park will be packed with families. Screaming kids, unruly teenagers. Men selling ices and water guns. This happens every Sunday. Saturdays too. Families spending all day in the park together. They don't look like they have any money. And sometimes you can hear a dad yelling at his kids or smell the marijuana coming from the bushes. But they carve out that time to spend together. Those kids might grow up to hate their parents, but I bet they'll know the reason they hate them.

I just wish I knew her. I wish I had a reason to hate or miss her. I wish she would have embarrassed me in front of my friends. I wish she would have insisted on chaperoning my first dates. I wish she would have told all her friends when I got my period for the first time. I wish I would have known her family. My family. But I guess I'm still pretty lucky. I have my sister and good friends and I know I need to be more grateful for that. I got to choose my family so I suppose that's pretty special.

Ding.

About me? Well, I find speed dating really hard. I know I need to be more honest and vulnerable during these interactions but it's really really hard. So, here goes. I am going to give it a try. Just be myself and if you like me, great. If not, it's okay too. I really love animals. I'm a pretty good cook. I mean, I think so. I work as a therapist. I've always loved hearing other people's stories. You know? And the thing is, everyone has a story. We have a concept of normal that we think everyone experiences. But the truth is everyone's experience is unique. There is no normal. It isn't an achievable thing. I like that. *(Pause)* I'm really close with my sister. Those are the highlights I guess.

Right now, I'm just really interested in hearing about you.

Coming Home
by Daria Miyeko Marinelli

Setting: An Herb Garden
Character: Regan

Gardens. A fighter. Steel wool porous but tough.

REGAN enters and kneels at the ground. She runs her hands over the rosemary plant. She inhales. It smells of Israel.

REGAN
When I was in the fifth grade Eleanor Lloyd wrote a poem about all the ways she didn't like me and showed it to the bus.
The whole school bus.
I was sitting in the front.
She was my best friend for the longest time
And then something just happened
A flip, a coin toss, the wind changed I don't know,
It's not important
I just-
I come to this spot
I come to this spot
Because here is where I first buried my first cat
And I cried and cried a thousand times
And my tears sunk deep into the earth
And that cat has been here, always the same
And my tears keep the dirt soft

As I grow older and cry less
And I come here
I planted some Rosemary
Because I went to Israel once
And it smells like that there
So now here it smells like that here
And all these people just want a home
And I found my home in that rosemary place in a small girl my height,
Maybe a little taller, with bold brass eyes and a smile that cut Chinese cheese
And then I left.
We didn't do anything, right, it wasn't about that, no.
It was just, sometimes you really see people.
And then I came home to a different home
With smells familiar and a body of all the curves I know
Elias.
She says we smell each other through the centuries, and sometimes I just wonder
What if I smell wrong
What if my smell is Rosemary

She runs her hands over the rosemary plant. She inhales.

Off the Edge without a Ruler
by Robin Rice

Setting: A zoo, a beach, and very flexible spaces between.
Character: A woman C.E.O.

This woman never paused in her rat-race climb to the top of the business ladder. She was tied in knots with organization and precision. The audience is people who need to stop and smell the roses before they crash as the woman C.E.O. almost did. Perhaps she is giving a Ted Talk.

C.E.O. is a woman who didn't pause in her rat-race climb to the top of the business ladder.
The audience is people who need to stop and smell the roses before they crash.
Perhaps this is a Ted Talk.

                            C.E.O.

The penguin is leaping. It's a rock-hopper penguin, so to be precise it's not so much leaping as hopping. Funny little tuft of fur or hair over his eyes bouncing up and down as he hops. I'd say he's 29 ounces, give or take an ounce, and 23 inches high. He sees me watching, but doesn't give a hoot. He's busy making sure he hops over every single thing on the ground.

I haven't been to a zoo since I was five and a three-quarters, but I've gained 1.47 pounds so I need to walk. I can't face an entire parkful of nature so here I am. I brought my ruler. I'll measure and record the distance between hops. Gather statistics. What's the longest hop? Will he hop faster and farther when it's 4:30 feeding time?

"Don't you know what year it is? Nobody's that precise. Live it up! Hop out of your regulated brain. Enjoy!"

Okay, this is a penguin talking to me. He's cute, but he has a very small head, a very small brain. He might hop off the edge -- not see it coming up, like a flat Earth. I wouldn't risk that. I have it all measured out. He's a bird. I respect science.

"I live it!" he chirps gleefully, hopping off the edge.

No more penguin. Not a splash. Not a sound. I picture him plummeting through space. I doubt he'll land on another planet. Chances are against it. Figure it out -- the ratio of open space to space occupied by planets to space occupied by a very small penguin. He's a goner. I take off my shoes and walk out of the zoo barefoot. I have no idea why I do that exact thing at that exact moment. Nobody's there to explain, or to remind me to take note of the length of my strides as I head home.

It's very quiet.

A padded "thud."
A very distant: "Yahoo!"

Where did I put my ruler?
I don't care.
Don't care? I can't go on without a ruler!

From far away in space comes a small voice: "Give it a try!"

This is getting out of control! Is that penguin actually floating around in space sending messages to me -- specific, unemotional, goal-oriented, rational me?

Frozen Women Flowing Thoughts

I've come too far to go back and find my ruler and my shoes. "Give it a try"? Give what a try? Bouncing off the edge of the Earth like he did? The weight of the world, which is round by the way, is on my shoulders. I can't simply smoke a joint, which I'm sure the penguin did, and hop away from responsibility. There's deception, improvisation, really bad stuff all around. If I don't deal with it -- "Stuff"? I don't use that vague word.

(hearing something:) What's that?

(listening:) Silence.

Silence.

Silence.

A distant cry: "I see you from afar!"
I don't see you!

"It will destroy you!"
What? Never mind. Out of sight, out of mind!

I check the ruler store. It's closed.

Finally, home. Wash my face with a cold cloth, change into pjs, lay out work clothes for tomorrow. Make half a cup of Chamomile Nights. Penguin logo. Bow tie. Silly cartoon. Never noticed. Not my penguin. The Ten O'Clock News? No. It's five after. Drink tea, put on shoes, set alarm, get in bed. Pull the covers up. Yes, I'm in bed with my shoes on.

Don't ask. I don't have an answer. All that's in my head is: tomorrow's another day.

Silence.

Far away -- far far far away -- there's an explosion.
The Earth shakes.

An Anthology

A tsunami! Grab bed post, hang on for dear life!
It crashes in. Up and over me. Back out.
My head spins. I'm drenched. Tomorrow's clothes are washed away.
The walls. The window.
Everything but the bed -- washed away.

Is this a bed? It feels like a listing boat.

This isn't my apartment; it's a tropical island. Oh great, now not only penguins will talk, probably palm trees and coconuts too.

Ukulele music. Hula girls. One dances over, puts a lei around my neck, kisses my cheek. The lei's smell -- so sweet I can almost touch it. Insignificant! Not measurable!

Soft waves wash soft sands.
I knew it. I've gone mad.

This is irritating as hell! I have deadlines, problems, a budget to balance, stuff -- stop it! -- things, so many things I have to do! It can't all have washed away. I'll be damned if I take my shoes off again. Seven and a half narrow. Three years and two months old. $275.99 on sale. People are counting on me.

A penguin is playing the ukulele. Wouldn't you know. He nods and smiles. He's tall and fat. He's not my penguin. The hula girls surround me, arms waving gracefully, knees bent, bare legs tan, bare toes... I admit it did feel good with no shoes. Don't tell anyone.

I'm not trying to figure out why a penguin is in Hawaii. I'm conscious of that fact. I'm conscious that I'm not dwelling on it. Even after saying it, I'm not hung up on it. How strangely liberating.

Sand... Sand... I never sit in sand. Or in the sun without sunblock. I never sunbathe naked. Naked! Sitting in sand naked except for, yeah, shoes.
Who took my clothes?
Why can't I move?

Frozen Women Flowing Thoughts

A coconut falls from overhead, missing me by inches. Hey! An alarm clock rings. I can't move. Am I in a hospital? Did I have a stroke? What's that small creature digging out of a hole... another... an army of -- sand crabs? Stay back. I'll smash you. Don't crawl... !

Surrounding me, each making a skittery sound with its mouth. A hundred beady black eyes, 800 spiny legs. Or more; or less. Dear God, I don't know exactly. Or even approximately. Sun beats hotter. They come closer. Okay. Okay. Nice crabs. Never eat crab. Allergic. But I like you! Nice little crabs. Do you have penguin friends? Crawl back in your holes please, okay? I'm not afraid of you per se. I mean, I'm big and you're little, but you're unnervingly spider-ish.

A shriek! A crab? Another shriek! A hundred shrieks! Electric pain ear to ear. You're demons sent by the penguin. Do you have my ruler? Did you send the wave? How much are you going to take? You can't have my mind. What? What?

Aska ranga ski ski ski skumbo bum bum

A sand-crab chorus.
I don't understand.

ASKA RANGA SKI SKI SKI SKUMBO BUM BUM BLAST! No, no! RIP! RIP! UNZIP!

Yes.

Yes.

The ice age has ended.

      (Pause. Pause. Pause.)

Slowly roll to my back. Luxurious. Heels, calves, thighs, butt, spine, hair pressed in sand. Roll. Face, shoulders, breasts, stomach, legs, toes in sand. Roll! Slow. Over, under, over, under, sand in mouth, eyes, ears, roll over, under, sand under nails, in folds of skin, in cracks and crevices. Comforting.

Palm fronds rustle up and down the coast. Sand-crab chorus, soothing now: *Aska ranga ski ski ski skumbo bum bum...*

Sit up. Or not. Or lie here with the sun going down -- ribbons across the water -- orange and yellow; thread of light outlining silver clouds. Huh. This is something that happens.

I want to toast the moment with coconut milk. I try to open the coconut, but can't. Find the soft spot and determine what tool is necessary. I could, but I won't. I... I don't want to move. I want to soak in the rippling reflection. The ocean understands. The sun understands. The crabs -- how I underestimated them! They're skittering about, writing in the sand, precise bodies moving like small miracles. If I squint I can make out what they've written....

Good thing you trusted the penguin.

Like a mountain with an unknown elevation, now leveled, I will unlace my shoes, slip them off and dig my toes into warm sand. I will throw my shoes out over the ocean -- beyond sizes, ratios and decimals -- beyond waves, beyond the sun's reflection, beyond the beyond. What size are they? How far is that? I don't give a damn.

(C.E.O. takes a slow, deep breath. Then: BLACKOUT.)

SUFFOCATION BAY
by ALANA VALENTINE

Setting: A kitchen, real or imagined.
Character: Liora, a woman of faith.

Suffocation Bay is written to be performed by an actor who can very carefully control their breathing and simulate the illusion of choking and almost suffocating. To do so without sustaining any damage to either their lungs or their person will be a virtuoso feat of performative control. There is also the invitation to a kind of magic trick in the work – where the performer pulls out larger and larger and more impossible objects from their throat (or pretends to). This should be done as convincingly as possible.

SUFFOCATION BAY
© Copyright Alana Valentine 2023

Note Well: This work can be performed with or without the detailed 'extrusions'. They appear in the script for the actor/director's discretion and can be 'imagined' or realised.

LIORA stands on stage, fighting for breath.

LIORA I think this breath may be my last

     I want to suck clean sweet air

An Anthology

But there is something...
Parsley from the soup?
A parsley stem from the bowl
Of garnish?
Trying to understand what this
feeling is of something caught
Trying to breathe
As I always do
As I have every moment
Trying to do one of the bodily functions that are
done without my conscious
will
Heart beating, cheeks blushing, eyelids blinking
And
lungs inflating
Like pink party balloons
Embroidered with bronchioles
The superb inhalation
Exhalation that has been consummated
From the day I was dragged by my feet
from within my mother
gripping with my hands not to come away
and tearing her youth and beauty with me

into shiny, shiny time
where from a young age I am taught that
merit
will be rewarded with attention
and acclaim
I don't know then
what a crock that is

But stop now
stop now
Because the thing is still in my throat
And I am standing at the sink
Choking
Breathing through some ragged gap

Frozen Women Flowing Thoughts

And my mind is saying
It must be the bay leaf stem
Caught
Across my windpipe
The stem, caught
So that I can't breathe
At all but

Cough

It must be bigger than a stem
Or a stalk or a

Cough

I cannot breathe
I am gulping for air
I pull at my throat and into the sink
Spins a heavy gold coin
My mother's jewel
Queen Victoria on the reverse

I have clutched at the chain and now it is broken in my hands
Oh and I have just had the gold repaired
I broke the clasp when cleaning it and the jeweller recommended that I have it soldered so that it would be safe
Soldered and strong
So when I clutched the chain has broken instead

All this I am thinking at the same time as I am still trying to get my head around the fact that I still cannot breathe
And thoughts are beginning to go through my head of people taken to hospital because of fish bones stuck in their throat
And how you can die if you cannot breathe

And I am breathing, shallow breathing and the thing
the thing
the thing is still in my throat
And the others are in the other room still eating their
soup as I stand at the sink and then I cough
And up comes a jagged edge bay leaf

The woman pulls a bay leaf from her throat.

It is out it is out
I have saved myself
I have cleared the blockage
I can breathe
Oh sweet sweet air
I fill my lungs with it
Grateful not only for the breath
But even more that I was not going to be on the
small kitchen floor
Staring at the vintage cooker that I had admired while
the soup was cooking kale and potato and chicken
Flavoured with bay leaves that were
not
removed before serving
And how humiliating it would have been to have
turned purple there
And an ambulance having to be called
How furiously humbling to have gagged so publicly
But all that has been
Avoided
Thank God
No really
Thank God
Who must have more for me to do
To dislodge that hideous flap of hard bay leaf
But when you were in it
When you were choking gulping
All those times that you are dominated by
Yes, you know

Frozen Women Flowing Thoughts

    Say it
    Say it
    Spit it out
    Like the bay leaf
    It is catching in your

Again she has trouble breathing

    But what is this now?
    Something else is lodged there?
    Is it
    Loss?

She pulls an object larger than a leaf from her throat now.
Perhaps a watch or a set of keys. Or pretends to.

    The number of times I have
    Lost
    Things
    And they call up in you the dominant
    Loss
    Of Mother

She pulls another object even larger this time.
Perhaps a pair of stockings or a hat. Or pretends to.

    Of Daughters

She pulls something else from her throat. Sometime impossibly large.
A book perhaps. Or a kettle or a teapot. Or pretends to.

    Of
    So many many many
    That now you try to keep in your mind every place
    Everything
    Every file and shelf and box and crate
    And all the keeping places
    Catalogued

So that you don't lose anything and the burden of all
that remembering so that you don't lose anything is

*She pulls something else out of her throat. Symbolic things.
A plastic childhood toy or a bar heater with a cord or a sewing machine.
Or pretends to.*

Even in that moment when you were choking you
were thinking of the misplaced beret and jumper
and receipt and photo that you have been looking
for and can't find
So much of your life on
Keeping
Instead of losing
That you are losing
Life
And choking
On chattel
Here now
Stop
Put it down
Put what down
Everything
Stop being the librarian of all your stuff
Let it go
Let it know that you are just leaving it
In situ
Can suffocation on a bay leaf give you that?

She pulls a long, long, long string of things 'out' of her throat. Fishing line, buoys, lobster pots, rubbish all mangled together, chip packets, pizza boxes, more and more and more rubbish seems to emerge from her throat. Newspapers, nuclear warheads, enormous inflatable toys.

She stares at the pile of it.

When I was choking
Suffocating

Frozen Women Flowing Thoughts

My life did not flash
But there were moments
My grandmother's eyes looking at me for the last time as I went down in the lift from the hospice
Even on the brink of death my brain was saying
but how could you have seen into her hospital room from the lift?
Memory is unreliable
But I can still see the look in her eyes, the knowledge that she would not see me again
And I think of the arrogant, stupid girl I was
Knowing that she was dying but not believing as I would now
Not accepting as I would now
Ignorant self-absorbed denial
And yet I loved her so much
She taught me love
Only she

She burps.

I did also flash on the
hundred dollar note I found in the wind blown rubbish while I was waiting outside the fruit barn
A hundred bucks! Among the dust and dirt and bits of blown around detritus and leaves
A hundred dollars in cash
And then the next time there was a maroon long sleeve t shirt with Warrior in black across the top
Things I found
Things I found I remember things I found
Such a wonderful feeling I've found a beret and a jumper too
Lost and found
Breath and death
Memory and masks

She removes her clothes, down to being naked or semi-naked (as the director prefers) and then pulls a small lit candle from her throat.

One day my friend asked me if I was a disciple of any particular religion and I told him I was a person of faith
And he said, 'Well I'm glad you've spat that out'
Then he never spoke to me again
It wasn't a dramatic rejection
Just a quiet nothing more
My faith stuck in his throat like a ragged edge bay leaf and made him unable to breathe I suppose
In any case what?
What do you mean you're what?
Yes.
Why have you never said?
I did say, when he asked I said
No, I mean, why have you never said that to me?
Are you a disciple of any particular religion?
No
I was scared you would reject me
I had a girlfriend who rejected me
Elizabeth
She made me a beautiful bag it was dark blue with a clasp and she embroidered a flower on it in sort of silver and pink to make it more personal
And I told her I was a person of faith and she never spoke to me again
Never called
Never texted
After I say it, I am erased

It's the secret that sticks in my throat
That I cannot spit out
But surely you're not ashamed of it?
No, I am not ashamed, I just don't want people to never speak to me again because my faith, my belief

sticks in the throat of others, So I want to spare them that
I see.
Do you?
Well. I don't know. I guess I'm going to have to think about it.
You will do it too.
You can't know that.
Yeah, you will
Only because you have lied to me all this time
It makes no difference, you would have rejected me years ago or today
Just as soon as you knew

She covers her nakedness (or semi-nakedness).

    When I go back into the other room
    After the bay leaf
    It's as if I've just been to the toilet
    No mention is made till one of them coughs
    Seems to choke
    But it's a joke
    At my expense
    My eyes are as narrow as a stiletto heel
    And as treacherous
    My smile is the rear vision mirror
    When the car behind you beeps

    And though the talk turns back to the business at hand
    I wonder would they have struck my back
    Like a big eucalypt tree limb hitting the ground hard
    Would they have acted quickly before the hypoxia cut the air to my brain
    "Can I trust my life to these people?' screams inside me like the high pitched wail of an inner city ambulance

Can I trust my truth to these people without choking on the assumptions and distortions and tribalism and us and them-ism and I haven't even said of which God of the hundreds of gods that people do worship on this planet
I couldn't even spit that out.
And I sit now in the deep chair
Breathing in and out
My airways clear
My secret safe
My breathing regular and calm
My breath
Keeping me alive.

© Copyright Alana Valentine 2023

TWO MINUTE AUDITION EXCERPT

I cannot breathe
I am gulping for air
I pull at my throat and into the sink
Spins a heavy gold coin
My mother's jewel
Queen Victoria on the reverse

I have clutched at the chain and now it is broken in my hands
Oh and I have just had the gold repaired
I broke the clasp when cleaning it and the jeweller recommended that I have it soldered so that it would be safe
Soldered and strong
So when I clutched the chain has broken instead

Frozen Women Flowing Thoughts

All this I am thinking at the same time as I am still trying to get my head around the fact that I still cannot breathe
And thoughts are beginning to go through my head of people taken to hospital because of fish bones stuck in their throat
And how you can die if you cannot breathe
And I am breathing, shallow breathing and the thing
the thing
the thing is still in my throat
And the others are in the other room still eating their soup as I stand at the sink and then I cough
And up comes a jagged edge bay leaf

The woman pulls a bay leaf from her throat.

It is out it is out
I have saved myself
I have cleared the blockage
I can breathe
Oh sweet sweet air
I fill my lungs with it
Grateful not only for the breath
But even more that I was not going to be on the small kitchen floor
Staring at the vintage cooker that I had admired while the soup was cooking kale and potato and chicken
Flavoured with bay leaves that were
not
removed before serving
And how humiliating it would have been to have turned purple there
And an ambulance having to be called
How furiously humbling to have gagged so publicly
But all that has been
Avoided
Thank God
No really

Thank God
Who must have more for me to do
To dislodge that hideous flap of hard bay leaf
But when you were in it
When you were choking gulping
All those times that you are dominated by
Yes, you know
Say it
Say it
Spit it out
Like the bay leaf
It is catching in your

Again she has trouble breathing

But what is this now?
Something else is lodged there?
Is it
Loss?

Frozen Women Flowing Thoughts

How to Get Married in Five Steps and 17 Years
by Kathleen Warnock

Setting: USA, present
Character: WOMAN: Late 40s on up, any color, any dis/ability.

Her dress should be casual. She might wear a leather or denim jacket with badges/buttons, and good sturdy shoes or boots
Monologue (cut and paste in Times New Roman 12):

>**Music up** *during scene change/pre-show: Something like Wilson Phillip's "Wouldn't It Be Nice," or another song sung by a woman or woman-fronted group. Actor or stage tech sets a music stand and chair.*
>
>**Lights up** *as A WOMAN enters, carrying a bag. She pulls out a folder, and places it on a music stand.*

>>WOMAN
>
>We met on AOL, which shows you how long ago this was.
>
>She was in Ohio. I was in New York.
>
>She was caring for her partner, who was dying of ALS.

An Anthology

Step 1: We fell in love.

We waited.

She asked me to marry her before the turn of the century.

Her partner passed away.

She moved here at the turn of the millennium.

Step 2: When she moved in, we went to City Hall and filed for a domestic partnership.

> Woman displays Domestic Partnership certificate.

It gave us visiting rights in city hospitals and jails, and inheritance rights for apartments, though my landlord would not put her name on the lease.

We found another apartment and both our names are on the lease.

Step 3: We went to Vermont for a civil union. August 15. My parents' anniversary. Feast of the Assumption. Her birthday. My mother gave us her wedding ring.

We bought a ceremony off the internet, as neither of us had ever seen ourselves as brides in a wedding. The local justice of the peace performed the ceremony. We played "Crimson & Clover" on a boom box. After, we toured the Ben & Jerry factory.

> She displays Ben & Jerry carton.

My sister in Baltimore threw us a reception.

We lived. We acquired pets. We paid taxes. We voted. We marched. We discussed going to Massachusetts to get married in 2004, but decided to wait until our own state, New York, would acknowledge us.

I've had to show the domestic partnership, the civil union certificate, and the health care proxy (she shows health care proxy card) at hospitals and other institutions.

In 2011, I gave our cable company more money on the day the State Senate voted on marriage equality so we could watch history being made on a high-numbered channel. When the act was passed, we held hands and cried. We made plans to marry on our anniversary.

Step 4: We went to City Hall and took out a marriage license. Our friends, a couple who'd been together more than 20 years, asked if we minded if they got married on the same day, and we said the more the merrier.

On August 15, 2011, we went to City Hall. A very happy man in a sharp suit with a snazzy mustache, acting for the GREAT state of New York! Pronounced us married.

> She displays the marriage certificate.

My sister in Brooklyn was our witness, and she brought flowers and took pictures. Later, she threw us a reception.

When we traveled, depending on what state (or country) we were in, sometimes we were not married. One of the states we visited had amended its constitution to recognize marriage as only between a man and a woman.

Step 4-1/2: In 2013, Edie Windsor was allowed to be a lesbian widow, as the Supreme Court overturned part of the Defense of Marriage Act. The part that defended inheritance from queer widows and widowers. This would have come come in handy when my wife's last partner passed away, as we're still in legal limbo over their jointly owned property.

Step 5: June 26, 2015: Just in time for Pride Weekend, the Supreme Court says we're married in all the states.

> As she continues to speak, she pulls out and holds up a protest sign.

It's not over. It's not going to be over for a long time. We'll keep voting. We'll keep marching. We'll keep yelling. You can yell, too.

> Fade in MUSIC: Something like Bonnie Raitt's "Burning Down the House" or another woman-sung anthem that implies breaking out/protest/breaking free.
>
> The woman chants the following, or another protest slogan, allowing the audience to respond if it wants to.

This what democracy looks like!
This what democracy looks like!
This what democracy looks like!

Thank you.

Portia
by chris wind

Setting: open

Portia protests the role Shakespeare has given her, in The Merchant of Venice. Which is ...

Her father, now deceased, left explicit instructions in his will regarding her marriage. Only a suitor who passed the test of choosing 'correctly' among three caskets (of gold, silver, and lead) was to be accepted by Portia as her husband. Fortunately, the ones Portia would reject fail the test (my list is fairly true to Shakespeare's), and the one she would choose, Bassanio, succeeds.

However, before the test and marriage, Bassanio had asked a friend of his, Antonio, to sign a loan for him, from Shylock; Antonio's own flesh would be collateral (the loan was needed to woo and impress Portia, who, Bassanio was well aware, was "richly left," I:ii, l.161). Antonio generously agrees to do so, but unfortunately all of his vessels are shipwrecked and he is unable to repay the loan; Shylock demands his flesh. Portia (now wife of Bassanio) offers to pay the loan, but Shylock remains firm in his claim. Bassanio leaves Portia to see what he can do for Antonio.

Believing Antonio to be as good a man as Bassanio (for they are friends), Portia disguises herself as a lawyer and appears at the court to plead for Antonio. Her lady, Nerissa (recently married to Gratiano, Bassanio's man) accompanies her, disguised as a clerk. The trial proceeds,

An Anthology

Portia speaking for Bassanio's friend (in spite of Bassanio's claim that he would give up his wife to save Antonio, IV:i, l.282-287), and delivering the famous speech about mercy ("The quality of mercy is not strained..." IV:i, l.184...). The Duke judges in Antonio's favour. Portia begins to leave, but Bassanio insists the lawyer name some payment. She names the wedding ring he wears (given to him by her with the words "When you part from, lose, or give away, let it presage the ruin of your love," III:ii, l.174-175); he is reluctant, but upon Antonio's pleading ("Let his deservings and my love withal, be valued 'gainst your wife's commandment," IV:i, l.450-451), he gives it. Nerissa, as clerk, also acquires the ring she gave to Gratiano. They part.

When all have returned, Portia presents the ring to Bassanio, telling him that she obtained it when she slept with the lawyer. Nerissa claims to have slept with the clerk, and she too presents her ring. For a moment, there is concern about being cuckolded, but Portia quickly tells the whole story, thus relieving the men.

Portia:
If I'm the one with the property
You'd think I'd be the buyer
Not the bought;
A lot of faith my father has in me:
He distrusts my ability to judge, to discriminate—
A decision made by chance,
A decision inevitably and ultimately irrational,
Is preferable to a decision made by me.
    But no, you say,
The decision was not to be by chance
But choice, and thus reveal the suitor's character—
That is, he who chose lead would be wise,
To forsake appearance, and realize its irrelevance;
True, but you forget the inscription:
To choose lead, to choose 'to give and hazard all'
Is to my mind *not* wise,
For its foolish risk (all!);
Is it not better to choose silver,
And 'get what one deserves'?
It seems to me a mature perspective;

Frozen Women Flowing Thoughts

So, to judge by appearance
(And thus forsake appearance)
Or to judge by words
—That is the choice.
Words have meaning,
And unless the words be false or deceiving,
Is it not better to judge according to content,
Than to judge according to form
To substance, rather than pretence?
So if it was to be a test of character,
'twas thus a poor test,
For who was to guess what my father intended:
The form did contradict the content;
And so choice becomes chance, after all.
That *I* am not allowed to choose
Is in principle, intolerable,
But in practice, just as well—
For there is really not a one worth choosing:
A prince who boasts of his precious Porsche
And can fix it himself;
The County Palatine, who believes
A real man never smiles;
Falconbridge, a pin-up boy
With a mind as two-dimensional;
A Scottish Lord interested in nothing
But a good fight;
An alcoholic (the duke's nephew, yes);
The Prince of Morocco, a blood-thirsty Rambo;
And Bassanio, attracted by wealth and beauty,
Willing in a moment to sacrifice his wife for his friend.
There is not one.
If I so despise men,
Why did I disguise as one?
'twas not my choice:
Shakespeare (a man) created my costume
(And that of Viola and Rosalind),
And in his cowardice, he refused to challenge the reality
That to be able to interact

Without having to defend against
Sexual or romantic intentions,
One must be male;
That to be taken seriously,
And to be exempt from compliments that essentially trivialize
One must be male;
That to be effective at an endeavour
Of the intellectual arts,
One must be male;
That to be dominant, influential, powerful,
One must be male
In patterns of appearance, behaviour, speech, and thought
    —Patterns of thought?
But didn't I put forward
The feminine concept of mercy over justice?
Didn't care and compassion win over fairness?
    No, look again:
The Duke first pleaded for mercy, not I;
My case was won on a technicality,
On the letter of the law.
(Though it is worth mention
That recourse to such a legal loophole
Was my last resort.)
The masculist mode won out;
But this is not surprising in a masculist court.
Where there is no challenge,
There can be no change.
For when the disguise is finally revealed
It is not recognized
That to be what I was (what I am)
    One can be female—
It is recognized only that I *am* female.
And their response concerns only themselves—
Relief, that they won't be cuckolds.

CHAPTER TWO

AGE OF THE MOTHER

An Anthology

Remember Me, Mr. Smith?
By Christine Benvenuto

Setting: An empty stage, character's home, or a street in the Chinatown of any American city

A woman late 20s or older, any race/ethnicity

GIGI

You called my house on my eighteenth birthday. Not my cell, that number wasn't in my school records. My mother took the call. I was with my boyfriend, smoking out back when she came to tell us. "Mr. Smith called," she said, because that's actually your name. "He is contacting his former students."

That's what you told her: I am contacting my former students. My mother tried to be precise when speaking to a teacher or even about a teacher, *hence* the stilted touch of formality. As if you could hear her. Would judge her for paraphrasing, using contractions. She smiled, delivering this message, proud to get it right.

My boyfriend groused, "I haven't heard from him." My boyfriend, to give him credit, was immediately suspicious while my mother was feeling good about herself and I was trying to remember whether I'd returned my textbook before graduation, suddenly sure it was wedged between the wall and my bed. But you weren't calling each new graduate to track down textbooks.

Frozen Women Flowing Thoughts

"Are you open to a meeting?" you asked when I returned your call. You said almost nothing else, just, "Are you open?"

I was open, oh yes, wide open, hearing a dog whistle to adult life. I told myself, *It isn't for sure he wants sex and nothing but.* I knew it, though. It would be easier to explain why I agreed if I'd been naive. Or if I liked you. Let me be clear. I didn't like you, Mr. Smith. I didn't find you attractive, not remotely, not in this universe. I didn't dislike you either. I'd never had a thought about you. I barely had one now.

We arranged to meet on a street corner in Chinatown. You arranged it. I thought we'd eat in a restaurant, but you wanted to buy things for a meal you'd cook, "authentic ingredients." I was supposed to be impressed. I was not. At 18 the idea that someone surrounded by some of the best Chinese food in the world would rather go home and create an amateur approximation didn't impress me (it still doesn't). I didn't say this. You were pleased with yourself, very, and you'd recently been my teacher, very. We went into a market and you bought whatever you bought. I don't remember the food. I remember the shopkeeper. You were friendly with her. Like you knew each other because you'd shopped there before. She didn't answer. Her expression suggested the sight of you caused her pain. She looked at me. I thought she was about to speak to me. Then reconsidered, and silently handed your bags across the counter. I thought, *He comes here with every high school girl he gets to meet him, she's seen him here with all of us.*

At your apartment, which you were also pleased with, you cooked what you'd bought, you were pleased with that too. I sat on your leather sofa, bored, and didn't offer to help. You sat down beside me. "How old do you think I am?" you asked. An inane question, the answer to which could only make you feel bad. I thought you were 45, 48. But girls aren't stupid, Mr. Smith!

I said, "No idea."

"I'm 33," you informed me. Then: "I think you might be open." 'Open' again, an important word for you. You meant open to sex, not unattached, you knew my boyfriend. I didn't ask why you thought this. I imagined you with a list of my graduating class, DOBs included, stars next to names of girls you thought were open. Open for business. Legally. Calling girls who'd turned 18 as they left school, others on their eighteenth birthdays. No longer children. No longer your students, now it was June and we'd graduated.

Would anyone blame you? Now, some people. Then? Before cases exploded in the news, raining words like coercion, grooming, pedophile? Though, of course, pedophile you were not. A pedophile becomes a normal man on your eighteenth birthday. Anyone would think, Fool. Slut. Loser. About me, not you. Only losers sleep with old men they aren't attracted to. Because, Mr. Smith, in your early thirties, hair and beard threaded with gray and already struggling to achieve and maintain an erection, you seemed old. I'd never seen a penis at half mast before. "Get me hard," you said in bed, "get me hard."

"Get you hard?" I laughed. I thought you were joking. I had to do something besides be? Besides be naked? You said things during sex that turned you on. I thought it was stupid. Embarrassing. I didn't say so. I also didn't say the words you wanted me to say. You squirmed on top of me and an animated clip ran through my head: the textbook from your class stuck beside my bed, shrinking, withering. Falling out. I laughed. I guess you realized I wasn't into it. Afterward you tried to gaslight me, a term I didn't know but a concept I recognized the instant the jet was lit: "Are you sure you aren't a lesbian?" you asked me. As if anyone unattracted to skinny, prematurely flaccid Mr. Smith must not like men.

I demurred, "I don't think I am." Did lesbian girls often agree to sex with you? Did sex with you lead to homosexuality in previously heterosexual girls? You said, "I thought you'd be different." You meant better. Rah rah go team. I'd done very well in your class. It made sense you'd expect me to do well here. Yes, I actually thought this.

Frozen Women Flowing Thoughts

I wish I'd answered you another way. For example, using the statement-phrased-as-a-question by which young females seek to disarm insecure men, I might've said: "I think the definition? Of lesbian? Is a girl attracted to other girls? Not girls who aren't attracted to prematurely flaccid Mr. Smith?"

What would I say if I saw you now?

Do you still have trouble getting hard? It gets harder to get hard. Time softens, the universal truth of manhood. You can have hips replaced, knees. Things that hinge and pivot don't seem to last. But they aren't replacing *that* yet, so far as I've heard. Are you married? That summer you were divorced, in a relationship with a student who graduated the year before. Not cheating on her, having sex with my graduating class. "We have an understanding," you said. "We allow each other." You didn't specify if she allowed you because she knew you'd do it anyway, if you allowed her because you knew she would. Did you realize at 19 she wouldn't be satisfied with a faulty penis, Mr. Smith? A few years later, when you became principal of that high school, you and this former student married. Are you still married? Still allow each other? Could you become principal today if you started a relationship with one student the moment she graduated and everyone knew you'd had sex with many others? Attempted sex; there was the problem of that missing erection.

You, Mr. Smith are a white man. What if a Black teacher, say, Mr. Chandler, tried this? Could he become principal? You called lots of girls, all kinds. I don't know your success rate based upon demographics. I only know what happened with Li. She and I compared notes afterwards.

You didn't call Li until August. Her surname fell near the end of the alphabet, it had been a busy summer for you. You met her at the same Chinatown street corner, led her to the same market, shopped for your famous meal. You went up to the counter where, as it happened, stood the same shopkeeper. She examined Li. Stared into the space between you and Li. Considering her options, Li believed. You were chatty. After all, you knew each other, didn't you? You said,

"How are you this glorious summer evening?" And, "These crab legs look amazing."

The woman spoke to Li. One short sentence.

Li had grown up hearing English and Mandarin. This was neither. Cantonese, Li thought. She didn't know the words but she understood their meaning, she thought I, too, would've understood. Even you caught the shopkeeper's drift. Became uneasy. "Hmm," you said. "Hmm." Holding your credit card, waiting to pay for your crab legs, splayed before you. The shopkeeper walked around the counter. You stepped back. She approached, very calm. Looking a bit sad, Li thought. She didn't say anything. Her small pistol, aimed at you, said it all.

A few years after, you became principal. You began giving talks about the amazing, unexpected things you've done during your career in education. I don't know if you ever mention that August night in Chinatown, how you amazingly hurled yourself through the shop doorway, unexpectedly landing on the sidewalk on your shoulder. The glorious summer evening crowds caved around you like a sink hole. You rolled until you hit the gutter, a man extinguishing himself. Then you picked yourself up and ran.

Holy Inappropriate
by Allison Fradkin

Setting: A conference for conservative Christian young ladies.
Character: Mary Jo (female-identifying, 40s, open ethnicity)

Mary Jo is addressing a crowd of teenaged Christian girls. She is modestly attired and the epitome of bonhomie.

Good morning, young ladies. Welcome to the first annual Pure and Simple Conference! Wooo! I'm Mary Jo Genesis, and I'll be leading today's first breakout session, The Birds and the Believers. So many disciples at my disposal. Not even Mr. Christ's crucifixion attracted a crowd this colossal. I see each of you is wearing her virgini-tee as required, with its promotion of celibacy as desired. Seeing the words *Cel Me More, Cel Me More* printed across each chaste chest, I've got chills—they're purifying and I'm oozing control. *Self*-control.

Ignorantly blissful and blissfully indoctrinated, and content with your mission in life: *sub*mission, you can't wait to create a family—nay, an army—for God. But you will wait. Not only that; you will throw your *wait* around. During the waiting period, you may find yourselves thrust into lust. These feelings you're experiencing are not unlike personal goals and higher education: they must be passionately denied. This is where self-control comes in. Along with self... something else. According to Proverbs 31:13, a virtuous woman worketh willingly with her hands. That verse calls us to use faith-friendly fibers in the construction of our modest attire. Taking the characteristics of a virtuous woman out of context—taking anything in the Good Book out of context—is...something we do religiously, so it's all hunky-dory.

If you are willing to work with your hands, as Jesus commands, waiting can be tolerable, pleasurable. Preferable. That's because a baby is not a female's only bundle of joy. She also has one generously applied to the exterior of her reproductive organs. It is called Clitoris. Repeat after me: clit-or-is. *This*, not creation, is our creator's most perfect design. Like you girls, Clitoris has a servant's heart: each and every one of its nerves serves the sole purpose of enabling you to experience the rapture righteously and regularly, thank God. *(prayerfully)* Thank you, God. Those unsaved unbelievers don't call us Biblical Cliteralists for nothing.

Inside your swag bag is a rudimentary replica of Clitoris in the form of a pom-pom ball. Let's expedite its excavation, for upon location, you will embark on your very first pilgrimage to exultation. Where there's lubrication, there's liberation! Well? What are you waiting for? If Jesus can turn water into wine, we can turn ignorance into bliss. Because the gospel truth, girls, is that the Second Coming belongs to Christ, but the first coming belongs to you!

THIS IS MY FIRST PANDEMIC a monologue from the play ANOTHER HOMECOMING
by MELINDA GROS

Setting: Spring 2020, during the COVID pandemic
Character: KATHRYN - Pulitzer prize winning journalist, late thirties this monologue opens the play ANOTHER HOMECOMING, revealing Kathryn's pandemic panic; she then retreats to the town where she grew up, to her parents' home and her about-to-be-married pregnant sister, to report on the zoom classes, the shuttering of downtown, the prom-in-a-parking-lot and the betrayal of the community when the largest employer closes.

KATHRYN

My family calls me - I hear their messages, I hear the confusion and fear in their voices. I don't know how to answer their questions: this is my first pandemic. Nothing has prepared me for this. Tell me: were you prepared? Were you? No, I didn't think so.

I never lived in an American city under curfew, before now. I never reported on a food bank where people lined up hours before it opened, before now. I've never heard my father scared, before now. My journalism training prepared me to be analytical: under these circumstances, this is the expected response. When people lose jobs . . . when the president articulates a vision . . . when people die . . . there are predictable responses. When the expected doesn't materialize, not in the way I expect, or you expect . . . when our world can't be easily deciphered . . . remember, this is my first pandemic.

I need to stay calm; people depend on my being calm, so I remain calm and go home and eat a pint of ice cream, have a glass of wine and a hot shower and another glass of wine. I walk through my home, touching and checking my stockpiles: toilet paper, soap, tampons, clean underwear, crank-up radio, bacitracin, fully charged battery packs, clean socks, extra chargers, band-aids, hand sanitizer, girl scout cookies, extra masks. I check my carry-on bag, packed with extra masks and clean socks and jeans and shirts and panties and a medical kit and fully charged battery packs and soap and tampons and crank-up radio and hand sanitizer and protein bars and a thumb drive with pictures of my family, whom I love. I check my backpack for my health care proxy and press credentials and insurance cards and passport and tampons and hand sanitizer and masks and fully charged battery packs and extra chargers and aspirin and credit cards and pens and notebooks and protein bars and sunglasses and medical kit. And a thumb drive with pictures of my family. To reassure myself, I check again. Knowing everything is organized calms me enough to lie down, read a few pages of <u>Jane Eyre</u> and turn off the lights. Most nights I lie in the dark watching traffic and I wonder how we got to this crazy place. Then I drift off and childhood anxieties of an incomprehensible adult world return and I awake to find that I am alone and the landscape has shifted around me. Other nights I fall into a blessedly innocent sleep and I dream of normalcy but when I awake - when I awake the world has not changed and I am overwhelmed by the chaos.

I am jealous of my colleagues with partners. When they wake in the night, as I do, sweaty and terrified . . . at those times I wish for the warmth of a lover's arms.

I am frightened for my colleagues with children. Do they wake in the night, sweaty and terrified, at the same time their children also awaken, frightened and crying? Do they wake in the morning, as I do, terrified by the world, the world we are leaving these beautiful children? They must. They must. But I am also jealous that they are nightly comforted by their children's gentle breathing and, by day, by their innocent laughter. These children . . . these children are why we get up each morning. These children's futures haunt us.

I am both jealous and frightened for my sister, my beautiful younger sister - she will comfort and be comforted by her child and her partner. I envy her that. I myself, I never wanted that life but now . . . but now . . . maybe I want that now. This is my first pandemic and I . . . I miss normalcy. What we considered normal but isn't anymore. I miss that certainty that tomorrow will be OK.

I know I am lucky - my sister is lucky - and perhaps you are also lucky - with jobs and work to shape our days and lovers at night. If my dreams, if my obsessive checking of my belongings, is the response of a lucky person, a person with a job she loves . . . what does everyone else do? What do you do? How do you quiet your fears and calm yourself?

Tell me - and help me quiet my demons.

An Anthology

The Sticking Point
by Fran Handman

Setting: Angie's living room
Character: Angie Holcomb

Angie, coming home from a boring day of work, plays a mind game that she is stuck wherever the bus passes her. The bus passes her before she can get home and it becomes a reality. She is stuck in front of a house and can go nowhere but in that house. The occupants leave and her options become narrower and narrower – even the walls begin to move – and in the end she is afraid she is disappearing.

Something weird is going on and I don't know who to ask or who to call.

Exactly six months ago today at 6:00 PM, I got stuck – not in one spot – I got stuck on the sidewalk in front of this house.

I know the exact time this happened because I always leave work at 5:00 o'clock. It takes me 55 minutes to get to my stop. And then there's the three blocks to get to my apartment, about 5 more minutes, give or take a minute or two and it's 6:00 o'clock.

And I was just coming home from filing all day on my boring temp job – walking the same boring walk home thinking about what I'm going to have for supper, what I'm going to watch on TV.

Frozen Women Flowing Thoughts

So I start playing a sort of mind game. Do you ever do that, I mean when you're bored – doing something you do all the time that you don't have to think about —you know, some kind of a game in your mind to liven things up a bit?

Anyway, going back to my walking home from work – and I'm thinking – If the bus passes me before I get home, I'll get stuck wherever it passes me – no rushing or anything – just walking normally.

So I'm playing this game about the bus passing me. I'm almost home. The bus passes me – okay – so game over and I keep on going home – but I can't.

I'm in front of this house, I'm trying to keep going – but I can't. There's some kind of an invisible wall. I can't get past it. So I go back, try to retrace my steps but when I do there's another invisible wall at the other end of the sidewalk in front of the house. I try to step off the curb. I can't do that either.

The only place I can go is to knock on the door of the house and hope they let me in. It's the end of November. It's getting pretty chilly.

I can see this young couple through the window eating their dinner. I hate to interrupt them but... I ring their bell. This young fellow comes and answers the door. I try to explain to him what happened. I tell him I live in the apartment building next door...he just cuts me off, tells me to go home and shuts the door.

I let a few minutes go by. I ring the door again. Nothing else I could do. I was getting colder by the minute. He comes to the door again. He looks really irritated. I tell him, look, I'm sorry. I don't mean to interrupt your dinner but I'm really stuck. It's getting really cold out here. Could you please just call the police or an ambulance or someone who might know what to do.

So he lets me in. By then, my teeth are chattering. His wife sees that I'm really cold. She offers me some coffee. He goes off to make the call. She introduces herself. Her name is Candy, short for Candace. Her husband's name is Bob. He comes back. The cops will be here in a few minutes. Before you know it, the doorbell rings.

Bob opens the door. A policeman and his partner, a woman, are standing there. They come in. They want to know what the problem is. They ask for some ID, my address. I tell them I live next door but that I can't go there because I'm stuck. They ignore that. They tell me to just come along with them. They'll escort me home. I wasn't going to say no. Maybe this wall thing doesn't work when the police are involved.

We start out. We get to the sidewalk. We start walking to my building. We get to the invisible wall. They keep going, but I can't. I'm stuck at the wall.

They look back and tell me to stop resisting them. I tell them I can't get through. The policeman, Stansky's his name, says, "give me your hands," which I do. "I'll pull you. Officer Janis will push from behind." So that's what we do. Nothing. They keep pulling and pushing until I think my arms would be pulled out of their sockets. They finally realize it won't work.

They decide to try going in the other direction. Sure enough, we hit that invisible wall again. It happens again when they try taking me off the curb The only direction I can go in is to the house. Nothing to be done but have me stay in that house until they could figure out how to get me out.

That doesn't go over too well, especially with Candy. I can understand it. It's like having a witch in your house. So, Jansky offers to stay over. He'll sleep on the couch until the next morning.

So the next day comes. It's me and Officer Jansky. Candy and Bob have gone to work. Jansky tells me – first thing – he'll walk me around outside just to see if that wall is still there.

Frozen Women Flowing Thoughts

That's what we do. Nothing's changed. I'm still stuck.

Oh, boy. I'm supposed to be at my temp job again that day. How do I explain this to them?

Jansky thinks this is funny. "What are you going to tell them?" I give them some cockamamie story about a sore throat.

The next call is to Edith. my friend in my apartment building. How do I explain how I got myself in such a fix? But I need some things if this is going to last a while. She has the key to my apartment.

When I call her, I don't try to explain about the wall. I just say I'm staying with the people in this house – I would explain later. Could she please bring me some clothes and a few other things. She just can't understand it – I'm only one door away - why couldn't I just come home, pick them up myself? I finally have to say, "I just can't. Please do what I ask. I'll explain when you get here."

And if this keeps on I still have to explain it to my daughters – well, Margie anyway. Clarice isn't talking to me. I know how she'll take it though. There's sad, helpless mom, making jokes again.

The doorbell rings. It's Edith. You should have seen the shocked look on her face when she sees Jansky. She turns her back on him and whispers, "What did you do? Are you under arrest?"

No, I'm not under arrest.

Angie, this isn't real, she says. Is this candid camera?" She looks around "Am I supposed to smile or something?" Hey, Angie, this isn't one of those games you play?

Yeah, Angie, it is.

It takes some doing to convince her that I'm really stuck. It isn't some kind of gimmick.

Anyway, in the following days, the news gets around about this woman who is stuck – me – it's even on TV – lots of excitement, reporters, even a man in outer space gear to see if I was a threat to the country. That's a laugh.

And a visit from a social worker. Since I can't get to my temp work and I don't have much capital, the landlord wants to know how he's going to get paid. I guess the social worker doesn't read the papers because she doesn't know about my being stuck. She finally figures out that the best place to put me so that I could get benefits was as a disabled person. You could say that in a way, I am.

And then, of all things, a parapsychologist comes to see me - that maybe I'm psychic or have some strange powers that made this happen. Can you believe it? Sure, I get hunches about people that turn out to be right, but after you've lived for a while wouldn't you pick up on clues about people even without knowing it. Or, they might be people I've known from another lifetime. He really latched on to that.

You believe in reincarnation? Why not, I tell him. It's nice to think that since I didn't do much this time round, I get another chance the next time. But, you know, what if it turned out that in whatever time I lived, I was a misfit – sort of a time-travelling nebbish? Like, I've always wanted long, silken blond hair. What if I get my wish? What if I come back with this gorgeous hair – and everybody's bald? Anyway, he gives me a few mind-reading tests. I must have flunked because he didn't come back.

And then comes the psychiatrist. He wants to see if maybe something I'm doing or thinking is making this happen. I tell him about my mind games when I get bored, but how my life is generally okay. Not much to look forward to but I've got my health, a nice apartment and make enough to get by. Just every once in a while for a little excitement I take out my diamond tiara to give it some air. He doesn't laugh.

Frozen Women Flowing Thoughts

He asks if I like my job. It's temp work. It's okay. Pretty boring but it doesn't tie me down so I can take off whenever I want. The joke is that I don't take off because there's always something unexpected I need money for. Like a weekend at the Hilton. He doesn't laugh at that either.

And so he wanted to know if I always make jokes about my life. Sure, I said. Nobody likes a complainer.

Then he asked if there ever was anything that I wanted to do with my life that I didn't get to do? Yeah, I had this crazy notion that I wanted to be a writer. I even took a creative writing class at the Y. I would get these assignments. My husband would come home from work and he'd want to go to a movie. And say, he was the one working all day, bringing in the money, how was I going to say no, so we'd go to a movie and I wouldn't get to do my assignment and I started falling back. Finally, I just quit.

So he asks, where is your husband now? We're divorced. He didn't ask why but I could have told him it was nothing personal. Barry just didn't want to be married any more – at least, not to me. And then he says, You have time now, you could take a class online and get back to writing. Yeah, I could, but how do you do that? I don't have an idea in my head that I would write about. I've spent most of my life doing for other people, where I was second fiddle and now, I go into an office – a temp worker – and I'm invisible. I don't have a clue on how I can even think that I have anything to do or say that is even worth trying.

Anyway, Candy and Bob moved out. I wasn't going anywhere. They wanted their own place.

Edith doesn't come anymore.

Margie comes once in a while when she can get away.

And something weird is happening. The walls keep shifting. I can't walk around the sidewalk anymore and I can't go upstairs. Even the living room is getting smaller.

It's a good thing there's a john down here. It's a powder room, really.

Today someone was at the door. I couldn't open it. I tried calling out to them but they couldn't hear me. That's happened a few times now.

    (Pause)

Do you think I might be disappearing?

Negative Is, Negative Does
by Allston James

Setting: **English Pub, Aardvark's Tonsils**
Character: **Unnamed narrator**

Thank Christ and the devil, I awake.

The Covid rain is coming down like ball bearings even though the sun shines bright and shiny as I duck into The Aardvark's Tonsils for first pint. Early, it is, but early is, early does, my first step-dad Airlanga Caniago liked to say regarding the considerable gravitational pull of a first pint in the A.M., especially on the outer edge of a nightmare.

I'll admit I am not in the finest of moods—having prayed serious as a widow, even in my sleep, all weeklong for a sign of some kind, a celestial signal to nudge me toward life-change action. Any action just so it be away from lost job, cracked molar, lost love—Samantha leaves me a one-sentence note to the effect no hard feelings, doll, but the flat is too confining for two pillow princesses. But lord have mercy, I say as I approach the bar, I be covid neg for the week.

Vax-Ine, on taps at Tonsils, nods. I am just settling upon my stool when through the open door I spy a very large frog on the opposite kerb, massive, lumpy and gray, like an escapee from a dreary-ass German fairy tale. And just behind him, creeping along is Miz Sandy Claws, Mrs. Milfred's jumbo calico, same-same, that copped honorable mention in Colchester Pride's Most Cantankerous Pussy event two years running. Now, the rain moving east, here is MSC going stealth-like on the amphibian as if she is auditioning for nature-show telly.

As Vax-Ine sets down my sweet stout, she sees what I am seeing. She comes from around the bar and slides a palm down the inside back of my jeans as she is wont to do, the tip of an indigo-nailed index finger resting on the crease of my glutes, and then places a chaste kiss upon my cheek. A girl like me likes a girl like Vax-Ine. Still neg-a-tory, as well, she reports. Our eyes are fixed on the street.

After taking all care, the calico pussy, all asshole and claws now, is righteously upon the thick amphib and I swear to Saint Erzulie Vantor, the feline simply disappears him, swallows him whole, taking him down the gullet sure as Jonah's whale, or non-Biblically speaking, sure as Mathew Cartright III can be observed to manage on the odd night in The White Swallow's backroom just around the corner.

Sandy Claws sits down on the cement and begins licking a fat paw when all of a sudden Miz Claws bounces once, then twice, metre-high into the sunlight. Then a third time, high as you please.

"Well, *she's* sure screwed," says Vax-Ine, no mean stranger to unforeseeable capers. Then a fresh bounce, a higher more violent arc launching calico Sandy directly into Mason Street on the path of a Guinness lorry, the tableaux doing a stage-right exit past our doorway's frame of reference, said pussy now well up a wheel-well, all in all putting a seal on my morning and signaling a largish imperative.

I sleep, absent nightmare, for the first time since birth.

Frozen Women Flowing Thoughts

The following morn, day one as it goes in the Year of the Cat, I decamp from Colchester and move straight away back to Indonesia, where my baby sister Amabarita has in a noontime voice message evening before, said that her band could use my bass guitar skills, limited in the extreme, at Surabaya Pride, a thing thus far existing only on paper, but a *'rally really ready,'* she sang to my mobile in broken English rainbow cheer. *'Rally really ready,'* she shrilled. *'Rally really ready,'* she cried.

The time to go home is when it is time to go home. And me, I am gone by half past two on the late-July afternoon in England, green and pleasant land, county of Essex, fourth long summer of the pandemic.

An Anthology

TEARING OUT MY HAIR:
and other ways to deal with life
by Moriah Joy

Setting: Standard Office
Character: Kia

KIA works as an office assistant, standard desk job. She's sitting at a desk typing or writing something she appears to be talking to herself when the monologue starts but then is revealed to be talking to the documentarian.

You work in this kind of environment and you'll see all sorts of things. I thought when I got this job it'd be a nice easy going office job. Some days are like that but more often than not it's a chess game. The only problem was I didn't know I was playing the game until it had already started. The first time I noticed it was when I came in with straight hair. Susan from accounting came in and offered her typical, "Good Morning" and then when she laid her eyes upon me it took her a moment to recognize who I was. I actually saw her do a double take like someone had broken in and taken my desk. Then as if I was watching everything like I was in Get Out, she goes-

(The following dilogue is said in slow motion as KIA mimes "Susan" reaching for her hair.)

"Your hair is so pretty like this. I wish I could get my hair to look like this."

Frozen Women Flowing Thoughts

(Before "Susan" has a hance to reach for her
hair, KIA swats her hand away.)

Oooh! What I would've given to actually smack her hand away. Like I thought we were past all this nonsense. We're not five year olds on the playground. Why can you not keep your hands to yourself? Oh and of course, I can't say anything to anyone about it because no matter how many times HR or management say they want you to come to them if you have issues, I look like the bad guy. I'm the one who's "hard to work with." Try telling that to your clients who love me. Some of them even bring me Christmas cards and presents. That's love right there.

Ever since that day, I've seen it creep in here and there so I've just had to put my walls up. Can only let people in so much when you can tell that they always think of you as a box to tick on their "I'm not a racist because xyz" list. I've almost turned it into a game by now after working here for so long. I like to call it, "What are the White People going to learn today?"

My favorite day I played this was the day I brought Indian food for lunch. Chelsea came into the break room and I could tell she had never smelled curry before in her life. So in trying to make conversation without being too obvious about it she says, "Mhmmm, what have you got there? It smells... different." "It's curry, do you want to try some?" "Oh no, I don't want to eat your lunch." "Oh, come on. You've got to try this curry. It's the best in town." "Alright, maybe one bite." When I tell you, her face turned so red from the heat, I thought we were gonna have to call the fire department.

I really try to find the good in being here but the truth is it's just a job. I should be able to compartmentalize but there's this burning feeling that sinks into my gut that I can't shake. It reminds me that I've been working here for five years and barely gotten a cost of living raise. But I know for a fact, that Chelsea has had no problem getting a raise even though for the first two years I was here, guess who was doing most of her work.

I have had to fight for everything I have in this world. Every day, every breath has not been gifted to me, it has been earned. When I decided I wanted to go to college, I didn't have a trust fund to rely on. And I have so much student debt my eyeballs hurt. Go to college, they said. It'll help prepare you for the real world. Ha. The only thing that college does is make people feel bad for being something they're not. Not rich enough, not cool enough, not smart enough, not having the right major. And don't get me started on the kids where their parents pay for everything and so they just dick around. "C's get degrees." Bullshit.I worked my ass off to get through college and I feel like I did everything right and I'm still drowning.

I was under the belief that if I got a degree in something I could build a career off of it, got lots of scholarships to help chip away at the cost of school, then I'd be good as gold. But no. Here I am making the equivalent of mortgage payments every month on an education that employers don't actually care about or use against me. Then when I do get hired somewhere, I'm severely overutilized and underpaid.

Why am I not allowed to do just my job? I could be focused on helping management take on tasks and organize everything, really be a motivator but no. Instead I get to read all the thousands of emails that come through about how people don't know how to do the basic duties of their job and get yelled at by their customers for things that aren't my fault and I can't control. There's so much unnecessary bullshit here and I'm trying my best to be organized and overcome but I just feel like I'm being pulled under a tidal wave with lethal rip currents. I hate this job. I'm tired of the passive aggressive tone that seeps into every conversation, like my existence is exhausting to them.

OH but my favorite part. MY ABSOLUTE FAVORITE PART!!! is having to put on my "white voice" to make everyone in the office comfortable. I can't get upset when they start talking about going to pro-white rallies, I can't lose my cool so the rage I have sits deep inside but comes in bubbles at the surface and I have to hold it down. But I can't. It comes through hot tears trickling down my face. Knowing that the only reason I'm here is because I'm the diversity hire. Not because I'm valued for what I can bring to the table. But because I'm the first thing they see when they come through the door and the image that portrays. So I have to keep my cool, can't lose it, can't falter. It sends the wrong kind of message that I'm weak. But I'm not. I'm so much stronger than people will ever know because they don't feel the weight of the world on their back every day. I do.

Black Joy
by M. Kamara

Setting: Here and Now.
Character: Katherine

Katherine explores what being Black means to her.
/ indicates that those lines are said at the same time; italics indicate singing

KATHERINE

It happens a lot. You show up to the function with homemade akara, bust out some legwork, and boom! You're Nigerian...sometimes, Ghanian. But me - I'm Sierra Leonean. The way I see it - well, you gotta get the full picture first to see it the way I see it. Both my Mom and Dad are from Sierra Leone, land of the Lion Mountains, Salone to the those who hold her dear.

(in Krio; to tune of Sierra Leonean National Anthem)
Sing bot yu gudnem, O netiv land.
(back to English)

I'm the first one in my line to be born and raised in America and so I think of it as home. Sometimes. It's the kind of home where you're not allowed to take your shoes off when you come in, and none of the pillows are soft, and there's always a strange smell in the air. Like you know how when you get used to your own house you don't smell it anymore?

Frozen Women Flowing Thoughts

"Star Spangled Banner" plays.

VOICE (O.S.)
And the rocket's red glare, the bomb bursting in air, Gave proof -

KATHERINE
I also think of Salone as home – I still got people there, both my grandparents are buried there. Sure I've never been and I don't really speak Krio, but I understand everything my mom say s. Even when she thinks I don't. I know the national anthem -
    (in Krio; to tune of Sierra Leonean National Anthem)
Wan we ge fet we de gi sens, Wan we ge zil we no de taya
    (back to English)
And every April 27 I don my best country cloth, wave my green, white, and blue flag, and party like there's no tomorrow. We did it! Salone is free!
    (in Krio; to tune of Sierra Leonean National Anthem)
Den il en den vali de ansa wi bak; Blesin en pis go de fo yu o; Land we wi lek, wi yon Salon.
    (back to English)
So I think I have some claim to it, right?

    A beat. KATHERINE considers her claim, then
    brushes the thought aside.

KATHERINE
My Mom and Dad both have good British Christian names cause of the whole divide and destroy Africa thing. M y mom's mom – my Titi – was raised Muslim and my mom's dad – who I never met so in my mind he's just Grandpa – was raised Christian. See there's this thing among Sierra Leoneans that goes if you ever meet someone raised both Muslim and Christian, they're Sierra Leonean – we got a reputation of mixing religions and being cool with it. It's a reputation that only exists among Sierra Leonean's but it's there. No one really knows what or where Sierra Leone is. One time I got asked if it was next to Haiti. HAITI! As in the one in the Caribbean which is not near West Africa. As a kid this wrecked me! Cause it wasn't like I was from one of the well-known foreign countries. Like nowadays

someone brings up jollof and people immediately think of Nigeria or Ghana. Watching one of the long distance races at the summer Olympics? Kenya! Which African country was never colonized? Ethiopia – and they will never let us forget it! First time I heard a person reference Sierra Leone was Frank Ocean so now when I say I'm Sierra Leonean I get met with

    (singing to the tune of "Sierra Leone" by Frank Ocean)
Sierra Leone.

                        (back to talking)
And no I didn't forget about Kanye's "Diamonds from Sierra Leone" that one just doesn't name us in the song so no lyrics for people to sing back to me. And I'm not mad about people singing Sierra Leone at me, it's just to show that outside of tiny coastal Salone we're nothing. So now think of little ole me being raised in the middle of white man's town America –

> A SEA OF VOICES offstage say the pledge. KATHERINE starts with them, holding her hand over her heart, but soon removes her hand and stops completely.

SEA OF VOICES
/"I pledge allegiance to the flag of the United States of America, and to the republic for which it stands, one nation under God, indivisible, with liberty and justice for all."/

KATHERINE
/"I pledge allegiance to the flag of the United States -"/

KATHERINE
With a good ole British Christian first name and a last name that's foreign that nobody can place because nobody knows anything about us and so it's often placed as white – I have no idea why! – so Miss-Mr.-Mrs. So-and-So teacher who looks nothing like me is expecting a hand that looks like them to shoot up and instead it's me.

> "Star Spangled Banner" plays.

Frozen Women Flowing Thoughts

VOICE (O.S.)
No refuge could save the hireling and slave from the terror of flight or the gloom of the grave, and the star-spangled banner in triumph doth wave O'er the land of the free and the home of the brave.

KATHERINE
And for a while that wrecked me too. Not knowing the language and the pillows are never soft and I call a country home that I've never laid my feet on and my hand was always the wrong color.

> KATHERINE ponders her place in this world, then pushes the thought aside.

KATHERINE
But then, in the middle of white man's town America, I meet the few other Black people that went to that school and we got each other K through 12 and beyond because Black is Black no matter where you go - at least that's how we saw it. Cause while my mom was making jollof, one person's mom was making jambalaya, another's was making red beans and rice or peas and rice depending on who you talking to. My Black is their Black is our Black. And ain't that something beautiful? Like how my Titi kept an elephant statue in each room of our house to bring us strength and wisdom and when I go over to my Black American or Afro-Latine friends' houses they got statues of animals in every room to bring they family whatever they family need in that moment. That's really the way I see it - that when I'm feeling like my Black ain't the right kind, I'm wonderfully reminded that to be Black is to take what you got and remix that shit and no matter where you are in the world another Black person will look at you and be proud of what you've done.

Big Bold and Beautiful
by JM Lahr

Setting: Anwhere in modern times where a woman is often told she is not good enough as she is.
Character: Mary

Big Girls need love too. I have always been big. bad and beautiful! When I was a kid, my mom would always tell me to make sure I learned how to cook and clean. You're a big girl, you better bring something to the table. If you can't be beautiful, you better be useful if you want a husband. I didn't say anything, but I always wondered why I wasn't beautiful. I have a pretty smile. I'm a good person. Shouldn't that be enough. As I got older and went to school, I found out what my mother meant. I got called names. Big fat Mary. Wide load, they had a nickname for me. Beast. I went home and cried a lot. Then puberty came. That was rough. My friends were getting all of these boys fighting over them and here I was still getting insults thrown at me. I wanted to drop out of school. Why am I not beautiful. No. I'm not a cheerleader. Now don't think it was easy. I was still self-conscious, I still cried myself to sleep most nights, but hey, fake it till you make it. It is hard to find size 22 clothes that aren't frumpy or too loud. Why do they think fat girls want to wear bright pink or leopard print? Most fat girls realize that they are fat and are trying to minimize that fact. They aren't trying to draw unnecessary attention to themselves by wearing obnoxious clothes announcing hold on, fat girl entering the room. don't get me wrong, it was not easy finding flattering clothes for a big girl. I would go from store to store

Frozen Women Flowing Thoughts

searching. Finding a top here, a skirt there, driving an hour to find a good prom dress. It was disheartening finding something in your size and trying it on just to find out it did not look as good on as it did on the rack. It was not easy for me to get the stares, the laughs and the dirty looks as I brought my outfits back to the fitting room. It definitely was not easy to look at myself in a full-length mirror. But what I realized was, I am not the only girl that has to deal with this. Every girl has had a good cry in the dressing room. Every girl has that tightness in her chest when she's about to try on an outfit. Is it going to look good? Is this even going to fit? I did it though. You could say a lot of things, but you couldn't tell me I didn't look good. Yes, I went to prom. I had a good-looking date too. He went to another school, and he saw me hanging out at the park with my friends. He walked up to me and asked If I had a prom date. I asked him if he thought this was a joke. He seemed offended. He said that he liked big girls. He thought they were pretty and a hell of a lot more fun. I said you are right on both counts. Yeah, I'll go with you. My friend's jaws were on the floor when I turned around. He is so hot! Not, I can't believe he asked you out. No, I think he's making fun of you and he won't show up. They were just like damn, he's hot. Like a matter of fact. But I was thinking about it though. He did show up and we had a blast! It was making everybody angry that I went to school with that this high school football quarterback was going to prom with me and loving every minute of it. I know what you are thinking. Yes, I gave it up. He was hot! I had to. And he was so gentle when he took my clothes off. He said, let me just look at you for a minute. You are so beautiful! I had never thought someone would see me as beautiful. Yes, I did know I was beautiful, but I always secretly wonder if someone else would know that too. We dated all summer and then we went our separate ways. I remember sometimes thinking, fuck you mom, I found someone who didn't care if I could cook or clean. So, I was 18 and empowered. I knew that there were men who wouldn't settle for me but line up to be with me. I have dated all kinds of men. Big, tall, short, fat, skinny. They were all beautiful to me. I knew what it was like to be judged on the outside, I was not going to do that to somebody else. So yes, big girls need love too. And you should go out and get it. As often as you can, as much as you would like. Not just big girls. Don't let anybody tell you what you can or can't be. You just be you and the world will follow. Baby, they can get on the bus, or they can fuck walk. Don't settle and no one will settle for you. Now there are so many stores that cater just to us big beautiful and bad ladies. Now I don't have to go to five stores to find one clothing item. I can find amazing clothes just by going to one or two. Like any other woman. I take care of myself. I eat right, I exercise. I'm still a big girl, but I am not unhealthy. Many of us aren't unhealthy. There are plus size models who look amazing, there are plus size women who are Oscar winners. We are big bad and beautiful. Even if you are not a size 22, you still are big, bad and beautiful. If you want to be.

I Hate Depression Screenings from Waiting for the GYN
by Helen Cheng Mao

Setting: *OG/Gyn waiting room*
Character: *NANCY, female, age 50*

Nancy explains why she finds depression screenings useless to her.

Augh, I hate filling out these multiple-choice depression screening forms. They leave you no space for explaining your answers. [*sees audience's puzzlement*] What do I mean?

Take this question for example: "Over the past two weeks, how often have you been feeling down, depressed, or hopeless?". The answer choices are: "Not at all", "Several days", "More than half the days", and "Nearly every day". If I were to answer this question honestly, I'd pick the choice "Nearly every day" because my father just died and I'm settling his estate while caring for an angry mom with dementia and two ornery teenagers.

[*Beat*] But how could you have known all this? I hadn't told you anything. So see my point? There's no room here for me to write all this down. If I answer every question truthfully, I'll probably be told I'm depressed. That may be true, but this screening doesn't consider what's going on in my life or address why I'm feeling depressed.

Okay, let's use another person as an example. Take a young mother of an infant and two toddlers. Suppose she were asked, "Over the past two weeks, how often have you been feeling tired or having little energy?". What if she picked the answer choice "Nearly every day"? She might be told she's depressed…but what do you expect from someone wrangling three kids under age four?

So how accurate is this depression screening, really?

There's <u>clinical depression</u> and there's <u>situational depression</u>, which I probably have given my current challenging life circumstances. But if I took this screening at a different time under better circumstances, would I feel and answer the same way?

Anyway, how can any depression treatment help me? No therapy or medication can bring my father back or cure my mother.

On the Greenbelt
by Karissa Murrell Meyers

Setting: The Greenbelt on the bank of the Boise River
Character: Jules

early 30's, she/her. Sarcastic, hardened, wounded, would rather self-medicate or run from pain than face it. Pansexual but hasn't fully "come out" yet. Works as a barista.

> JULES stands on the bank of the river,
> holding her mother's ashes.

JULES
….okay, well –
Mom, uh…well, she was always a lot of fun.
Growing up with her was kind of chaotic all the time, but we were never bored. One time she told the school Jake and I were sick so we could have our own personal snow day. We drove up to McCall and went sledding in an almost blizzard, it was awesome. She used to say, "life is for living, not sittin' on your butt!" and she would show us her scars and tell us these amazing stories about where they came from.
Biking through the Outback.
That time she fought off a wolverine with a rake.
She called her scars a map of her adventures, remember that?
You just seemed bulletproof, Mom - like you could take leaps even if you didn't know where you were gonna land.
And I loved that about you. I always wished I could be like that.

There is so much I felt like I couldn't tell you, and I wish I had. I couldn't even tell you how relieved I was when I got kicked off the volleyball team in high school because I secretly hated the sport, even though you and Jake loved it.

I just - all I ever wanted was for you to be proud of me, and I was so scared to tell you who I really was and what I really wanted because what if, WHAT IF you didn't approve and then I lost your love because of it?

Or maybe I wouldn't have, I guess I'll never know.

But I do know that she wanted us to live.

You wanted me to live.

So, even if it's scary, and even if it hurts, I want a map of my own adventures.

The Love of my Previous Life
by Elena Naskova

Setting: Empty Stage
Character: Emma

EMMA

I couldn't sleep last night. Maybe it was the bottle of wine that I opened after you went to bed. I was going for a little buzz to help me fall asleep ... but ... I didn't stop drinking soon enough. The bottle was empty before I remembered to pay attention. My mind went somewhere far away, and it returned to me, too late. So when I finally went to bed, my head was banging, instead of buzzing. You were sound asleep. I could hear you breathe next to me, and like almost always, completely oblivious of what I was going through. I tried to lay still and ignore the banging in my head, but I couldn't. So I sat up and turned on the nightstand lamp. You didn't budge. You were where you were, and you weren't going to join my drunken party. But you were the only one there, and right next to me, so I ... watched you sleep. And as I watched you sleep, I started wondering, 'Who's this man sleeping next to me?' The more I stared at you, the more I felt like I had no idea who you were. When I was just about to start panicking, a weak voice in my drunken head spoke to me: 'He's the love of your life', the voice said. 'Oh yeah', I thought, 'this man is ... was ... is ... the love of my ... previous life'. The life that is no more. The man is still here, the bed is still here, and the room and the house ... everything is still here, but ... it does not belong to ... this life of mine. ... anymore.

(pause)

I jumped out of bed alarmed and started searching for anything that belonged to my current life. I checked my closet. My closet too was full of things from my previous life. Dresses, skirts, high heels, tops, bras, business suits. Things that I haven't put it on for a long, long time. I felt as if I was going through a dead woman's closet. I quickly left the bedroom and walked around the house, disoriented. As I walked into the kitchen, I approached the recycling bin and opened it. There it was, the empty wine bottle. I picked it up and held it, asking myself: 'Is this empty bottle the only thing in this house that belongs to my current life?'

(pause)

I put the wine bottle back in the recycling bin. 'Tonight there will be more empty bottles in the bin', I thought, and that thought terrified me and made my skin crawl and my stomach cramp.

(pause)

A sudden urge to flee overwhelmed me. An unbearable urge to run away, and leave behind the sleeping man in the bedroom, the empty bottle in the recycling bin, and all the wine bottles that are yet to be finished alone. Run away, but where to? What is there but the present and the past? I asked myself.

(pause)

'Just run away, no matter where?' And there in that question was the answer, and that was that. I went back to the bedroom, I scooped my clothes from the floor and put them back on. As I was grabbing my purse, I wondered, 'Is this all that I need?' My passport came to my mind. 'My passport? Do I need a passport to where I'm going?'. I dug out my passport and my reading glasses too ... and ... as a little act of kindness, I wrote 'Sorry and goodbye' on a piece of paper that I found on the kitchen table, ... and ... I walked out of my life into the vast nothingness.

She Got the Movie
by Dorian Palumbo

Setting: A seedy apartment, somewhere in West Hollywood. Lots of light, not much in the way of furniture

Character: Viviana Burgos, early 30's, standup-turned-actress

Sweet, until she's not, and kind, until and unless you cross her, at which point she'll mock you without mercy. When she says she's your best friend, she means it.

>Enter Viviana, 30's, Latina, She's carrying a plastic bag with a bottle of wine inside.

VIVIANA
I brought champagne. Because we're celebrating. You remember when I had to go to the Warner lot last week? I got the movie.

>Viviana pulls a bottle of cheap champagne out of the bag and shows it off.

VIVIANA
I got the movie, Marcus. I'm gonna be in a movie with Viola Davis and Denzel Washington. How amazing is that? It's amazing, don't you think so? Do you have any clean glasses in here? I mean, I guess we can just drink out of the bottle like maniacs too, right?

An Anthology

   Viviana starts peeling the paper off the neck of the bottle.

You know, at first I just thought, well, why should I invest any energy hoping for this, you know, I've never been in a real movie before, I've just been in, you know, indie stuff back in Austin a million years ago, and, like you always say, life gives you this "Here, kitty kitty" and then you fall for it and start hoping for it and then nothing actually happens. Right? Especially actors, 'coz you audition your ass off and then its just "no" and "no" and more "no."

Oh, and I forgot to tell you, this is so good, when I was coming out of the callback I saw Selena Gomez going in after me, and I thought, well, she and I are the same type, so, obviously I'm not gonna get it if Selena Gomez is-
      (Beat)
Markie, I'm going to be in a movie. With Viola Davis and Denzel Washington. It's a greenlit movie. I booked a job, Markie. I'm playing Denzel's daughter, Markie, I'm going to have scenes with him.

We start shooting in Vancouver on the 10th. Look, what the hell is wrong with you? This is the best news I've gotten in my whole life. Markie, this is a big deal, are you not happy for me? I mean, I know we talk about it all the time, how hard it is to be happy for other people, but this is me, this is my life, don't you care? Am I not your friend all of a sudden, Jesus Christ. Markie, you can't just treat me like other people. After eight years.

After eight years, really? That's what I am to you? Other people? Do other people stay on the phone with you for two hours at three in the morning because you're bored working at Ticketmaster? Do other people let you stay on her couch for two weeks because Gerard was cheating on you with that pendeja who worked for the travel agency? Do other people go with you all the way out to the fucking Ozarks to pretend to be your girlfriend just so your great-grandma can think you have a girlfriend? A sane person would have said "no" to that last thing at least, but I didn't. Because you asked me.

Frozen Women Flowing Thoughts

Was it just easier to be friends with me when my life was crap? Just one episode after another of trying to do stuff and never getting to really do it? That was okay with you, right, but this, this Viviana who actually gets to be an actor, is suddenly not your friend?

(Beat)

You know, I didn't even call my Mom yet to tell her. You were the first person I wanted to tell. I guess I'm an idiot.

Viviana exits

An Anthology

The Annual Staff Retreat
by Jass Richards

Setting: open
Character: Brett

Brett has just been hired as a relief worker at a halfway house run by the Mental Health Association.

    Unfortunately, it turned out I was hired just in time for the annual staff retreat. I suspected it was an office party disaster waiting to happen. I didn't want to go. But I also didn't want to be reprimanded, yet again, for not being a team player. Damned if I do, damned if I don't.
    So Friday evening, six of us piled into Kathy's minivan. We were obviously going to get a headstart on the group bonding thing. I asked if that was fair. They smiled indulgently and said, "Oh you just want to drive down on that new Harley of yours instead of being with us." Well yeah. Duh.
    We arrived at the retreat site, which was well off the highway, and for a second I was glad I came – it was beautiful. Forest as far as the eye could see, in orange and gold and scarlet, a sparkling dark blue lake, a couple canoes on the shore, gentle babbling from a stream that fed the lake… We spent the entire next two days inside. Replenishing our inner spirits.
    Saturday began with a pre-breakfast yoga session, a breakfast get-to-know-you, two morning sessions, and a lunch mixer. So I was told. I don't get up until noon. (Well, unless I work the midnight

Frozen Women Flowing Thoughts

shift. Then I don't go to bed until noon. Which means that on any given day, or, well, on any given night I guess – oh never mind.)

At around 1:00 p.m., I found myself being hustled to the first of three afternoon sessions by one of my coworkers, Clara. Who was way too chirpy. Obviously a morning person. I grabbed a carafe of coffee and a cup from the lunch table as we passed it, and stuffed some creamers and a plastic-wrapped egg salad sandwich into my pocket. She led me into a roomful of people, and to the corner occupied by the 602 staff.

"Hello again," the session leader at the front of the room said, and beamed. "Wasn't that a fantastic lunch?" she asked, and everyone applauded. Applause? For egg salad? Plastic-wrapped egg salad? I looked around. A lot of people looked suspiciously beatific. Did I miss something spectacular? Were the leaders that charismatic? No wait, I've seen that look – they're fucking all on Prozac! I missed the free samples!

"What we're going to do first this afternoon," she continued as if she were about to present a won-der-ful gift, "is something called 'What Colour are You?'" You've got to be kidding. I had finished my first cup of coffee and had poured a second, but was still way too tired to run through my Meyers-Briggs critique, and anyway these people should know better, this is all so old, and lame, " – but with a little twist." Her eyes twinkled. Mine twitched. "I want you to think about what colour each of your coworkers is. Then we'll have you pow-wow in your work groups to share your perceptions. Be open. Be honest. Remember, those are the building blocks of a good team..." Yeah right. Like I'm gonna fall for <u>that</u> again. (When did you stop hitting your wife?) Director Jean, you're airhead blue. Kathy, you're – oh my god. They're <u>all</u> airhead blue.

"I'm going to pass on this one," I said, "I really haven't had time to get to know any of you," I tried to smile. "And I really have to pee," I pointed to the carafe.

When I returned to the room, I discovered that things could indeed get worse. Each session ended with a group hug. I looked around. Surely they don't have enough Academy Awards on hand to cover this performance.

The next session was a 'revitalizer'. Up on our feet, stretch up, that's it, one arm, skyreach, the other arm, skyreach, now climb that ladder into the clouds – I can't believe I'm doing this. I imagined myself presenting these warm-ups to my old track buddies, started to laugh, caught Clara's glance, then imagined myself packing it in right then and there and going for a long run through the forest. That's it, now exhale, and blow those clouds away! Good! Now stand on one leg and lift the other, from the hip, that's it, how do you feel?

"Like a dog taking a piss." Oops. Jean gave me a look of disappointment. As did Kathy, Clara, and Lynn.

And then it was time for another group hug.

Cat Lady
by Chloe Selavka

Setting: An apartment somewhere in a city somewhere. Not New York, or Boston. Maybe Providence? Seattle? Somewhere that is somewhere but not the center of the universe.
Character: Honey (36)

Honey copes with what it is to be a woman, a queer one who likes theater, at that, while cleaning up cat puke.

[*Low lights up. HONEY enters. Sighs. She flicks on the lights, kicks off her shoes and drops her bag. She walks forward, probably to scream or drop herself down on the couch but stops short when she sees the rug. Cat puke. The kind that you can't just scoop up. It's permeating the carpet. The NEW carpet. God. FUCKING. dammit.*]
HONEY
SHIT. FUCK me. SHIT.
[*She exits and re-enters with cleaning supplies.*]
BALLS. ASS. FUCK! Cunting, mother, shitting me right now.
  [*She continues swearing (actors choice, get creative. Make your grandmother turn in her grave, or in her bed, I won't make any assumptions about your grandmother's relationship with life. Just, make MY grandmother turn in her grave, if that's easier). She sets down the supplies. She sets down herself. She takes a deep breath, stops swearing, and begins to scrub, vigorously.*]
HONEY

Ungrateful witches.

[*Beat. She looks at the audience.*]

My family started warning me about the adverse effects of becoming a crazy cat lady when I was 15 years old. [*beat*] They said I had too much ahead of me. [*beat*] I wanted to be an actress then. I'd been in one high school production, but I had too much ahead of me. [*beat*] Honestly, I peed myself onstage. I had, at most, a failed community theater career ahead of me. [*beat*] I don't really think it was about the cats. I never liked cats. [*beat*] I think they were just telling me not to become an unmarried spinster. [*beat*] Or worse. A lesbian. [*beat*] I had too much ahead of me to become a lesbian. Too much what? Disappointing straight people sex? [*beat. Vigorous scrubbing*] I had begun to amass a disturbing amount of cardigans, I guess. [*beat*] Unsurprisingly, this advice did not guide me away from the path of homosexuality. [*beat*] The cats aren't mine, though. Just, for the record.

Crazy. Cat. Lady. What does that even mean? Crazy for cats? The cats make you crazy? You're already crazy and you begin to attract and amass cats? You know, I don't like the word crazy. In reference to a person, I mean. A woman, actually. People use it too much in reference to women who aren't crazy. To women completely justified in their actions. I'm sorry, you know what, that was a generalization. Not all people do that. [*beat*] Men. MEN use the term crazy like it's interchangeable with straight jacket insanity when they don't want to own up to the fact that they suck.

You know, my first and only boyfriend, Adam, I dated him when I was in that show. That show that supposedly put so much ahead of me. He helped me memorize all my lines, and it was Shakespeare, so he gets some credit for that. Not as much credit as I get for memorizing it, but, still. And, you know, he came to opening night, the night, coincidentally, I pissed myself on stage because I was so nervous, and he A) didn't bring me flowers. And B) When I told Adam, in secrecy, I had pissed myself walking onstage to deliver the monologue he knew I had stayed up night after night reviewing and forgetting and stumbling over, when I told him that my underwear were frankly, very uncomfortable to be in, he did not console me, or even at least, keep his disturbingly large mouth shut. That prepubescent ass LAUGHED at me and then TOLD HIS FRIENDS, who proceeded to tell everyone, and I became fondly known to all as "Puddles".

Frozen Women Flowing Thoughts

And when I told him I was angry, when I began to cry after the **dean of students** referred to me as Puddles, he told me I was acting crazy. Acting CRAZY? Would you like to see me act crazy, Adam? I'll give it my best shot. I could tell everyone to call you Floppy, for reasons I won't disclose as to not bruise your ego. Or, do you think Tiny suits you better? OR, in a homewrecking twist of fate, I could sleep with your surprisingly built divorced mother. She could tell me all about your birth. The damage it did to every part of her. I could become well acquainted with that damage. And then, I could come back to you, fake an orgasm, and shout her name instead of yours. [*long beat*]

I'm not saying I've thought about what I'd do if I were to act in a way that actually <u>earned</u> the classifier "crazy". I'm just saying, I could do worse than crying. Much worse. Most women can. Most women know crazy like the back of our hands, but you know, by a different name. [*beat*] Existence.

Anyway. Adam broke up with me after I shouted his sister's name during sex with him, and I realized that straight girls don't hook up with their boyfriend's sister. Adam and I have bad blood now. Because of the Puddles thing. And the cunnilingus with his sister. Thing. Not that we talk often. It's been fifteen years. But I'm pretty sure that my bridges with Adam have been burned. Woe is fuckin me.

[*Beat. The stain is coming up now. She moves to dabbing lightly.*]

I was actually in acting classes for a long time after that. Like yeah, I pissed myself, but I think that shows a certain commitment to the craft. That's what my mom said. She was desperate for me to have a passion that wasn't googling "girls kissing" on the family computer. I wasn't half bad. I've played half your favorite Shakespeare heroines. Absolutely devoured Lady Mac. My acting teacher, she was this crotchety old lady and smelled like this rancid mix of moth balls and sweat and she wore water shoes indoors, she said to me that "death became me" like murder made my skin glow or something like I was this succubus. I think she might have been high when she said that but it stuck with me. Is that why I look so tired all the time now? My skin care regimen is missing retinol and… bloodshed?

The point is, now, I'm sitting on this rug scrubbing out what my cats chucked up, no, not my cats, my wife's cats, what my wife's cats

117

chucked up. This brand fucking new rug, first new thing I've bought in years, the first new piece of furniture I've bought since. Since. Since I moved out of my college apartment.

You know, I went to TARGET. I walked through the rows and I talked to an employee and I carried that damn thing to my car. This rug was expensive and nice and really all I had going for me. This rug is a woven interpretation of my will to live. And the most fucked up part of all of this is that I want to be pissed at the cats, or my wife for adopting the cats, but I can't, because the cats are all sick and old and near death and I can't blame them for their tendency to upchuck. If I was sick and old I would want to throw up everywhere too to grasp onto some form of control over my feeble, hairball filled life. And no, I can't find it in myself to curse out Bridget for her insistence on adopting the sickest, most near death, and honestly, ugly, creatures she can find. I should be angry at her, or the cats, I should be seething, but I'm not. All I can think as I scrub this cat puke out of my carpet is "out damned spot". It's playing on a loop. Out damned spot, out damned spot, out damned mother cunting spot. And that makes me angry, not at the cats, not at Bridget, not at Adam, that douche, and not even at the Target employee who guaranteed me this rug was stain proof. It makes me pissed at, of all people, my mother. Because in all her panic I would end up a lesbian, she made me into something even worse. A lesbian who enjoys theater.

Carhenge
by Samara Siskind

Setting: 3 miles north of Alliance, Nebraska.
Character: GWEN: female, thirties to forties. A mom looking to make memories.

A single parent on a road trip tries to corral and connect with her kids.

The time is now.

Lights rise on GWEN, fortyish, staring in awe at the beauty of the natural wonder that stands before her. She wears shorts, a tee shirt, some kind of cap or visor. Perhaps a fanny pack around her waist, but a cool one. Suddenly, her reverie is broken.

GWEN
LIAM, NOOOO!!! STOP STOP STOP! DON'T PUSH THAT!... BECAUSE IT COULD ALL FALL DOWN!! BECAUSE, BECAUSE SANTA'S WATCHING!...YES, EVEN IN JULY! Tess, a little help here?... TESS! REMOVE THE AIRPODS. TESS! *(Miming removing pods from ears)* AIRPODS! Thank you. Could you please just, grab your little brother before he-? What? What's with the face? Ugh, nevermind. LIAM, C'MERE!
GWEN bends down, speaking at the eye level of a little one.

Okay, Liam, here's what I want you to do. I want you to run a giant lap around this whole thing *(Miming perimeter with her finger).*

Yeah, yeah, as fast as you can. Totally, yes! You're an Avenger protecting it all, yeah! Okay, ready? On your mark, get set, GO! *(Beat)* Whew. That'll keep him busy for a hot minute. *(Back to taking in the view.)* So, Tess. This is it. What did I tell you? Amazing, huh?. . . What do you mean a big pile of junk? Are you kidding me? This is epic!. . . No, not Carhinge, Carhenge. It's an exact, to scale replica of Stonehenge. . . You know, Stonehenge. The monument. In England? Didn't you ever learn about it in school? . . . Uh, because it's one of the great ancient wonders of the world. . .Well, look it up on your phone. *(Beat)* Tess, c'mon, why can't you just- . . . Yes, yes I know you voted for the National Forest, but I wanted to stop here. Just give it a chance, okay?

GWEN unzips her fanny pack, taking out a touristy book or brochure type thing.

Here. I think there's a blurb in here somewhere. Let's see. . . *You don't have to travel to England to behold the wonder of Stonehenge when you can visit its quirky American cousin, Carhenge. The structure consists of 38 vintage American automobiles arranged in the same formation as the mystical Stonehenge. . .*

Wow. It says here it aligned with the solar eclipse in 2017. . . Tess?. . . Did you get any of that?. . . Can you just quit texting for a minute? Because, just look around you. Check out the scenery. . . What? No!. . . Because we just got here! Why do you have to be so- . . . Then fine! Fine! You know what, just go! Go sit in the car!! *(Beat, putting on a smile)* Yes Liam, yes I saw you! You were SO fast! Yes, they are all real cars. Cool, huh? Have some water. Hey, do you think you can do it again? Even faster? I dare you! Okay, one more lap and I'll let you eat all the M&M's in the trail mix. Alright, GO!

A few beats.

Look, I'm sorry. I know you'd rather be spending this summer with your friends, or with your Dad. Instead you're stuck here . . . with me. I get it. I just thought it would be a cool adventure. Like we used to take when you were small. The Three Musketeers, remember? With Liam strapped to my chest? This road trip was supposed to be special. Just us.

GWEN takes a seat on the ground.

Come. *(Pats spot next to her)* Come sit by me. *(Beat)* Y'know, your Grandpa brought me here once . . . I was about your age. . . Some random stop on a road trip to my Grandma's. Just him and me. I don't remember why Mom couldn't come. Anyway, you remember what a car geek Grandpa was. We just walked around in awe. Dad told me about each model, we picked out our favorites. Let's see, Dad's was . . . that one. The 1945 Jeep Willys. Mine was . . *(Shielding eyes from sun)* There. The Cadillac, with the fins. . . That one? That's a, hmm, Ford Thunderbird. That summer Dad taught me how to change a tire, check my oil. Yeah, we bonded a lot during that trip. . .Well, you know. Good question. It's. . .it's actually a memorial. This guy built it as a memorial to his father during a family reunion. Isn't that something? I wish we could've done something like that for Grandpa. *(Beat)* You know, it may not seem like it now, but you'll remember this one day. You'll remember that time Mom forced you to stop in the middle of nowhere in the Sandhills of Nebraska to see a bunch of cars stacked on top of one another. Liam probably won't. But you will. And you'll tell him about it, and you'll remember me. Just like I'm remembering Gramps right now. What's that Dr. Seuss quote? You never know the value of a moment, until it becomes a memory? . . .Something like that. . . Anyway.

GWEN stands, dusts herself off.

Where are you going?. . . *(Surprised, smiling)* No, no, sure. Yes. You should definitely get a few snaps. If you didn't take a picture, it didn't happen, right? I'm just impressed this place is cool enough to make it on your Instagram feed. We can totally get a selfie, with all of us. Yeah. I'd love that. *(Beat)* WHOA, LIAM! That was SO FAST! You are SO awesome, my man. . . Well, which one is your favorite? Tess likes the Thunderbird. . . Ahh, you like the Gremlin, huh? Good choice. *(Beat)* Hey guys, look. See there? That car on the top of the hill? We can all autograph it before we go. Leave a message for Grandpa. . .Who says we don't have a sharpie?

GWEN opens her fanny pack, producing a permanent marker.

Don't ever underestimate the power of Mom. Tell you what, I'll race you both up there. Whoever wins gets a pressed penny from the gift shop. *(She puts away Sharpie, zips up fanny pack and assumes a runner's stance)* Ready Musketeers? Okay. On your mark. . . get set. . . GO!

Eight Ways to Plead with a God
by Kanika Asavari Vaish

Setting: *Mount Darshan (DHAR-shun), a (fictitious) sacred mountain among the Himalayas. Based on the real-life Mount Kailash.*

Character: *AMAAL, W, 30s-40s. An undiscovered photojournalist striving to capture the first ascent of the mountain. Blunt, ambitious, independent.*

Synopsis of Play – Six tourists and a local climbing guide set out to summit a historically unsurmountable Himalayan mountain believed to be the abode of several Godly presences. As their physical limits, relationships to one another, and perceptions of reality are tested with each meter they climb, they must find a way to achieve their new collective goal: survival.

(Elsewhere on Mount Darshan.

The altitude ticker reads: **6,333 m / 20,778 ft**

Lights up on AMAAL trekking alone.

She slips, and falls, and gets back up.

She walks over the same part, and slips and falls again.

She gets back up.

She tries again.

When she falls this time, she stays down.

She closes her eyes and breathes for a moment.

She slowly sits up.)

AMAAL

If I were *really* scared for my life, maybe I would pray. To you.

But I don't need to.

This is fine. This is doable. This is where I'm meant to be.

Because I worked to get here. Me, not fate, or God, or anything like that.

It's easy to believe in fate and life after death and all of that when you practice a religion that is…I don't know…more palatable? To everyone else.

And it seems like all religion does is make people soft. Why do we need to believe in something bigger in order to get anything done?

This is why I have to go after things myself.

(A beat.)

Frozen Women Flowing Thoughts

Look, those guys were never going to make it. And the only guy who could just…called it off. Like that. Like none of us have anything else at stake.

I mean, yeah, it's not like…my daughter is dying. Or that I even have a daughter. But Maggie could have come with me. She's the only other one who seems like she can put up a good fight out here.

(A beat. She stands and looks to the sky.)

It's not like I don't believe in anything.

But it's hard to believe anything…anyone else…is out there. Looking out for us.

Mama believed. I mean, you know, she believed in you more than anyone…until it stopped being about hope and faith and strength. And more about giving everything we had to the mosque.

Because of *you*.

Do you see what you do to people?

None of that money was put to good use.

(A beat.)

But if you don't exist…then I guess it's not your fault?

I don't know.

(A beat. She sits.)

They all must think I'm selfish.

But I need this. I need this footage.

I left home for this.

Baba asked me if all of this was worth it. I told him I needed to share the world's stories. Our stories. He asked me why can't we just live in our story, why do I have to tell everyone else?

(She considers this.)

Maybe because so many people have the luxury not to hear anything. See anything.

I need them to know what they're missing out on. All those people, who are too comfortable to leave their homes. Or take a trip only to stay at the hotel, or spend money on expensive food, or treat the locals like shit.

Or make everything in their life about one thing.

Their worlds would become so much bigger, and they would become so much smaller…if they knew something like this was possible.

(A beat.)

And, more importantly, it's for the people who can't afford to do this.

I mean, look at this place. If a God were to exist anywhere, wouldn't it be here?

(She looks back up at the sky.)

Even if it is all made up. Everyone needs something. For me, *(holding her camera)* this was my hope.

Those people deserve to feel hope, too. And I can give it to them.

If I can just make back to the others. And not die.

Baba, if I see you again, I'm taking you with me next time.

And you'll see everything.

> (The same comforting sound of gentle wind chimes.
>
> TRISH, the snow leopard, appears.
>
> She begins to approach AMAAL, who does not back away.)

AMAAL

Ya Allah…

An Anthology

How to Not Die Horribly in a Fire
by Chloë Whitehorn

Setting: Anywhere someone might be proposed to
Character: Claire, a young woman engaged just a moment ago

Claire stands surrounded by rose petals staring at her left hand ring finger, making the engagement ring on her finger sparkle in the light. She has just been proposed to. She does not look enthusiastic.

Claire: My mother has slept with a platoon of men. I can't think of any context in which I would want to know that information. She told me this the day I lost my virginity to Zach. She took me to that ice cream store, 167 Flavors or whatever, and she started by saying "Claire, men are like ice cream." I thought this was going to be some sick mother-daughter fellatio lesson bonding moment, but it wasn't. It was worse. She started pointing to the different flavors of ice cream and naming them. The caramel crunch was Derek, sweet personality but way too sticky in a needy way. The peppermint was Hugh, cool and unsatisfying. When she got to the ice cream cake being her high school football team I intentionally gave myself brain freeze so I wouldn't have to hear anymore. I think my mom was trying to tell me I was young and I shouldn't get hung up on one person. I should experience the world. One hundred and sixty-seven times apparently.

After Zach, I went through a phase where I started going to night clubs every night and picking up. Different place every night. Well,

Frozen Women Flowing Thoughts

not at first, but after I went home with this one guy, Tom, he was an engineering student, the next night I went back to the same bar and he came up to me and was all sexy and stuff and I thought maybe the night before hadn't been a total disaster, 'cause here he was flirting with me again so hey... And I brought him home with me, and we're making out on my bed and he stops, and he looks at my duvet cover and he's like "I know this blanket". It was then that I realized that he didn't remember me. At all. Well, I'm sure he remembered that he'd had sex the night before, but he didn't realize it was with me. It was that night, lying in my own bed feeling out of place that I decided I wouldn't do that again. I don't mean him... that's obvious. It wasn't even good the first time. Let me tell you, practice does not make perfect 'cause, well, you don't need the details, but it was like leftovers.

Anyways.

I kept a book. I wanted to be able to remember, not remember ... ummm, keep track of, all the guys. Just 'cause I felt like I should you know. It was the responsible thing to do. I even bought some gold stars, you know for like a rating system. But I decided against that. Mostly because I couldn't decide what to base it on. That and when I cut the stars to make 1/2 stars they just stuck to the scissors. Turns out I didn't really need a book. I mean, I went out on plenty of dates... but they didn't all end well. Like this one guy Eva set me up with. We went to this party, one of his friends, having this great conversation... then out of nowhere, this girl, she was just sitting there real quiet the whole time, she absently says, kind of quietly—I only really heard her 'cause I was sitting next to her, she says "I don't want to be here" and she just stands up and walks into the kitchen. I'm like, whatever, and we continue talking. A few seconds later out of the corner of my eye I see her come out of the kitchen and go into the bathroom. And then I didn't see her for awhile. The conversation digresses into a discussion about tv so I wander into the kitchen to get another drink. I walk in and all the drawers are open, which is a little strange right? Not like poltergeisey strange, just not normal you know. And they have one of those wood blocks with the knives of various sizes in them and I notice that the middle knife is missing. So naturally I'm thinking... maybe something is up with quiet girl. I knock on the bathroom door. No response. And just like in the movies I gently push the door and it creaks open. So here's the thing about that knife. We used that knife to cut cheesecake with. It was the "cheesecake knife". That was its purpose. It was thin enough and wasn't serrated. When you use a thick knife, a lot of each slice of cheesecake ends up on the knife and then you have to smooch it off the knife and then it just doesn't look good on the plate. And if you use a serrated knife you waste a lot of the cheesecake too—you can't even lick it off or you'll cut your tongue. Anyways, so I push open the door and I totally expect to see her—God I don't even remember her name—completely expect to see her sitting on the floor with both arms hanging into the bathtub with her wrists slit and the knife covered in blood. Makes you realize how insignificant life is. Ending your life with a cheesecake knife. What I don't get is, if you are going to be considerate enough to bleed into the bathtub and not all over the floor, why not go all the way and be considerate enough to not kill yourself in someone else's bathroom?

So I'm opening the door and I'm thinking, I wonder if she thought to leave a note. You're supposed to leave a note. That's like a key ingredient. Except this one suicide pact I heard about. These two actors were in love, and I don't know the details of why they killed themselves. Maybe life was just too mundane for them. Anyway, they were in this very Baz Luhrman-esque adaptation of Romeo and Juliet and on the last night, the final performance, when the characters kills themselves, they actually did. Nobody even realized at first. Mostly because the rake of the audience was so bad you couldn't see anything that happened on the stage floor. So nobody noticed the blood seeping across the stage from Juliet's body. Not until the actor playing the prince slipped in it walking downstage for his curtain call. They didn't leave notes. But they did it in public so people actually saw them do it. That's kind of like a note. I mean they told people exactly what they were doing. "then I'll be brief. Oh happy dagger, this is thy sheath. There rest and let me die." And a suicide note written by William Shakespeare is pretty much the best explanation out there.

Frozen Women Flowing Thoughts

But she wasn't dead. She was on the toilet, and since I'd sort of expected to find her dead in the bathtub it took me a minute to collect myself and close the door. The rest of the night was pretty awkward.

So my book only has four entries. Well, three really. I counted Tom twice. The other one was Josh.

Ooh, good story...There was this guy my best friend Eva was into. He was an artist. Really huge paintings, the kind that take up your whole wall. You ever see one of those in somebody's house and stare at it, colors everywhere, real expression of something that you're sure is supposed to be deep and meaningful, and you're staring at it with this intense look of wonder and somebody walks by and says "oh yes, this is our PicassoGoghWarhol. Isn't is marvelous?! It's the only one of its kind. Martin went to the wall for that one. The artist's funding was getting pulled all because of some endangered rabbits the government said were being threatened by the artist's process... You know he spent fifty-three days in a trench listening to recordings of bomb testing in Bikini Atoll before he even lifted up a paintbrush for this series." And all you're really wondering is... how did they get this enormous painting through that little door?

So this guy, what was his name? It was some real pretentious artsy name with all sorts of extra letters and those little dots over them like a sideways colon. What are those for anyways? People are going to pronounce your name however they want to, regardless of how many squiggles you add to look exotic.

That's the only thing Zach and I used to get into a screaming fights about. Like there was one about the pronunciation of Angelica Huston's last name. 'Cause it's pronounced Houston, like the city, but there's no O in it so he was saying it was "Huston".

Fred! The artist's name was Fred. So Fred was doing an exhibition and he wanted to make sure that SOMEBODY came so if other people came they wouldn't see the empty gallery and feel awkward and think he was a complete loser so Eva said she would come and bring some friends, but then she got invited to Las Vegas by this Elvis impersonator. Well, he wasn't really an Elvis impersonator, he was more like an Elvis copier... wanted to live the same lifestyle and stuff. He even made it into the top ten finalists in the look-a-like contest in Vegas, and that's a really big accomplishment. Especially for a guy with a blond buzz cut.

So, Eva couldn't make it to Fred's show 'cause she was going to be in Vegas. She promised she'd scout out the best hotel for us to stay in when we went together. I told her she has to find one with one of those martini shaped hot tubs with the spiral staircase going up to them like the ones the burlesque dancers are always photographed in. So I had to go by myself. And that's where I met Josh. I walked in and across the gallery I saw him. Fred had run into him at the convenience store down the block just before his show and Josh was dressed all in black and Fred thought it would fantastic to have someone who looked like an art critic wandering around exclaiming magnificent things about his work so he hired Josh to stand in front of his paintings staring at them and remarking how brilliantly they juxtaposed the light and dark elements of life blah blah blah. And that's how I met Josh.

We don't really have anything in common, but he's cute. And he gives good presents. There are some really bad present givers out there. For Valentine's Day, Josh took me on a hot air balloon ride and we had a picnic up in the sky. Eva's boyfriend gave her a copy of "He's Just Not That Into You". I suppose she should have taken that as a hint. As far as I can tell he's okay in bed. Josh. Not Eva's... Not that I have much to base that on. But I wouldn't need to cut any star in half for him. So, that's plenty of reasons right? I mean, you got to marry someone right? And you're not really supposed to marry your first love. What does that say about your experience of life? I mean, it's not one hundred and sixty-seven, but it's not one either. And at least this way there'll always be someone there to make sure I don't sleep through the smoke detector and die horribly in a fire, like kindling. And really, isn't that the point of getting married anyways? So this is good. Perfect almost. Now if only I can talk him out of wanting an ice cream cake at the wedding.

CHAPTER THREE

AGE OF THE CRONE

The Loopin' Ladies of Loredo
by Ben Beck

Setting: The porch of a small farmhouse in Nebraska. August 1942. Evening.

Character: Annie, 60's, far from "lady-like"

Somewhere before it turned 1900, Omaha started somethin' up called a "Wild West Show". Like some sort of carnival with horses and people doin' shootin' tricks with their guns and folks dressing up like cowboys and Indians fighting and pretendin' to kill each other. My baby sister Ellie and me joined up when I was nineteen and she was seventeen. Every cent we could spare went home to mama. Ellie and me had our own ropin' act. They called us "The Loopin' Ladies of Laredo". We wasn't from Laredo but it sounded good with all the L's. Now, I love my baby sister. But she ain't nearly as spinning like I am. She could spin a regular flat loop but it wasn't worth a nit. Thing kept bouncin' up and down and kickin' up dust and eventually it'd just shrink up and plopped on the ground like a dead snake. I was the only one who did the real spinnin'. Texas skips and verticals and butterflies. No one in the crowd ever gave a fig though. Nope. They just liked her 'cause she was taller than me and…well she's real pretty. So long as she was smilin' and winkin' and wigglin' her tail all the boys were hootin' and hollerin' for more. She'd strut around all over the arena. More like skip though. She couldn't dance for nothin'. You'd never think it to look at her but my baby sister had the biggest feet you ever saw. Now, not just long. Big. Like the way a baby's foot looks when they're first born, but then growed up. All because of her

Frozen Women Flowing Thoughts

feet she couldn't dance, she sorta just skipped around back and forth. So then they decided to put her up on top of a big round step. Like the stump of some giant tree hat got cut down. They painted pictures on the sides of cowboys rustling cattle across orange skies. They perched her up top of that step and she'd start wigglin' up there and singin' "She'll Be Comin' 'Round the Mountain". They'd leap outta their seats and cheer for her like she was the queen of India. Shoot, I could loop Ellie blindfolded from twenty feet away and I bet you a million dollars there's no one else in the whole world that can do that! But, I'll tell you something, she never, not once, treated nobody different. Far as she was concerned, even though she got all the attention, she wasn't no better than me than nobody else. Touring all over the whole country. She never got a big head. Then one morning I wake up, in the bunk we shared together… and Ellie was gone. The bed was made like no one slept in it in all. All her stuff was still here except for a little lace pillow that she had since she was a baby. She never went nowhere without it. I looked on the ground to try and see if it'd fell on the ground or somethin'. But instead of a pillow, I saw a folded up piece of paper with my name written on the front in gray pencil. I opened it up. There weren't much written… "Annie, Me and Frank have gone away to get married. We're going to live in California where it's warm and sunny everyday. He makes me happy he'll take good care of me. I'll write back to you soon. Love, Ellie." Frank. Frank was a… boy. Frank was part of the show. He was in a big act called "Custer's Last Stand". He played an Indian and would rub red makeup all over his face. His job was to run around wavin' a tomahawk shoutin "WOOP WOOP WOOP WOOP WOOP WOOP!" That ain't hard. Hell, that was easier than Ellie's job; at least she had to sing. I waited for weeks but Ellie never wrote back. I don't know if they ever made it to California. Everyone kept asking about her. People in the show. People who came to see the show. I dunno. My guess it that she shacked up someplace and just, I dunno…forgot to write back. She was so dumb. With Ellie gone, I didn't have nobody to do my act with. No pretty little thing to wiggle while I spun my rope. So they cut my act and put me standin' out front of the main tent, spinnin' with one hand and wavin' to all the different folks as they came in for the real show. After everyone came inside, my job was all done. Nothin' to but count the change that people would toss to me as they walked by. Like they felt bad for me and thought they was bein' nice 'cause they thought the only reason I was up front was 'cause I wasn't good enough to be inside. I wasn't in the center ring no more. After a while it just… just felt like it was my job to feel sad. But then, one day, something came along that made me really... glad. I was sittin' at a picnic table in the way backstage. By myself and eating somethin' for lunch, I don't remember exactly what it was for sure. Probably a sandwich or something. But there I am, all by myself and someone claps me on the shoulder and says, "No lady pretty as you should ever eat by herself." Before I even turned around to see who it was, the first thing I did was look around for my sister. I'd heard a buncha dumb boys say things like that to her all the time. But Ellie wasn't around anywhere. I turned around finally to see who it was. Owen. Now, Owen was actually a girl. She was in all the same shows that Frank was in. Except she didn't play no damsel in distress. This girl could ride. She could shoot. She was strong like an ox. So instead of putting her some frilly dress, they made her one of the cowboys. She wore clothes that were real loose and she stuffed all her hair up into her hat and she didn't wear no makeup. If you was in the audience watching the show you'd never think she wasn't a boy. Anyway, everyone just called her Owen. I ain't sure why. Owen said I was pretty. Owen wasn't really that much to look at so I figured she must've been a kinda right. So we started eatin' all our lunches together. Then we'd go walk around outside when she wasn't doin' her part of the show. Finally we was spendin' the whole day together everyday. Sometimes girls kiss other girls. Owen kissed me real quick. Then again. I didn't know if I was supposed to say somethin' but She said it's okay to kiss somebody if you really like them and how it feels nice when you doit. She kissed me again but this time she stayed there for a little bit longer. So then we kissed for a while. Owen. I could spend all day kissin' you. Not too long after that, the show got boring. I was only there for Owen but then I found out that Owen was only there 'cause she thought I didn't want to go. We decided we didn't like being in the show no more. We wanted to go someplace else far away where could spend our whole lives together. Just the both of us. But we didn't have no money to get any house. We were stuck there livin' on what they gave us week after week. Then one day, outta nowhere, Owen says. "Maybe we could go live with your mama." Now, what in the goddamn hell was she thinkin'? I didn't want to go back to that little shack. And what'd she mean "we"? I didn't want to say it in from of Owen, but I was scared. What would mama think about me bringin' another person along to live with us? Some stranger from a Wild West show she ain't never met before. I told Owen that I'd think about it and Owen said she understood, which was weird 'cause she always poked and fussed until she got her way. The next day, THE

Frozen Women Flowing Thoughts

NEXT GODDAMN DAY, they brought me a letter from my mama sayin' how happy she was that I was comin' home, and thankin' Owen for convincing her, and saying how excited she was to meet him. Well, I threw a fit right there in front of everyone. Not only hadn't she waited until I made a decision, not only had she written to my mama behind my back, but I screamed, "YOU DUMBASS! YOUR NAME IS OWEN! SHE THINKS YOU'RE A BOY!" Owen made a weird face and she didn't say nothin'. I don't know if it was because she didn't think that's what my mama would think, or if she didn't think it made no difference. The thing is, whatever that face meant, it just made me love Owen even more. Sometimes girls love other girls. So we left the show and came back to Nebraska to live with my mama. At first she was surprised that Owen wasn't a boy but then she liked it and thought it was real funny that there was a girl with a boy name. Owen made her laugh all the time and even though I knew my mama missed Ellie; she started to love Owen like she was one of her own daughters. Turns out mama hadn't been spending none of what me and Ellie had been sending her. She'd just been doing odd jobs mendin' and sewin' and she insisted we use that money to stay with her. We wasn't gonna say no. During the day, me and Owen just sorta pretended like we were sisters, gigglin' and braidin' each other's hair and stuff. We slept in the same room that Ellie and I used to share when were kids. Mama still slept in her room, and when all the doors were shut, and when we knew she was asleep, I'd climb out outta my bed and settle in with Owen in her bed. All cramped up. It went on that way for a few months until mama died. It was her heart. It got weak or somethin' like that. It couldn't beat like it was supposed to. But she passed while she sleeping so I guess that's good. About a month after she died, Owen and me moved into mama's old room. It's nice 'cause we can still hold each other but we can also stretch all the way out. We've got this little shelf in the bedroom. I've got two pictures sitting on it. One's a fancy one they took of Ellie and me for our poster for the show. The other is a picture of all the folks in the show for advertising. Everyone is posing in front of a big tent. The whole group of us. It's the only picture with Owen and me together, even though she's on the whole other side. I don't mind it though. It's just as good as the one with me and Ellie. Just 'cause you're far apart in the picture don't mean nothin'.

She looks through an imaginary window. She'll be gettin' home soon. Owen. Thirty-nine years ago that girl clapped me on the back. I ain't never eaten alone since.

The Good Wife
by Liz Coley

Setting: A bedside in an institutional setting
Character: Mrs. Banks, 75-78

An abusive husband, near death, lies helpless as his "good wife" tends him and speaks her truth

Have you heard what they call me 'round here? I mean besides "Hey, Mrs. Banks!"

When did folks start yelling "Hey" at people? Pop always said "Hey is for horses." You mighta heard him say it a time or two yourself. At least they say Mrs. — not sweetie or hun, like cash register people. So, it's a half-measure of respect, I suppose.

Oh look. Your eye—in the corner, you've got a sleepy seed . . . there. Should I call —no— I can. There. Better? All better.

They call me "the good wife." To be sure, just one of the "good wives." We're the ones who come and visit every day even when our—I won't say loved ones—our husbands are long gone from responding. See how lucky you are? I'm here. Every day. Rain or shine. Better or worse.

I can't tell if your eyes are working any more. They're open, but. I don't think so.

Frozen Women Flowing Thoughts

Still, you look terrible, Frank. To be frank, you look terrible, Mr. Banks. What, not even a smile? Course not. You never liked my jokes. That social worker says you can hear me. Right up until. Hope you're listening, someways.

Lord, your hands are so chilly. I'll tuck 'em in. They're all purple-like. But not cold purple. More of a two-day bruise purple. And look at your toes. No, I realize you can't. They're quite white. Bloodless white.

They say you're closing in. Minute by minute. Retracting to your core, they tell me. What exactly's at your core, I wonder. Is that your heart? Your mind? Your soul? What is the last thing?

Recall that TV show we saw? About the death of stars? First they blow up real red and hot, like you in a temper. He's a Red Giant, I used to tell myself. Just means his energy got all used up at work. Just means you ran out of gas, Frank. But patience, girl, I told myself. In the morning he'll be a white dwarf. Tight and spinning. Dense. But smaller. Safer for this little planet in orbit.

Guess I've orbited you going on sixty years. Going where you go. Doing what you do. Like I promised in church. What choice when you've stood up in front of God and everyone, holding in your tummy bulge, and promising to be a good wife forever, for better and worse, sickness and health, till death.

And Jenny came so soon after, and, Lord, she was sweet. She was like gravity pulling us all together. Jenny was the apple of your eye.

So I slowed up my plans, slowed up the idea of college and travel and taking what I learned on the high school newspaper to a grown-up career. Couldn't go to journalism college with a baby. Couldn't leave you with a child to follow a story. And then she left this world.

How could you've said what you did? When she went to God, how could you've said to me, "Get over it. It was an accident." Except that isn't even what you said. You recall? Do you? "Get over it. *She* was an accident." That's what you said to a grieving mother. To me. Lord, how I hated you.

I expect you knew that. I expect you felt it, even though I was a good wife. I expect that's why the long, cold winter of our life. Look. You're glaring at me even now. You probably want to strike me. That's not going to happen. Ever again.

Maybe one of us should've given up and gone away? Any case, it wasn't gonna be me. At seventeen I'd promised till death in front of God and everybody, and I don't break my promises.

You recall, when I was just pulling out of my grief? You didn't say, "Now go get your dream and heal." You said, "Act your age. You're too old for this shit." I never said a single swear to you, in all our years, no matter what you did, but you called my dreams shit.

Know what I say to you Frank? I say . . . "Fuck you." That's what I say. Goodness! I've never said that word aloud before. It feels mighty powerful to say it now. "Fuck you, Frank."

Well. So long as we're being honest, I've got one remaining fear of you Frank. I'm afraid you're going to keep on haunting me. Your shriveled unshriven soul is going to haunt me when you're gone because there's no way heaven will have you.

Recall the end of the star? When the star core shrinks down and down and down to a black hole. Heavy as a dozen suns and smaller than a moon. Time itself stands still. Cold as it's possible to be. Nothing moves. Nothing changes. I believe Hell is a black hole. Not a fiery place, but a black hole of nothingness. I fear that is your fate Frank, for all you've done to me, to Jenny.

I ask myself why God appointed me to be companion on your terrible path. But mysterious are His ways. I have been a good wife. That's all I can say.

Frozen Women Flowing Thoughts

I'd like to forgive you Frank. I would. I think that might release you from the black hole, release me from the haunting. But Pop told me, you have no business forgiving someone who isn't sorry. That's not your place. Repentance must come first.

Were you ever sorry, Frank? You never said so. You never showed it. You just blustered on day to day dictating terms to the world until this final stroke felled you. Then you dwindled into this white dwarf I see before me. Whom I visit every day. "Hey, Mrs. Banks. Here you are again. You're one of the good wives."

If only you'd ever showed one drop of remorse or sorrow or even understanding, I could have forgiven much. All. And we could both be free.

Oh look now. Your eye—is that—is that at last? A drop? Let me—let me dab that for you, Frank, sweetheart. Let me wipe your cheek.

An Anthology

It's Big and Red
by Kristen Lowman

RITA is in her seventies. Her bouffant hair is styled in the front and sides. The back is a tangled, matted mess. She smokes a cigarette and is seen sitting in her wheelchair, in her living room, peering between the blinds. With her back to the audience, curls of smoke rise as if from the top of her head. With a clatter, she releases the blinds and wheels around.

It's still out there. Just sittin' there.... My god it's big.... I like big but that's BIG. *(She peeks quickly through the blinds and groaning, wheels to the other side of the room.)* I like red too but that's RED.... My nerves, my nerves can't take it. First Tom dies and then this! I... am... oh yes... having... a GD drink! A.A.? AS ALWAYS. Then I am going to call that little miss educated daughter of mine, the snoot, and tell her to have someone come and get it. That! *(She clutches the bottle.)* Not the gin! Have to be careful what you say. Have to clarify your pronouns in this world. She– *(catches herself)* Adelle-Who-Doesn't-Smell—doesn't do a damn thing for me except lecture when I call. What does she know about suffering? She lives a high falutin' life in wacky Los Angeles! Just points a finger. *J'accuse*! Thinks I killed her father. High drama! Just her excuse... for abandoning her mother. *(weepy)* Her mother, who was left a widow – three times! Her mother, who made sure she got an education. Don't drop out of college like your mother, I told her. And what does she do? She graduates and defects to Germany!... Wellesley, believe it or not.... Me! Not Adelle.... Wellesley. The War. The Waves. The Wife. The Widow. Wow. My Life.

Frozen Women Flowing Thoughts

How do you, I ask you, kill someone who kills himself! *J'accuse*! And she's the lawyer. Says I made him so miserable, says I broke his heart. My dear, if only I had that kind of power. Luke – Adelle's father – was my first husband. Married twenty years. Had it all! The house, the cars, the parties. Then he wakes up one day out of the blue like he's Joan of Arc or something, and says, tells me he doesn't want that. 'Oh, what does it all mean?' It means, Luke, you work hard and make a lot of money. You want to quit? Quit, I told him. You climbed your way up the executive mountain, go ahead, throw yourself off if you want to get down.... He took me literally. It was his last hurrah. A big Fuck You Bash. *(Rita pours more gin into her glass.)* ... 'Fuck' I do believe is an old Welsh word that means to till the land. Oh, he did. He tilled it alright. With his head! Right off the 16th floor of the Texaco building. Now Luke is the saint. Luke the Saint! Uh-huh, fooled everybody, including me, with his secret love shack. I, frankly, don't know how he had the energy for two lives – it's hard enough with one! A regular Walter Mitty.

I worked hard, too, you know. Raised two girls. Gave the fancy dinner parties. Yes, Luke Hamilton, go ahead, throw it all away. Yes, my dear enlightened CEO, go wander the land. Wanted to read and think and swim in the ocean. What are you talking about? You can read and think here and swim in the goddamn pool! ... You never think things are going to change because... basically... we never change. But maybe that's why. That's why life changes. We don't.

I can feel it staring at me. It appeared yesterday. They just left the red monster truck sitting in my driveway with a big card. 'CONGRATULATIONS! From the Piggly-Wiggly Grocery!' Well, let me congratulate you, Piggly Wigglers, for BLOCKING MY VIEW OF THE FINKLER FAMILY. I use them like a night-light. I like the flicker of their TV. I get scared, you know, now that Tom is gone. ... *(tearfully)* Tom's last words to me were, "Rita, Rita, you're my gal." ... THE BASTARD. The Finklers are good company too since Johnny retired from the TV. Used to love to get cozy and settle in with Johnny. *(Rita hums the Carson tune.)* Now he was a class act! Won't find him crying and carrying on. Which is something I cannot say for The Oprah. Everything gets discussed on The Oprah. Wants everybody to get out a journal, oh, if life were only that simple, dear SIMPLE Oprah. Wants you to write down how many bags of potato chips you stuffed down your throat. And then go clean out your garage. Everybody's depressed. You want depressed? Try THE DEPRESSION. Want to lose some weight? Get in a BREAD LINE. Put that in your journal... and eat it. Wants to know everybody's business and then get some quack swami guru – Mr. Deep-pocket Choke-ya – then rake you over the coals! What happened to live and let live? Speaking of which I almost called the police a couple of weeks ago for sweet Juney Finkler. Saw her being tied up to her bed. I thought she was being abducted or something peculiar and awful. But apparently it was just... peculiar. I don't know, in my day we didn't do those wacky things. Ah gee jiminy in my day Artie Shaw was about as wild as you got. Ahh, Juney's a good egg. My day you GOT YOURSELF THROUGH A WAR!

(Rita wheels toward the window, giggles nervously.) It's like a goddamn total eclipse! I could kill Tom. He was my third husband. You know he had The Cancer. My god, what I went through. I'm still recovering. No I'm not kiddin', no foolin', it took it out of me. Don't get me wrong, I know he was suffering, oh god, was he suffering but they gave him painkillers. I nearly took the whole bottle myself! You know why? He was a PAIN. God bless him, a GD pain! *(As she lights another cigarette—)* Throat cancer. I don't know why, he never smoked a day in his life. You won't find that in my family. Good, strong Yankee stock. My people hail from England and Ireland. Where I got the gin gene. ... Yes, he was my third husband and he will, no doubt, be my last. Luke. Fred. Tom. All of them. Dead. Gone. Good. Yes, I'll be the last one... sitting.

I am going to call that spoiled rotten Adelle-Who-Doesn't-Smell. Miss Smarty-Lawyer-I'll-Have-You-Committed. Over my dead body. I have all my faculties. Hm-hm. I got my checkbook, I got my Depends. And I got my wheels. And I can roll right on out of here.

Where oh where is my girl? Wacky Cathy. Before I let her in, I always ask her if she has taken her medication. No, seriously, she gets nutty acting. When Wacky Cathy gets Chatty Cathy, watch out. I had to call her father one night. She was dancing around the room playing my hi-fi. My Julie London record. You know what she called me? She called me a b-i-t-c-h. That's when I wheeled over behind her during her Gypsy Rose routine and just rammed! Brought her to her knees like a GD camel. Well, I'm sorry. She had to be subdued, she's a maniac depressive. No, Cathy's a good egg. Shops for me. Helps me with private things. I slip her a couple of extra bucks to make sure she keeps the libationary larder loaded.

I used to run over to 'Liz's Hideaway' for a nightcap... when I was ambulatory. Liz keeps poppin' in my mind lately... BOO. I found her place, by chance. This was after Luke took his swan dive. I think 'Liz's Hideaway' is now called Bubba's or some name of refinement, they, someone, Bubba, I guess, rebuilt...years ago.... I was going to stop by the night she died... oh that storm, my god.... The others were— *(As if interrupted, she turns to the window, turns back to the audience.)* Well, you know how cruel people can be in these small towns. I've always wondered if, maybe if I had—excuse me a moment. *(Wheels around to the window.)*

WHAT? *(turns back)* My apologies. Now where were we? No, I'm no Philadelphia lawyer but one thing I can say for myself is that... I may have my obiter dicta but I don't judge. No, I'm not looking back until it's all said and done. I'll pay when I'm finished spending. I get all eternity to pay it off.... THE BASTARD. Now, Dead Fred Number 2 is in Hell. So I don't have to worry about that. Believe me, I would have killed him myself if he hadn't crashed that fancy sports car. That I bought!! Big freeloader. Adelle had to take a student loan because of Dead Fred. My other kid— *(with difficulty)*— got all lu-lu la-la, and runs away. I have my suspicions.... Let's just say he had a predilection for... well, I won't go into it.... Never heard from her. And you know as a mother at the time I thought, let her go on out there, let her toughen up, do her good! What is it they call it on The Oprah? Tough love? She was soft, that kid.... She had a flair for dramatics. I'm talking talent! You know, I look for her on the TV shows... my baby. To tell you the truth, when Dead Fred died, I thought maybe she'd come back. But maybe she... maybe...Violet never found out he was gone...Violet....

—Now how's Wacky Cathy going to take me for a walk with the Peeper out there? *(Rita wheels back to the window, drinks, peers outside.)* 'Jeepers creepers, where'd you get those peepers?' They're enormous, I think it's got a thyroid problem. And look there, it's lifted up off its—what the hell are those? Its haunches? Dear god, it's ready to attack.

(She wheels downstage. Rita, on second thought, wheels back to the window.) I'M ON TO YOU. *(Agitated, she wheels in circles. Somewhat calmed, she turns back to the audience.)* Oh-ho-boy, the Piggly Wigglers love me. What the hell was Tom thinking? It must have been his medication. He buys seven hundred raffle tickets, ten dollars apiece, proceeds going to the VA. He was— 'feeling sentimental about having served in the Armed Forces,' they tell me at the Piggly-Wiggly. "Put them in my wife's name," he told the Wigglers. "In Rita's honor." Said he wanted 'a little something for me to remember him by.' Told them all, "Rita's going to be the winner!" Told everybody and his uncle how he had SERVED.

I served too! A Wave! United States Navy! I shared a taxi with Gene Kelly, in Washington, DC. Sometimes I dream I'm dancing... *(sings)* "Poor little rich girl, don't drop a stitch, girl/Better beware, better take care./ Cocktails and laughter but what comes after? Nobody cares." *(Rita starts to cry, then whips around to the window.)* I HEARD THAT. Think you're King of the Road, do you? I could take you for a r-i-ide. *(She wheels over to the phone and dials.)* Operator! Get me J. Edgar Hoover! .... What do you mean I have to call Information, that's why I'm calling you. .... Just put me through. I'll pay. I'll pay whatever you want, you big fascist. .... —Please, I'm sorry. *(whispers)* Big Baby. *(to window)* You are going to have to hit the road, Jack! .... Not you, my perpetrator! .... Information? Get me J. Edgar Hoover. .... What do you mean 'what city?' Washington, you big idiot! .... I'm very sorry. ... I have to dial 555-what? ... I don't have a pen! I have a stroke! Information, it's outside, I need to report– ... I don't know what to do... do about my baby– .... Yes, my baby Violet is missing. She's only fifteen. .... The police? .... It's too late. .... Oh, she's been gone for years. .... I know you can't help me. .... *(Rita holds the phone. We hear a dial tone. She hangs up and smokes feverishly.)*

It's called in these modern times – HARASSMENT! NOW TAKE YOUR BIG TRUCK SELF AND HAUL ON OUT OF HERE. *(She picks up the phone and dials.)* Oh no, no – The Machine. *(Adelle's message is heard. Rita speaks into the phone as if it is an instrument of great complexity.)*

Hello. This is a message for Adelle. NOT George. I would like to say: I'm a winner! It's big! Boy, is it big. And red! It's-it's too much, honey, for me to handle. I'm not up to it. Are you there? ... *(whispers)* Adelle, listen carefully. It's got me cornered. Make it go away. I would also like to add: Adelle...I'm all alone. Over and Out.

(Rita takes a gulp, slams her drink down. She wheels over to the blinds and defiantly pulls up the shades. Huge headlights pop on. A blinding light floods the stage.)

Hot Milk
by Sherry MacDonald

Setting: A kitchen

ALMA, a woman in her sixties, stands at a stove stirring a pot of hot milk.

ALMA

The secret to making hot milk is to keep the temperature low, so it doesn't get heated too quickly. Means standing at the stove for a good fifteen minutes.

And it's fifteen minutes every morning. Seven a.m. On the dot. Have to have the hot milk ready, upstairs and on his bedside table before he opens his eyes. The first thing Robert wants to see in the morning is his cup of milk. If he wakes up, turns his head and doesn't see it, his day is ruined. And if his day is ruined, mine is ruined too.

He likes it with a little sugar. And it has to be a cup and saucer with a spoon for stirring. Never—god forbid—in a *mug*.

So I get the milk ready, take it upstairs, place it carefully beside him, open the curtains and quietly leave. He's awake. But he keeps his eyes closed, just the same. Pretending. And I let him. We have the whole day to talk. No need to start any sooner than we have to.

Frozen Women Flowing Thoughts

It's important to keep stirring the milk. Otherwise a skin will form. And if there's one thing Robert cannot stand, it's a skin. He'll blow a fit. I won't get a minute's peace for the rest of the day.

First of all, he won't have his milk. Because he'll insist I've ruined the pleasure for him and I'll be out that part of the day. The part where I'm guaranteed to be alone for an hour so I can have my coffee and read without someone calling my name, asking me where the toilet paper is, or the towels or the shampoo, even though these items are always kept in the same place and have been since we moved into this house thirty-two years ago.

It's not like I know I'm going to get a skin. That is, it doesn't always form in the pot, but later on in the cup. If the cup is already on his bedside table, it's too late. He's awake. And before I have time to do anything, it appears. Mottled and lumpy.

I can't pick the cup up and leave the room, make another one. I know, I've tried it. His eyes will snap open like roll-up blinds and his hand will reach out from under his quilt and snatch me by the wrist.

"Alma. Where are you going?" he'll ask. Knowing full well where I'm going and why. Then he'll peer down into the cup with his watery, lash less eyes. Searching for the offending item. The evidence he can use against me.

It's more challenging now. With the both of us at home. Robert is long retired, but I was still working until recently. So, now we're both at home. Together. All day . . .

My mother warned me against marrying a man fifteen years older than me. She said, "Oh it's fine now. He's still relatively young. But wait until he gets closer to the end. You'll still have life, but you'll feel like it's being sucked right out of you." And now that Robert is closer to the end . . . an end that never seems to come . . . I'm beginning to see what she meant.

My mother was not speaking from experience. No. She and dad were only two years apart in age. They had what I would call a passionate marriage. They had their differences. Mom was city. Dad was more at home in the woods. He'd take my sister and me camping every summer. Believed us girls should know how to rough it. Mom, of course, stayed home. But summers were for Dad and the woods. The sound of the birds waking us up in the morning and the crickets putting us to sleep at night.

One time my sister and me–I was only ten and Aggie was seven–we took the hand-drawn gondola across Cheakamus Creek and we got caught half-way. We were so scared sitting there in the little car with the wooden benches, thinking Dad's never going to find us. And then suddenly he appeared as if out of nowhere. Wading in up to his chest, the creek rushing all around him, calling, "Alma, climb out. You can do it." And I did. I climbed out, reached up and I grabbed the pulley and got back into the car. I pulled us back to the shore and into Dad's waiting arms.

I can still smell the wood smoke in his black and red checked woolen shirt.

He taught Aggie and me all kinds of survival techniques. How to build a fire from nothing. How to trap and skin small animals. And we did. Once anyway. We packed all kinds of food with us, but Dad wanted us to know that if we needed to we could survive . . . He taught us about different plants, berries and mushrooms. Which kinds were safe, which were poisonous . . .

It's a nighttime drink, don't you think? Hot milk. Like hot chocolate is a nighttime drink. Something to sip under the stars by a campfire. Who the hell drinks hot milk first thing in the morning? Robert. That's who.

I wonder what my bear of a father would have to say about a man who drinks hot milk in the morning. Served in a cup and saucer, no less.

Frozen Women Flowing Thoughts

And what's wrong with a skin? For Aggie and me skins on a hot drink were a bonus. We'd heat our hot chocolate up over and over just so we could pick the skins out of the pot and fling them at each other.

Maybe Robert's hatred for hot milk skin has something to do with the hatred he feels for his own skin. Every day he stands before the mirror, inspecting the little wattle at his neck, the fleshy jowls. I've even seen him hold his arms out–I'm not kidding you–shaking the loose skin. "Chicken flesh" he calls it. He's obsessed. Convinced it's going to fall off. "Like blobs of wax, dripping off a candle," he says. 'That's impossible, Robert," I tell him. But he continues on, pulling and pinching. "You wait," he says, "You'll see."

I've gotten pretty good at making sure Robert doesn't have to look down into his morning beverage only to be reminded of his decomposing body. But there is the odd slip-up . . . One time, after I'd placed the hot milk on his bedside table. His eyes still closed. His mouth open, breathing in that labored, wheezing way he has. I look down and there it is, a big thick skin. I can't retrieve the cup. Any second now he'll be opening his eyes.

So I take the spoon and pick up the skin. Careful not to make a noise. If I can just make my way quietly out of the room . . . But no. His eyes flick open. His head snaps around. And I . . . drop to all fours beside the bed, still holding the spoon with the skin.

"Alma?"

Silent, silent . . . If I straighten now, he'll see me. See *it*. Hanging from the spoon. He pokes his little turtle's head around and peers down.

"What are you doing down there, Alma?" I make like I'm searching for a lost item. "I dropped something." And before he can crane his neck down for a better look, I deposit the skin into the closest thing I can find: the heel of one of Robert's slippers.

The thing is, he doesn't even notice. He puts his slippers on, shuffles into the bathroom for his shower. So I follow him and retrieve the slipper only to find it's empty. Thinking maybe I have the wrong one, I pick up the other slipper, but it's empty too.

Just then, the shower door snaps open. "Alma!"

"Look at this. Look!" Robert's face is filled with fear. He beckons me over to the shower stall. I look down at the drain. And there bubbling under the water, stubbornly hanging on for dear life, is the milk skin. It must have stuck to the bottom of his heel. 'This proves it,' he says, "I am losing my skin."

Two weeks ago, last Saturday, Robert and I attended the funeral of Sam Turner. Sam and Margie are old friends of Robert's. We spent Christmas Eve with them and two other couples, where we played charades. I'm up having a hell of a time trying to act out "Deep Throat", when Robert blurts out, "For god's sake Alma, sit down. You're making a fool of yourself."

Standing graveside while they lower Sam's body into the ground, I look over at Margie who's twisting a light blue handkerchief about in that nervous way of hers–Robert standing next to me wheezing away, and I begin to seriously imagine what it would be like to have the house to myself.

Maybe I won't even stay in this house. I'll head to the woods. Sleep in a tent in the warm weather. Find a cabin for when the cold sets in. I'll get a little camp cooker for my coffee and a whole stack of books. I can drink coffee and read till noon. Or all day if I want to.

A few days after Sam's funeral I took a quick trip into the woods. Sort of a dry run. Well, I was on a mission. I bought a tent from Mountain Equipment. It was just for one night. Robert practically blew a gasket. But I went. Had to get a girl in in the mornings to make Robert's hot milk for him.

Frozen Women Flowing Thoughts

I pitched my tent, built a fire, put a pot of coffee on, and went foraging in the woods. It all came back to me the lessons Dad gave us. The plants that have medicinal value, the ones to avoid . . . If you want to avoid them.

Nothing that would be too painful. Or leave a trace. If I add extra sugar it should cover any tinge of bitterness Robert might detect.

ALMA sniffs the contents of the pot and adds more sugar.

Just to be sure. He might notice his hot milk is a little sweeter than usual. But only a little.

At least it won't have a skin.

ALMA continues to stir the pot.

The sound of birds start. As the lights fade to black, the sounds of birds turn to those of crickets.

Nest
by Jennifer O'Grady

Setting: The place where she lives now.
Character: Madelyn, 65+, an artist

A woman struggles to remember the son now lost to her.

(MADELYN. She speaks to us.)

MADELYN

Can you see it? Outside my window. Four eggs the color of a spring sky. Cyan. A member of the cyan family. Each color has its own frequency and wavelength, does different things to the eyes. This one in particular makes us look.

I discovered it by accident—a fluttering just beyond the glass. I went to look and a robin was climbing through the leaves. She's placed it in a rhododendron—sturdier branches, broader leaves for camouflage. The mother spends much of her time keeping the eggs warm. Untouched houses for little bird bodies. Unmarred. Waiting to exist.

They've told me to talk, so I am. It isn't like I have much else to do. They say writing can help too—helps to fix things here *(her mind)*, or at least create a permanent record. The trouble is I'm not sure which things I want to make permanent. Or if anything can be fixed.

Frozen Women Flowing Thoughts

It begins probably in the hippocampus. Little things: keys, the name of your childhood dog, a street you once lived on. Once it's well advanced, you don't know who you are. There's a woman here, she sees no problem in parading around nude. They'll bring her back to her room but she'll say, "No! I want to go outside." What does it matter what you do if you don't know who you are? There's a man who mostly sits in the TV room and drools, and he...No. That isn't anything I want to make permanent.

I haven't told anyone about the nest. They can see I'm holding something back. "What is it, Madelyn? You seem happy." Well, screw them. You need something of your own here.

When I first arrived, there were still garlands in the hall. Gone now, thank god. You'd need to worry about a place that keeps Christmas cheer until springtime. Emerald, completely the wrong color for garland. Not that anyone else would notice. I have few visitors. Well, I mean...

(Looks around)

Not a place *I'd* want to come. Frank is gone, pancreatic cancer eight years ago. My sisters, older friends. Few of them suffered.

And Alex...We named him Alex. Frank was a history teacher. "Alexander the Great." One expects great things from one's children.

He was born on a spring day very much like this one. Cobalt sky, zinc-white clouds. No one thinks childbirth will be easy, but he almost slipped out in the Volvo on the road to the hospital. I was lucky. That's what they told me: You're lucky, Madelyn.
Having a child changes things. Frank went to work, of course. Some days I would really rather have been painting. He was an accepting child. Found things to do until I'd finished. TV was probably on a lot. When I was done, he'd come and look at what I'd done. Just gaze at the canvases. One wasn't always sure what he was thinking.

Sturdily built, strong, like his father. Long eyelashes for a boy. And a dimple here—it's clear as day, even though I'm in twilight. Floppy blond hair in his eyes. People called him beautiful. Well, that type of appearance…I was after the abstract, the essence. All the girls adored him. They chased him around at recess. He once asked me what to do and I said, "Well, Alex, just tell them to stop." But telling, speaking…It's why I painted, why Frank taught history. The things you understand later, as if a shadow you'd never noticed suddenly lifts and there's a valley beneath you. *(Beat)* Don't know if there were others—girls, I mean. I never asked. I assumed he'd say.

And when he entered school, well, they all played it. Begins with T-ball then rises through high-school varsity. Frank and I…sports weren't part of our existence. I couldn't have told you the difference between a strike and a ball, what type of glove to use for anything. But when we have an aptitude for something…They made him a catcher, right behind home plate, crack of the bat and a ball flying straight toward his head, over and over, my heart! He wore protective gear but still. Those were nerve-wracking years.

They gave him an award senior year: Most Valuable Player. Frank and I didn't quite meld with the other sports parents. But there was Alex, beaming, the coach shaking his hand…Naturally he was recruited. Not quite the college of his choice, but he seemed…

I didn't do portraits. Tried a baseball painting once: blur of colors, whirling shapes. Can't paint unless something matters to you. Baseball…I found it slow, tedious. Sometimes rather pointless.

It's afternoon, isn't it? Usually a time when the babies get fed. Didn't I mention they'd been born? They look like a dust bunny, soft-gray mass against the brown of the nest. They have the instinct to duck down low to avoid predators, whenever the parents are out shopping for food. They regurgitate into their young, did you know? The babies take in whatever the mother vomits. Eventually they mature and go and vomit into other little birds. It's a cycle. An unending cycle.

If I could paint it, perhaps Cadmium Light, Transparent Orange for the breast feathers, Asphaltum for the wings, Raw Umber for the nest. The young a mixture of grays—soft, not like the last. Slashes of black, reds, the color of burnt metal…No idea what I was thinking. I never showed it to Frank. Cut it up and threw it out, into the trash. The garlands here have the same opacity, same darkness. I don't think they realize. What most people know about color would fill a thimble.

That Christmas Alex drove himself home in his used Toyota, a gift from Frank. I always felt Frank was spoiling him. No jacket—well, it was a mild winter. I waved to him through the window. It registered that he looked thin, but well, college. Frank came home early, a supper of some sort. Alex cleared his throat and then spoke. Of course we immediately said no. "You were recruited to play ball, it pays your scholarship, so no, Alex, you can't just quit." Frank was upset. A high-school teacher's salary…I'd sold a few paintings, not nearly enough. Alex offered to drop out for a year, get a job, but in Frank's and my families you finished school at twenty-two and then went out into the world, so no. We told him no.

He didn't say much after that, which we thought was best.

Years are like straws—you gather them into your hand and they jumble, some slip away. But this was twenty years ago, of that I'm certain. A mild Christmas. Not a speck of snow.

The groundskeepers are out there. They're always doing something—cutting hedges, digging up flowerbeds, weed-whacking weeds. Sometimes they spray, I assume it's a sort of poison. I ought to tell someone. You can see they have feathers now, their wings fledging out.

I can smell cooking. Smells help too: meat smells, lunch or dinner; eggs and toast, breakfast. The light tells me, though sometimes it's deceptive—darkness, dimness, doesn't always equate with evening. Might just be a rainy day. I do wonder on such days whether it's out there or in here *(her mind)*. The dimming. The dimming light.

In the morning he came downstairs with his duffle. Frank was already at work. He kissed me then got behind the wheel. He was wearing a red tee shirt, some sort of writing on it, I can't make out what it says, though I see him clearly through the window, fiddling with the dashboard. A scratch on the fender. I thought, "If Frank sees that, he'll be angry." The car began to move. I waved. He didn't see me. He was focusing on the road.

They called us. Well, Frank, actually—the phone was on his side of the bed. It woke me too. I watched him listen. I saw his face. The rest of that night a hole, a black slash.

In the morning they came, two of them, fresh out of cop school. They looked embarrassed, twisting their caps in their hands. I invited them in. I made tea. I served them tea while they told me about my son.

I visited, eventually—just tarmac and a guardrail, somewhere in godforsaken Pennsylvania. Was there ice? Presumably. Maybe a sudden squall. Drugs, possibly, not that we'd have noticed. We chose not to have an autopsy. It seemed…

When they hand you the book, the big thick binder of photos, all different, varied shades of whites, browns, mahogany, the inexpensive pine, glossy or matte—little…decorations I suppose they are, brass handles and whatnot—you turn the pages and think, "This one? Can we afford this one?" Somehow you know you'll never paint again. How can you without browns, whites, rectangles, how can you? I packed up my paints. I never looked back.

When Frank got sick it was almost a relief to him.

At some point I began hearing—noises, restless sounds. Something might not be where I'd placed it—a prescription bottle, a hairbrush. Things vanishing—backdoor key, the name of my childhood dog. I sold the house. I moved in here.
"Early onset" they call it. As if I'm in any way, shape or form "early."

Now I talk, or I write. Not sure who there is to hear or read. Nancy perhaps, I believe her name is. Ugly blue uniform, or is it pink? She seems kind, a listener, making her daily rounds, but will she remem-

Frozen Women Flowing Thoughts

ber? Of course it's my view of him anyone would receive. Not the same as remembering *him*, is it?

I have this window, a nightstand, room for a few trinkets, some clothes I rarely wear. Where is he now, my son? Is he in my hippocampus? Soon he'll be with the lost keys, the names of the streets we lived on. Something distant and dim, without features— just the back of his red tee shirt, growing smaller as he walks away and the sun disappears.

A few minutes ago I looked out the window—they were all balanced at the edge of the nest: four speckled bobbins of red and brown, bright persimmon beaks. Not moving, just standing as if listening. A few minutes later they were back in the nest again, biding their time. For what, I'm not sure. They seem ready.

Very soon now. Very soon they'll all be gone.

DON'T LOOK AT ME LIKE THAT
by Marj O'Neill-Butler

Setting: Somewhere in Carol's home
Character: Carol, a woman over 50; any race or ethnicity

Don't look at me like that. You know I did what I could for your father...until it became too much for me. Even he recognized he needed help. I needed my life, the end of my life, to be more than as a caretaker for an old man. I was worn out after being locked in with him for more than two years. You saw what I looked like. I love him, will always love him, but he's not the same person anymore. Not even close.

And I've met someone...a man so loving and understanding. He treats me gently and with such kindness. He found me on a dating site. My friend Pam told me to try it. It's fun she said. A lark. So, I signed up, not expecting much if anything, really. I thought I could use my experience as fodder for my writing.

But then Edward sent me a smile. And I smiled back. And the next thing you know, we're writing to each other...giving last names and sharing things about my husband and his wife. About how she suffered through years of cancer. About how your father, the smartest man I'd ever met, the most affectionate man, turned into a monster who lashed out at me. Physically. Someone I couldn't take care of anymore. I didn't want to be afraid of him. I didn't want to spend the end of my life being afraid.

So yes, I have met and spent some time with Edward. And it's…I've found laughter again. And romance. And I'm not afraid to be with him.

Please, don't look at me like that.

Please Marry My Dad
by Kathryn Rossetter

Setting: On the phone, a treadmill at the gym
Character: Brenda, 58

Having made it to the last round of screenings for, "Please Marry My Dad," Brenda looks for support from her best friend as she outlines her desperate preparations to impress the Producers.

> AT RISE: We hear, the beginning of "GONNA FLY NOW", The theme song from, "Rocky"
>
> LIGHTS UP: BRENDA FRANCIS, 58. Cell phone earbuds in place, and phone on her waist. She runs in place as if she's on a treadmill throughout the entire piece.

Brenda

Meg, oh thank God you picked up. I made it to the in-depth screening for the show, "Please Marry My Dad!" I can't believe it! I'm at the gym… Treadmill. It's cardio day. No, I saw on Instagram that two days off between weight training is recommended at our age. I was so relieved because weights are heavy and boring. So, the selection committee is coming to my apartment to check out how I live and decorate and cook and everything about me. They only pick 16 women for the show. The guy we're competing for is like late 60's, and I'm up

Frozen Women Flowing Thoughts

against it because they'll still pick women in their 30's and 40's. They all act so desperate. What do they know about desperation?

(She runs a little faster.)

I haven't had sex since Christ left Cleveland. I'm tired of hearing that it's my fault if I'm alone. "What's wrong with you, Brenda, after all, he's available." Yes, but he can't see his shoes over his 'Dad bod' and he mansplains over everything I say. Why am I the one who's expected to settle? Why is winning restricted to youth and beauty? "American Idol" won't even let you be on it if you're over 28.

(She listens.)

Sure, lots of other shows let older folks on but they are never really in contention. Even Susan Boyle didn't win. There's so much I have to do. I have to plan a menu… yes, they come for lunch, get my roots done… I'll have to skip Mindfulness Goat Yoga and go straight to Home Depot. I need to get those shelves I saw on "Bargain Block" last night. Didn't you love them!? And those cardboard walls were genius. Those buyers were so provincial. They didn't like it because I'll bet the wife smoked and was afraid to light up in it. Those lines around her lips and her yellow teeth? Dead give-away. That's why God invented White strips and collagen. She looked ten years older than me, and she was half my age. It never ceases to amaze me that women like her have men. Dr. Phil would have called her on her bull. Like that woman on his show yesterday whose husband walked out on her at 40. Like she's unique. Boo Hoo. She's lonely. Boo Hoo. She doesn't know who she is. Boo Hoo! I could tell her. She's a middle-aged woman on the fast track to becoming a cliché. She needs to get off the Prozac, off the therapists' couch, off her ass and just take action. Look at me, I'm multitasking as we speak. I'm exercising, watching the food network, and talking to you. For some of us, this is 'having it all'.

(Another call comes in.)

Oh damn, another call… I may cut you off, this phone is new, and I can't see shit without my glasses. It's an iPhone 13, 14 5G, 10K A S S or something. It does everything except wash the dog. I love it! Everyone has one. But I feel like it's watching me.

(Brenda nearly falls as she tries to answer the call with her earbuds) Damn. Hello? Hello? Meg? It's still you? I don't know. I lost the other call. I press a button and it all goes to hell.

(She listens and laughs.)
Oh, Wait! Turn on the food network, Meg. Kelsey Bernard Clark is making the most divine Salmon! That's what I'll make for the TV interviewers. Gourmet, classy, hip, healthy and effortless. I hope I'll have time to at least paint my living room. My colors are so dated. It's all low carb colors now. Celery, watercress, mushroom, salmon… oh yeah, salmon is everywhere…Eat it, wear it, rub it on your ass. And I need new window treatments. I saw the most amazing fabrics on Nate and Jeremiah's show. A combination of organic cotton and the foreskins of baby yaks. It's the purest you can get! … It doesn't hurt them at all. It's like a group yak bris. A Tibetan Monk performs the procedure on a hilltop facing the sun, on the third Tuesday of every month. It's very spiritual Feng shui. Blah, blah, blah. And it's my angle because I'm betting no one else will have them… Of course they're expensive, but I'm worth it. It's an investment, no different than Facials, Botox, Collagen, or all that therapy we did in the 90's.

(She listens and speeds up a bit.)
Easy for you to say. You have a husband and family. You matter. Yesterday these two girls were next to me in Yoga, loudly complaining, about how they can't walk down the street in their summer belly shirts and "Daisy Dukes" without being assaulted by men's grunts and hoots. They were so earnest and self-righteous, going on and on about how disgusting it was and how their rights were being violated, (she is running even faster and faster) and all I wanted to do was my sun salutation, and they were violating my right to a peaceful class. Suddenly, I'm screaming, "It's so easy to be outraged when you think it will last forever. I want to thank every man who grunts at me, "girls", because it's only disgusting until it stops." Then they threw me out of class. For life. Unbelievable…

(A call comes in again.)
Hang on Meg, another call. Tying again.

Frozen Women Flowing Thoughts

(She does it right this time.)
Hello? Yes......yes....yes.... of course, I can...absolutely. Thank you.

(She clicks back to Meg.)
Meg, Meg, I couldn't have planned this if I tried. I just got hair and make-up appointments with Nick and Carmandy, remember from the old "What Not To Wear!" I've been waiting months, but they just had cancellations so I'm in! I used to love that show. Stacy and Clinton are geniuses. "Their rules" for dressing were easy if you didn't let your own taste get in the way. This is such a good omen; I can feel it. Once Nick and Carmandy are through with me, I just know they won't be able to reject me from, "Please Marry My Dad".

(She is running full speed.)
I'm going to be living proof that 58 is the new 30. I have the wisdom of aging, the courage of my convictions and, I'm not high maintenance; new shoes, a martini, and a great lip color. That gets me through the day. This is my comeback, like Martha Stewart! Oh shit, I just ran 5 miles. I'm an animal. I should take a selfie and post it on Instagram. I need more followers. I just started Tic Toc, but it confuses the hell out of me. I'm a late bloomer, but I feel like I'm finally getting it right. Send good thoughts, Megger. This has to work...

(She starts to slow down, trips over her own feet and hits the floor. Dazed she starts to crawl off.)
No, no...all good here...Of course he'll be a great guy. They only pick the best. It's TV.

(She collapses onto her face.)
WE HEAR the chorus of Katy Perry's song, "ROAR", the lyrics, "cause I am a Champion and you're gonna hear me roar. (Lights start to fade) Louder, louder than a lion 'cause I am a Champion and you're gonna hear me roar."

An Anthology

The Happy Place
by Joyce Newman Scott

Setting: Disney World back office
Character: Ethel, 60s a widow looking to bury her husband's ashes in Disney Land.

She is confronted by and detained by one of the Disney police officers who is dressed as Woody from Toy Story.

The woman, ETHEL, (60) once a beauty in her early days, has perfect cupid lips and sparkling eyes. She has come to the Disney Park with the intention of scattering her husband's ashes, until she gets apprehended by a guard.

ETHEL
How long do you plan on keeping me here ... Officer Krupke?

You have no legal right to hold me. You're just a Magic Kingdom custodian dressed in costume. Who are you supposed to be, anyway, Woody from "Toy Story"? (Beat) So, Woody, do I need to call my lawyer? After what they charged me for a ticket to get in here? I still have a half day of rides and shows. Look, I'm just a widow trying to find a "fun" final resting place for my husband's ashes. How's that disturbing the peace? He loved It's a Small World. Used to sit on the platform near the head-spinning bird. Always made him laugh. And how are my husband's ashes contraband? I couldn't very well carry

Frozen Women Flowing Thoughts

around Fred's urn of ashes out in the open, now could I... at the happiest place on earth? It would have depressed the other park guests.

How could I be a terrorist? I'm a housewife... (points to a stuffed monkey) That's where I placed Fred's urn. Anyone can see it's a stuffed monkey, for goodness' sake. Fred liked to hide his money in the zippered belly-pocket. Pickpockets.

You can never be too careful. Pickpocketing is heavy in the park. Almost an epidemic. And if cops weren't out harassing innocent housewives ... There wouldn't be as much crime in the Small World. (Beat) Fred thought I was passive- aggressive. Fred loved that stuffed monkey. Unfortunately, I was a little slow on the zipper ... And slow at decanting him.

I had it all planned. First a trip to the Pirates of the Caribbean, for a goodbye. Then a last stop at the moat underneath the flying elephants of the Dumbo ride. I was busy. Reading group. Knitting group. Yoga. Boxing group for seniors. The usual. Then last week I was cleaning out the China cabinet I thought, today's a good day to fulfill his dream. And everything was going perfectly... until Snow White tackled me. That broad's got a mean left hook. Then Dopey jumped in with his floppy ears. . . and all hell broke loose. (Beat) Look, it's obvious your cops aren't coming. Why don't you just let me go? I'll leave quietly. I promise. I'll never darken their kingdom again.... (under her breath) Happiest place on earth, my ass.

If Only I Had Married Aiden Fuller
by Germaine Shames

Setting: an office anywhere in the post-industrial world
Character: Daisy: a '60s flower child turned business executive held hostage by her own romantic obsession and whose liberation comes at great cost

There can only be one first love…

Daisy, dressed in business attire and looking frazzled, gets up from a desk chair and stretches. Her electronic devices all buzz and ding simultaneously; she gives up trying to attend to them, tosses her headset onto the desk, and lights up a joint.

I met Aidan Fuller in a cave. On a Greek island. Freshman year. There were a dozen or so of us broke Hippie wanderers crashing in that cave, having run out of Drachmas for a room. As fate would have it, Aidan's sleeping bag was next to mine, and while we lay surrounded by snoring adolescent bodies, we had our first whispered conversations about—well, I don't remember now exactly what they were about, though I'm sure they were deep and terribly earnest.

(*her hand absently gravitates to her heart*)

Aidan was a well-bred well-muscled Cambridge student majoring in History, but what first attracted me was his Sir Galahad haircut. Everything about Aidan perfectly accorded with that knightly coif—

his gallant manner, his chivalrous abstinence in the face of mounting lust.

(*AMBIENT SOUND of rough seas segues to dreamy BACKGROUND MUSIC*)

When the time came to leave the island, Aidan and I boarded a ferry for Athens. It was an unseasonably cold night and Aidan, being a knight, spread out his coat on the filthy deck, bundled me into his arms, and held me for the duration of the voyage. Once on the mainland, we rented a tiny room with a bed the size of an army cot and snuggled until the idyll ended. I left Aidan at a noisy bus stop, where we kissed goodbye. Only after the bus had receded from sight did I realize that this was our first kiss—and likely to be our only for a long time. We corresponded by air letter, giddily hatching plans to reunite at semester's end. I bought a motorcycle and wheeled off on new adventures, but always, hovering near my heart, was Aidan Fuller, with his man-locks and waiting arms.

(*bittersweet beat*)

Our story didn't end there—though I sometimes wish it had. Come June, I made a beeline for Cambridge. No force on Earth could have kept me from Aidan Fuller, who by this time monopolized my young imagination. Had he suddenly galloped up on a white steed, it would not have seemed the least contrived. Tingling with anticipation, I arrived at Aidan's student flat in Cambridge, only to find that he had left mere hours earlier to spend a couple days at his mother's home in the Cotswolds. I journeyed resolutely on, arrived at the quintessential country cottage, and presented myself to a very proper lady whose eyebrows rose at the sight of me and who made little effort to veil her disapproval. Okay, so I was a bit tatty from the road—my tie-dye dress threadbare, my toenails unclipped. But I sensed it was my freedom that most offended her, the fact that I had biked and hitchhiked across a continent to be with her son, whose innocent kiss I still carried on my lips. Aidan settled me into a guest room and tucked me in. He had left a single yellow rose on my pillow and a note on fine linen stationery, saying—well, I don't remember now exactly what the note said, though it had to have profoundly stirred my hormones. I barely slept. Next morning, Aidan's mother brought tea to my bedside, eying the rose with bitter resignation. And here, memory grows hazier still… Was it at breakfast that Aidan told me he would be leaving for the States the next day to spend the summer as an exchange student? He'd never mentioned it before. I'd just assumed, having come so far… Aidan left me in the London flat of some medical students and stole off in the pre-dawn penumbra to catch his plane. As the sun rose, my young self pondered how easily the bottom might fall out of a person's world.

(*realizing that her joint has gone out, relights it*)

When did it begin, my obsession with Aidan Fuller? Not in a Greek cave, nor in a Cotswold cottage, but gradually, as the Sixties faded and men cut their hair and put on suits, and women put on suits and sallied forth to pursue careers. At each blind turn, whenever the way felt harsh or empty, I would pause and think, "If only I had married Aidan Fuller…" I wouldn't be carrying this briefcase and racing for a taxi, late for another business appointment I dreaded. No, if I had married Aidan Fuller, I would live in the countryside and bake scones and tend the garden. I would lie in Aidan's arms and reminisce about dancing barefoot outside a taverna and riding a donkey back to a cave with just a sliver of moon to light our path. If only I had married Aidan Fuller. If only… and so went the refrain through my twenties, my thirties, my forties… What had become of Aidan, I had no clue. I only knew that my life was passing, my youth gone, before even a fraction of my adolescent fantasies had come real. There had been no more Sir Galahads, though men were willing enough to share my bed. If only I had married Aidan Fuller, I'd have spared myself a seemingly endless string of one-night stands, decades of post-coital depression.

(*takes a last deep drag of cannabis*)

It was inevitable, I suppose, once the Internet came along, that curiosity would get the better of me and I'd Google Aidan Fuller and send him an email, nothing heavy or desperate, a few friendly lines.

Frozen Women Flowing Thoughts

He promptly responded, only too happy to recount his personal history. Not long after our parting, he'd gone off to India and become, not a university don or historian, but a swami. When, at last, he returned home, he struggled with erectile dysfunction, but gradually recovered—enough to father swarms of children with several women. He had married in the end, remained married, the youngest of his children only two years old. Aidan Fuller, then in his mid-fifties, parenting a toddler. He offered to meet me somewhere to continue our chat in person, confiding that he'd need to keep the rendezvous a secret from his wife. I thanked him for offering, but declined. He then admitted he was a bit sloshed when he proposed the idea. For a few bittersweet hours, we sat at our respective keyboards and sifted back through our idyll. He remembered every minute detail, seemed to savor this disembodied trading of memories. Once we'd come to the end of them, there seemed nothing more to say.

(*beat of, "Oh well"*)

Had I married Aidan Fuller, my life would not have been any less perplexing nor any more fulfilling. I'd have given my best years to baby-making and diaper changing only to watch my husband ogle younger women. At fifty, I would likely have been replaced by a Gen X version of myself with bouncier breasts. Our children would have borne the scars of our failed marriage. Could I ever have forgiven myself?

(*beatific BACKGROUND MUSIC softly fades in*)

And yet, had there never been an Aidan Fuller, I would not have known that purest of loves and sweetest of aches. First love can keep its hold on a woman for eons. But if there must be a first before there can be an ultimate, who better to fill the role than Aidan Fuller?
Daisy puts her headset back on, and the CACOPHONY of electronic devices resumes.

An Anthology

Carla Keeps Talking
by Julia Weinberg

Setting: A small cluttered apartment in Los Angeles
Character: Carla, 60's, opinionated, stubborn, brilliant and angry. Also generous, kind and caring.

This character is based on my friend Cynthia Szigeti, a brilliant actor/comedienne and a famous teacher of improv in Los Angeles. Doctors told her that she would lose her ability to speak in short order because her disease would make it more and more difficult to breathe and talk. It was destined to end her life in months. She fought those odds and lived and TALKED for several years beyond anyone's wildest expectations. She drove me mad and I loved her. She called herself (and me and others like us) the "scary smart women".

Carla, seated next to her oxygen tank with tubes in her nostrils, watches Maria carefully, as Maria cleans her living room. Carla rarely moves out of her chair. She moves her hands expressively.

CARLA:

I'm glad the agency let you come today. Had a bad day yesterday - pretty bad. I did something - I need to ask you about it. You're a medical professional - Can't ask my friends - they know nothing. (watches Maria) Don't worry - it's not that serious - no, keep going. You only have a few minutes. I'm sorry about the commode and this mess. I'm okay. You know -- good days - bad days. You understand it. My so-called friends - they call - they don't know what to say to me. They say - "How do you feel today, honey?" I feel like shit - just like I did yesterday. Then they argue with me. Don't fucking argue with me. "You're doing great - you sound great." (sarcastically) Hello? I'm sitting down. I sound okay when I'm sitting down. I can't even walk five feet to the commode without gasping for air - even with the oxygen at full blast. I cough and I pee all over myself. Oh yeah - nobody wants to hear about that. I'm sitting in a pool of pee right now. How's that sound - that sound good to you? Oh - and this is my favorite question - "Do you think they maybe misdiagnosed you?" No - I don't. I'm not misdiagnosed. I'm dying. I'm worse every day. There is no Dr. House for me - this is it - and it's idiopathic. In other words, the doctors are all idiots -- nobody knows shit about this disease. Oh - I know nobody fucking wants to hear that. You know what else they're all saying to each other - what the fuck - she was supposed to be dead a year ago. So - then they ask me -- "How about lunch at Bootsy Bellows or the Ivy?" Are they fucking serious? And if I say "lunch, fuck lunch" -- I need help. Take me to Costco. Yeah - right. They're off the phone in a shot. Now the phone -- not ringing much. All day long - the sounds of silence.

Let me tell you something. You, Maria - you're my best fucking friend - I kid you not. Look - over there - I put some stuff in the corner for you - for your daughter. (she raises her hand in the air to stop Maria from replying) No - don't thank me. You've got 5 more minutes and you've got to go. I know hospice care only pays for the two hours, and you need to pick up your daughter. I don't want you to leave her alone at the school for even ten minutes. Bad neighborhood -- not safe for her. (beat)

This thing that happened yesterday - before you go - I need to know if I did the right thing. (looks at Maria)   Good. Okay - so I'm just sitting here and all of a sudden I can't breathe. Weird - right? Comes out of nowhere. I'm sitting here in front the TV, watching Ellen, and then I can't take a breath. I'm stuck. Nothing going in and nothing going out. I say to myself - Carla, this is it. You can't take a breath in - well that's it - blackout - show is over. Then I say to myself - fuck that shit. I pound on my own chest - that's what I do - I pound and pound - as hard as I can. I'm strong - you know that. I can lift my own wheelchair into the trunk - my pussy friends can't even do that. I pound and pound. I had to make it change - so I could take a breath. (more exposed) Maria - You know me - I am not scared to die. I've got all that morphine stashed away -- enough for an elephant. When I'm ready - I'm going to take care of business. On, come on, don't look at me like that. I'm prepared - that's all. But not for that surprise shit. I'm not ready for that. I did the right thing, right? I just pounded like a crazy person on my chest - and it changed - and I took a breath - look at me - I'm still here. (looks at Maria) Don't do that. Oh Maria - you can't cry if I can't cry. Takes too much air to cry. (short beat)

Okay - I guess it was okay what I did. Maria - you're a good woman. Thanks for coming to see me. I want you and your daughter to be okay. You take that stuff with you. Take all of it. (watching her). Good. See you tomorrow? Great. Bye Maria.

(She waves goodbye. The phone rings. She looks in the direction of the ringing)

CHAPTER FOUR

AGELESS AND ARCHETYPAL

Power Pose
by Allie Costa

Setting: Anywhere
Character: Hera

Female. Getting ready for an unexpected job interview. Excited and nervous.

HERA

I had an interview last week for my dream job. Totally out of the blue, utterly unexpected, I got a call from someone I worked with on a project however many years ago who said there was an opportunity and they thought of me and was I available to come in today at eleven-thirty? Of course I said "yes" and "thank you" and then I was out the door and on my way, and before I knew it, I was telling a security guard, "I'm on the list" and showing her my ID and then I'm through the gates and up the stairs and I get to the right floor and I sign in and that's when I notice my hands are shaking. We're not talking a little tremor. We're talking San Andreas Fault. We're talking Shake Shack. So I clasp my hands together and realize they're clammy. I cross my arms – my armpits are sweating. I wipe my hands on my pants and see a ketchup stain. It looks like I'm bleeding. Clammy, shaking, sweating, and stained - I'm gonna make a great first impression.

Frozen Women Flowing Thoughts

Then I remembered this article I read that said to strike a power pose before interviews, to stand like this (she demonstrates, putting her hands on her hips) to boost your confidence. So I do that, and the Wonder Woman theme song starts running through my head – you know, (singing) "All the world is waiting for yooou – and the power you possess" – and I'm thinking, You can do this, you're gonna get this, you're gonna get this, get it - and the door opens. As I lock eyes with the person who can change my life – or at least, my career - I realize not only am I clammy, shaking, sweating, and stained, I'm also singing. My ears don't recognize the words - am I still warbling Wonder Woman or am I chanting, get it, get it? As my future boss raises her eyebrows and says my name with a huge question mark at the end, I keep my hands on my hips and say, "That's me," then I stride into the room, ready to take on the world.

An Anthology

MODERN GODS
by Vivienne Glance

A Dramatic Poetic Monologue

Various Settings: Jane's home, a lingerie shop, a gym, a doctor's surgery. Modern day.
Character: JANE

Another morning and another boring shift in a shop selling lingerie. But today Prince Charming walks into Jane's life and she does everything she can to turn into his beautiful Snow White. Using symbolism, song, humor, and dramatic metaphor Modern Gods tells the tragic story of plain Jane who longs to be beautiful. She grew up with stories of witches casting spells and so tries to cast her own modern magic to transform her body and create the current ideal of outer beauty. Her story weaves in and out of fairy tales and memories, as Jane endures her transformation into both a fragile and a grotesque princess, chasing her dream of perfection.

Beauty is not constant, and each era has redefined and questioned it again and again. In our modern times, beauty has slipped and morphed to suit current ideals and to fit in with new marketing campaigns to sell beauty products and clinical procedures. I have noticed how young and older women, and increasingly men, may be subtlety pressured into transforming their outer appearances, often at great cost both financially and emotionally, and this inspired me to tackle this challenging subject. I hope the themes and dilemmas of Jane will resonate with you, the reader, and with audiences and perhaps contribute *in some small way to encourage people to recognize their own individual beauty without succumbing to an often-unattainable ideal.*

JANE

'Criss-cross apple sauce give a little clap.
Fold your arms together and put them in your lap.'

Be a good girl, not now, dear, I'm busy.
Sit still, be quiet, I'm talking.
Don't you look pretty in your pink dress.
Be a good girl, not now, dear, I'm busy.
Sit still, be quiet, I'm talking.
Don't you look pretty in your pink dress
… dear… good girl…still… quiet…pretty… pink…

Sugar and spice and all things nice, that's what little girls are made of!
Wine before beer, makes you feel queer. Beer before wine and you'll feel fine.

Slag! Look at her.
She shouldn't wear that dress with her figure. No fat chicks allowed.
She'll go with anyone; if they'd have her. Wouldn't want to wake up to that.
Slag! …her figure … fat chicks…if they'd have her…wake up to that …

Slugs and snails and puppy dogs tails, that's what little boys are made of.
Leave me alone!

An Anthology

Birth date 21 06 1987. Weight 3.79 kg. Length 51 cm. Head circumference 35.5 cm. From Day One the measuring up begins

---

Once upon a time there was a little girl. She lived with her mother in a cottage by the lake. They had everything they needed. They drank cool, fresh water, they gathered fruit from trees that grew in the rich, dark earth and each night they cuddled up in front of the fire to keep warm from the cold wind. And her mother made up stories for her. They were so happy together. Ahhh!

One day a handsome fisherman came to their cottage. He was big and strong and spoke with a firm, but gentle, voice. He had caught salmon from the lake, and he offered them the pink, soft flesh to eat. The little girl didn't like it, but her mother did. And that night the little girl was left alone in front of the fire to warm herself and make up her own stories… as the fire crept out from the fireplace and began to dance. It danced around the little girl who danced around with it. And they danced, and they danced…..

And when the fire had danced itself to ashes there was no cottage, no fisherman, and no mother left. So the little girl was sent away to live with her grandmother deep in the forest.

--

Shit, no it can't be! Just another hour, please. *Arrrrgh! I don't want to go to work! Can't I stay home?* Ok! Ok! You win. You win. You always win!

Coffee! Coffee! Coffee! Shower. Brush hair. Clean teeth, don't want smelly breath. Minty breath, sparkling white! Deodorant and perfume. Roses float unseen into my world. Civilise the senses, civilise the sensual. No room for bad smells. No place for real smells. For as long as I can remember…

Frozen Women Flowing Thoughts

(As GRANDMA SOPHIE)
Hello sweetie! Come and give your Gran a hug.
Had an accident, sweetie? Come on. Let's clean you up. Don't want to be a smelly girl. Don't want to be a stinky girl.

(As JANE)
In front of my friends. Thanks Gran!

Stinky! Stinky! Stinky! Stinky! Stinky! You smell.
Smelly Jane. Jane the Pain.
Smelly Jane. Jane the Pain.
Smelly Jane, Jane the Pain.

I hate mornings. They're too early. There should be more night - I like the night. The time when dreams are created from the mystery of sleep.
But I conform to the day Nazis. I rise at 7 get to work by 8 and function in the civilised world - of retail lingerie.

32 34 36. Lace. Black. B cup C cup Double D. Satin. Red. Under wired, support, sports. Cotton. Grey. Teddy, baby doll, full length. Silk. White.

Yes, ma'am that looks great. Just your colour. Need any help Sir? Very sexy! Shall I gift wrap? Of course she can change it if it's not her size. Or her taste.
Men …… Words of advice …

(as GRANDMA SOPHIE)
Don't set your sights too high, dear. Trust and friendship are the best things to look for in a man. It doesn't matter that you're not as pretty as the others. Beauty lies within. You'll do fine...

(as JANE)
But of course we all know that's a lie. Beauty matters. It opens doors, it gets you noticed. It means that even if you fail, you haven't failed. It blesses you - you are God's gift …
And there was I Plain 'ole Jane. Surviving school – rather than attending it. No cheer leader attraction, no confidence, no ambition. And absolutely no personality.
This is my niche. Working in a shop where the merchandise is centre stage. Where no one looks me in the eye or really listens to what I say. That's 38 dollars and 27 cents. Thank you. Have a lice day!
See? A place to go unnoticed.

--

Once upon a time, in a land far away there lived a wicked witch. She used her magic to make herself beautiful, so beautiful that the king fell in love with her.
and made her his queen.
Mirror, mirror on the wall
who is the fairest of them all?
The king's first wife died, many years ago giving birth to their daughter who was now grown up. Oh, she was so beautiful with long black hair and full red lips and skin as white as new fallen snow. And her name was …. Jane.

Frozen Women Flowing Thoughts

The Story Book... my Bible. Witches, my disciples. Fairies were too nice and – well, floaty. I was floaty in life, I needed my stories to be firmly grounded, to be solid black.

(Imitating a FAIRY TALE WITCH)
Woman of the Hearth, Woman of the World
Of health and birth, of pot and broom.
Pills and lotions, pills, and lotions
I make the potent potions.

Woman of the Night, Woman of the Woods
Of the dark places, the mossy beds.
Secrets and spells! Secrets and spells!
I hold the secret of spells.

Every one of us has a story. Every story casts a spell. If you dream of magic, beware, careless dreams become nightmares.
Come here, little girl, I'm going to eat you up. Ha, ha, ha, ha!

(As JANE)
Witches always have a good laugh, loud and strong. Ha, ha, ha, ha! Women with loud, strong voices that are heard in the middle of the darkness.
Scary.

32 34 36. Lace. Black. B cup C cup Double D. Satin. Red. Under wired, support, sports. Cotton. Grey. Teddy, baby doll, full length. Silk. White.

(SINGING) There was an old woman tossed up in a basket
Seventeen times as high as the moon;

Where she was going I could not but ask her
For in her hand she carried a broom.
'Old woman, old woman, old woman,' quoth I
'Where are you going to up so high?'
'To brush the cobwebs off the sky!'
'May I go with you?'
'Yes, by-and-by.'

But of course witches were never like that. That's the stuff of fantasy. The winners write the past, the losers – well, they just live with it. Think about it -if witches could do that sort of magic, they'd reign supreme. Those witches never existed. Except in my dreams. Pity. And old women don't have adventures or fly to the moon, they just complain. Like Grandma Sophie with all her words of advice....
Skin sags, belly sags, arms sag, eyes sag, arse sags. Heart sags. The unrelenting pull of gravity on flesh.

(As GRANDMA SOPHIE)
Hello dear. Taking care of yourself? You're looking pale. Never listen to me. Ahh! Wisdom comes with age when your too old to enjoy it. It's a curse. It is. You fight the same fights I did, cry the same tears. I know, I was young once. Still, as I always say and as my mother before me said and hers before that - 'To thine own self be true'. It's the only way that works.
To thine own self be true.
Oh, sit me down. Take the weight off my feet. Aches and pains are my constant companions. My body and my heart.
I see the way you look at me. I see the pity and disgust that age brings.

Frozen Women Flowing Thoughts

So I live with my memories. More memories than ever, my mind replaying my life, things long forgotten come flooding back, clear as the day I lived them.
Memory …
Warm, woollen blankets and Mother's good night kiss. And happy dreams.
Memory …
Hot steaming mashed potatoes, a mountain of it, with butter and salt. And thick, brown gravy...
Memory ….
His letters… written in an uncertain hand from a place far away. Never forgotten ….
'Sophie, my love,
I think of you every moment of the day and night. I long to be with you. I know that when I am back in your arms you will rid me of the memory of stinking mud and blood and my constant fear. I have witnessed the evil in men's hearts, but I know it can be conquered by love. And my love for you Sophie, gives me the strength to endure this pit of hell. I will love you forever,
Your husband, Joe'

Grey mud. Black hearts. Red blood. White fear.
And, like his love he will never grow old.

Alright are you, dear? I just wanted to look. What is all this anyway? Underwear? It'd never keep you warm.

(As JANE)
Blah! Blah! Blah! … Always the same. Is that all I have to look forward to -a decrepit body and wrinkles?

To thine own self be true. Blah! Blah! Blah! ... Anyway what 'self' do I have as every day I sell the stuff of fantasy? Unnoticed.

Let me take those for you, Sir. White. Cotton. Soft. With little white roses. White rose. The Virgin's flower. I fall in love with his romance. I fall in love with his possibilities.
Gift wrapped?
His face is full of desire. I want him and all his heart beating, grasping, slippery, pumping desire. But he looks beyond me to the poster on the wall.
Satin, red and shiny, she gazes out onto the world...Black hair falls long and silky down her nameless, perfect body. Her snow-white face adorns the busy street, the movie screen, magazine. Frozen in the moment twenty times larger than life, looking straight at me. No awareness of her near nakedness, oozing sensuality, selling sex. Saying 'Be like me. You want me.'

Mirror, mirror on the wall, who's the fairest of them all?

I am bewitched. Above me she towers, shiny and slim and before me Prince Charming. As untouchable as the father I never knew. The man of my many dreams with white roses -his kiss will free me from my frozen sleep.
But in this forest my Prince rides on by, never noticing me. Have a lust day!

(SUNG IN A BLUES VOICE, LIKE BILLIE HOLLIDAY.)
I long to be beautiful! I long to be thin!
I long for love! I long to be beautiful!
I long to be her! I long for him!

Frozen Women Flowing Thoughts

There is always longing!

Lunch break. I buy white cream to delay wrinkles, red lipstick to seduce, black mascara to ensnare and colour to cover the grey. Potions and lotions and balms and creams and perfumes and dreams! Modern alchemy. Transformation. The power to become something other than me -to make my magic!

Mirror, mirror on the wall, who's the fairest of them all?

I join a gym.
Ten minutes…. Nearly done. Keep it up. Check calorie count. That can't be right!
9 and half minutes… Fasting. That's the only way! Oh, I'll miss my food! But the pounds will fall off. One by one, then two by two, three by three, four by four, five by five, six by six, seven by ….
Seven minutes… Still?! Will it never end? Without food I'll feel drowsy. I do feel lousy. I'm starving. No! I must suffer. I must control. I must… I must…

Possession. Obsession. Possession. Obsession.
My desire possesses me. It seeps into me. Eats me up from the inside. I am possessed by the devil of longing.
Only 3 more minutes to go… I will make it. I will…
Muscles scream, chest hurts.
My life is dripping out of my pores. My fat arse, my flabby thighs, my plump belly. It is melting as I run. Stumble. Push one foot in front of the other. I will be the adoration creation I dream of.

Mirror, mirror on the wall, who's the fairest of them all?

Chasing hope and desire, chasing hard, staying still. I will get there to my goal weight, my perfect shape! He will love me!
    Grandma! Gran. Will I ever be beautiful?

(As GRANDMA SOPHIE)
Come here, dear. There, there. Come on. Just be yourself. Like me and my Joe. I never looked for him, we just happened. I wished you'd known him; he was a good man. And I know even as he lies in the cold Earth, he still loves me. That's the kind of love you need.

Grey mud. Black hearts. Red blood. White fear.

(As JANE)
But life's too short. I can't wait for true love, I pursue it. I use the ultimate weapon. He will notice me.
I call upon the serpent and the sword. Once symbols of wisdom and healing now become modern Magic. A helping hand.
Stretched out, a virgin sacrifice, scared and excited, cloaked in cleanliness.
The blue coats and masks, eyes peering down at me. Clinical smiling eyes.
Drugs numb, bright lights blind. Devoid of sensation, I am floating under the knife. Cut! Tug! Cheek lifts up. Pull gently. Oh, so gently, pull beauty into place. I am a sacrifice on the altar of beauty.
Beneath the bandages my red skin swells, puffy and sore. For weeks I hide awaiting my transformation. And like a serpent I shed my old body to reveal my new.

Frozen Women Flowing Thoughts

Hi! Isn't it wonderful? And he's so reasonable. Invisible scars. Can't see a thing. Only a couple of weeks to recover completely. Oh really? Do you think so? Thanks! Just need the rest of my body to catch up. I'm having lipo. next week. Belly and buttocks. Then the breasts. Keep it balanced, if you know what I mean.

Belly! Buttocks! Breasts! Shape shifter! Shape shifter!
Belly! Buttocks! Breasts! Shape shifter! Shape shifter!

New garments shape my breasts and firm my waist. Almond shaped eyes and teeth like pearls. I am pressed and pulled and pushed into shape.

Belly! Buttocks! Breasts! Shape shifter! Shape shifter!
But still he doesn't notice me!

(As GRANDMA SOPHIE)
We all love, we all lose love, and we all look for love again. The circle forever turns. To thine own self be true. Remember? Have patience, and love will find you.

(As JANE)
Yeah, yeah, but I want it now. I can't wait. I am filled to the brim with longing.
So I stop selling lingerie and start selling dreams…

Powder, rouge, powder, powder. I am fussed over like a princess. Everything is perfect. Every hair on my head in place, every other hair removed. Smooth, silky skin, yards of it, from my fingers to the tips of my toes -long, and lean, long, and lean. Lips, cheeks, eyes shine!

I am called. I am ready to work my magic. To grace their product with the power of the feminine. The compelling force that binds us all -the bottomless pit of desire. I love this! In this moment all their eyes are upon me. Look at me! Look, but don't touch.
And now he looks at me. He looks and he is filled with desire. I have become his red satin beauty. And like a high priestess I administer to the faithful. One man after another comes to worship at the temple of my body. They kiss the cold statue, whisper adoration, and leave their offering.

Ahh! He is here. My Adonis. My inspiration! He comes to me with white roses.
We dance the dance, and he draws me close. His strong limbs and hot breath encircle me, and we are one. So easily the others are forgotten. His love is all mine now. So easily it is given. And he kisses me.
It's nice. It's warm. But it's not breaking any spells.

Mirror, Mirror on the wall, who's the fairest of them all?

Gran!
He stands beside me and shares my light. He stands before me and casts his shadow. And now he wants more - more than just me.
For only so long can I beat my body into submission, stretch my face like canvas over a frame. My bewitching charm fades.
But I am more than just my body. I have become everything you wanted me to be - vision of perfection. I am trapped in a circle of perfection.

You won't let me grow old, as moment by moment I age. Minute by minute my time ticks away. Every cell in my body waits for its des-

tiny. Its programmed time to self-destruct. Inevitable. Every single cell.
And youth goes by so fast, so fast, you hardly notice. Where did the time go? Where's that beautiful woman who used to be me? Her young skin, firm cheeks, a strong and hopeful step? The world was a giant game…

Gran?! Gran?! Help me! He despises me now. Spits on my scars. Throws my image onto the fire. I am condemned by his fear. He tortures me with neglect. Starves me with loneliness. I was his burning desire, now his indifference burns me. So easily love turns to hate. Gran? I know you can hear me. Gran? Gran? I know you can …
He left me. They all left me. Even you will leave me. So easily love turns to hate.
I became his red satin beauty when all I wanted was his white roses. Grandma, I'll miss you! I wish … I wish I'd … I love you Grandma! You were always true. 'To thine own self be true'.

(As GRANDMA SOPHIE)
How my old body still craves a lover's touch even as I stare at death! To lose myself in a passionate kiss and feel ecstasy ripple through me. Another's life wrapped in my arms, flesh on flesh, another's scent. And death does not mock me. It's ever-present stench does not strip me of my humanity. My desire for love still burns deep inside me. Up until my last breath, I am a woman.

(AS JANE)
Being exists only as a series of instants. Time exists only in the moment of its perception. That instant is the realisation of being. That instant is ultimate compassion. And compassion is the seed at the heart of all magic.

Shit, no it can't be! Just another hour, please. Argh! I don't want to go to work! Can't I stay home? Ok! Ok! You win. You win. You always win!

Coffee! Coffee! Coffee! Shower. Brush hair. Clean teeth ….
I … I dreamt I was a white rose. Now I'm not sure if I'm a woman who dreamed I was a rose, or a white rose now dreaming I'm a woman. If we learn from anything we must learn from our dreams.

32, 34, 36. Lace Black… black hearts, red blood…
To be different has always been dangerous. To think beyond accepted thought is to invite scorn. To speak of possibilities for true freedom…

B cup, C cup, DD… Satin…
I see myself. As I am. The healing inside begins.

Under wired, support, sport…
Speak the truth, always. The magical power of the Word.

… Silk. White.
To thine own self be true.

Life is our only 'Once upon a time' our chance to tell our story. And they are all the same old story because every story must have an ending and every ending is a new beginning.

Mirror, mirror…

And beauty lies within for all the world to see.

Blessed be.

Salt
by Judy Klass

Setting: In the Jordan Rift Valley
Character: **IDIT:** *SHE is Lot's wife, and she stands alone: a pillar of salt.*

Almost immobile, IDIT addresses the audience.

IDIT: If you've ever visited the Holy Land, you may have seen me. I stand near the Dead Sea. I have been here a very long time. The Dead Sea is harsh to swim in. Or, rather, to float in. The salt will creep into your every crevice, and cause every cut and abrasion to hurt. Wounds you did not even know you had will smart and sting, as soon as the salt crawls into them. Salt is bitter to the taste, and I should know. All I am, and all I have been for thousands of years, is salt. *(beat)* They say my husband was a good man. The only good man in our city. God wanted to wipe out the whole city, but Abraham bargained Him down. Abraham was my husband's uncle, you see. And he and God were very close. And when God said He would destroy our city, Abraham asked – well, but what if there are fifty righteous men who live there? Will you kill the righteous, along with the wicked? God said no. And Abraham asked: What if there are only forty-five righteous men? Or thirty? Or twenty? And he haggled with God, until he got Him down to ten. But the only righteous man in the city, as it turned out, was Abraham's nephew. Lot. My husband. *(beat)* So, God sent two angels to our house. And my husband – he was a very righteous man, Lot was. He greeted them. He let the angels know he was their servant. He had me wash the feet of these two beautiful young men, in a basin of water, with a clean cloth. And I made those two men an enormous meal. Unleavened bread, and wine, and roasted lamb, and pastry filled with cheese and a rose petal jam – every dish that I knew how to prepare well, Lot ordered me to make, and I set it all before these two shining, beautiful young men. But our neighbors were rough and crude. They resented the righteousness of my husband. That was not new. That had been going on for some time. And they had seen these men arrive. And they banged on the door, demanding that Lot send the men outside, for our neighbors to rape. Well. My husband would never do that. He would never turn on a guest like that. My husband understood the rules of good manners, and hospitality. *(beat)* My husband was a righteous man, after all. *(beat)* So, he told the crowd outside of our house: I have two unmarried daughters, here at home. Virgins. I will send them outside to you. Gang rape them, he said, instead of the angels, my visitors. *(beat)* Now, those of you who read the Bible – you generally assume that when the crowd continued to demand the angels ... that no harm came to my daughters. That my husband's generous offer was refused by the crowd. *(beat)* I will not ... I will not discuss what I think may have happened. The truth is – I am not sure, exactly, what happened. I objected to what my husband was saying, you see. For the first time in my life, I stood up to him. I was wild. I was shouting and pleading, and grabbing at his clothing. And so, he locked me in a back room. And I could not really hear, for a long time, what occurred. My daughters were screaming and crying in terror, you see, and the crowd outside was jeering, and threatening, and calling out obscenities, and laughing, and my husband was shouting at them, righteously, and I myself was screaming, and pounding with my hands on the door that I could not get open ... This went on for a long time. Endlessly, it seemed. *(beat)* When, at last, that good man Lot allowed me out of the room where he had locked me – things had changed. The angels had brought blindness down upon the men outside the house, and those men were no longer a threat. My daughters were huddled in their room, consoling each other, and weeping, and they would not talk to me, or to anyone, and my husband told me to gather our things, and pack. To take everything I could carry. My daughters had to do the same. Once we left the house, my husband led us to the homes of my

Frozen Women Flowing Thoughts

married daughters, but our sons-in-law jeered at him. He was a very righteous man, you see, and that caused some people to dislike him. Some saw him as proud, humorless, priggish and smug. So, my married daughters – they were left behind in Sodom. While we headed down the road, toward Zoar. And Sodom ... you must understand that I had grown up in Sodom. I had friends in the city when I was young. Once I was married, I was not allowed to leave my husband's house. And my daughters, the unmarried ones, rarely left the house, though I don't know if he threw them outside that day, to the crowd ... but in any case, I remembered. I remembered my parents, and my grandmother. I remembered childhood friends and playmates. I remembered my married daughters and my grandchildren. And as we headed down the road to Zoar, the town where my husband planned to hide ... that was when God chose to smite the city of Sodom. He rained down fire and brimstone on the city. Fire and sulphur. There were sparks and flames, and lightning bolts in the sky, and a horrific smell in the air. You could smell the sulphur and acrid smoke. You could smell the sweet, seared human flesh. You could hear the screams. You could hear the buildings collapsing, caving in on the people inside, all over my city. The ground trembled as they fell. And I was walking behind my husband, and he had ordered me not to look back. But I heard a scream – it sounded to me like my oldest married daughter ... and I looked back. And so, he left me there. Left me here. And here I stand. I was deemed unworthy, you see – I looked back, so I must have been lusting for a wicked way of life. *(beat)* So, I stand here now. And many tourists visit this place and gawk at me. People from different faiths and sects. From all around the world. With cameras and with prayer groups. And sometimes they pray by me. Sometimes they read aloud from the Torah. And that is how I have come to know what happened to my family. *(beat)* My husband and my daughters went on to the town of Zoar. But then, my husband took my two young daughters away from the village, and up into a cave in the mountains. I don't know why. And I don't know the state of their minds. I don't know exactly what happened to them when I was locked in that room, pounding on the door until my hands bled. I don't know how it affected them – the destruction of our city, and leaving our relatives behind, and leaving me, their mother, behind, here, as a pillar of salt. I do not know if they were still thinking clearly. But what I have heard read in the Torah ... is that they thought they must lie with my husband. Perhaps they thought that every city, everywhere, would be consumed in flames, as our city was. Perhaps they thought that he was the last man on Earth – this one righteous man that God had spared. Perhaps they went a little funny in the head. *(beat)* They gave him wine. And he got drunk, and he lay with one of them the first night. And perhaps he was aware of what he had done, when she got up and left. And they gave him more wine, and he lay with our youngest daughter the next night. And after my husband had sex with our two daughters ... well. He impregnated them. They each had a son. And there was no punishment for him, from God, for doing that. Because ... because Lot was still good in God's eyes, he was not wicked and sinful like me, or like my city. Because my husband, after all, was such a righteous man. *(beat)* I have lot of time to think, as I stand here. I may not look recognizably human to you, when you visit, but I can still see and hear you. I can feel the sun beat down. And I have a bitter taste in my mouth, always. It is the taste of salt. All I am is salt. All of my memories are crusted and preserved in salt. And it stings.

THE FAT LADY SPEAKS
by Judith Pratt

Setting: A gym, today

Character:. The Fat Lady, an avatar of The Goddess. The actress need not be fully "fat," but should definitely not be thin! Six feet tall and stacked is good. So is round and firm and fully packed.

> *The Fat Lady is working out. She wears a sweatsuit and a headband decorated with an ivy leaf print.*

God this is boring. Boring. Bore. Ing. Bore. Ing. Bore. Ing
Snaps her fingers. Loud aerobic dance style music comes on. She boogies as she steps or walks.
Ah, hell.
Finger snap, music stops. So does she.

Why do you folks <u>do</u> this?

> *If she's on a workout machine, she gets off. Snaps fingers. Aerobic dance music again. She does dance calisthenics awhile in front of a "mirror" that is the audience. In rhythm with the music.*

Tedi-<u>ous</u>. Monoto-<u>nous</u>. Repeti-<u>shous.</u> Tedi-<u>ous</u>. Monoto-<u>nous</u>. Repeti-<u>shous</u>. Tedi-<u>ous</u>. Monoto-<u>nous</u> . . . PAIN IN THE ASS.

Music stops.

So why? Feels so good when you stop? Better than this was bungee jumping. At least that gave me a thrill. Zing. Snap. Splat. Thin layer of fat lady. Whooee.

> *She gestures. Belly dance music. She takes off her sweatshirt, and is wearing a belly dance bra and bangles underneath. She dances.*

Now this is dancing. The old way. All day, all night. Drink wine, make love under the moon. That's a thrill. Tit-til-ation. Oh yeah.

What. *[Considers her expanse of belly.]* I don't do this kinda dancing in a sweatshirt, that's why. Now you all listen up. You dance for fun is why you dance. Not for mirrors. You dance for sex, power, ecstasy. You dance for the hell of it.

You got some serious issues here, you know that? Little shakin gets you all nervous. Little jigglin. Little jelly. *[Jiggles aggressively.]* Lotta wimps.

And what's up with these machines to work out on, hah? They power something, that's it, right? Run the lights, the windmill, the dishwasher? Don't see no dishwashers here. No windmills. Lights still on.

Oh, it's healthy? Crap, if you'd a told me that. Like the stuff you eat. Jamaican grilled tofu on a bed of arugula with miso-tahini sauce.

Compost.

Tell you what. You find me a nice pig. Feed him arugula. Then we eat the pig.

What are you talking? Pigs don't make you sick. People been eating pigs for thousands of years. Roasted on a spit, mmm-hmm. Cooked up with some rice, few vegetables, lotta garlic. Mmm. Split pea soup with a good juicy hambone. Mmm-mmm.

Frozen Women Flowing Thoughts

No? Okay, how about some cheese? Goat cheese with fresh bread. Melt up some Swiss with a little wine, twirl in some toast, get it on your chin. Yeah. Just a plain old cheese omelet, few scallions, fries. Mmm.

Oh-kay, yeah, I get it. *[some kind of bad Eastern guru routine]* Right eating is right living. Right living avoid suffering. No suffering, no Death. You are immortal. You are . . . skinny, righteous, and <u>bored</u>. For a looooong time.

What we need around here is a little more whipped cream and a lot less righteousness. Because I'm tellin ya, honey, I clip when I clip. *[Takes a pair of scissors out of a pocket. Starts pulling threads from her clothes, snipping them.]*

You don't know about the three thready sisters? Nah, course not. Who cares about a bunch a has-was goddesses these days. Okay, here's the deal. Clo spins out your life thread. Lakeisha measures it. Addie clips it off. Only what with all this downsizing, Lakeisha's gone into marketing, and Addie took early retirement. Now I got to do both their jobs and my usual harvest-fecundity-roast-pig gig too.

And I clip when I clip. *[Pulls out and snips off threads as she speaks.]* Mr. twenty-year-old athlete. Missus sixty-year-old eater of high cholesterol foodstuffs. Mr. thirty-year-old vegetarian. Missus eighty-year-old madam. Some of 'em had fun. Some of 'em didn't. *[gentler]* Here's a sweet thing. Fell for the wrong goddess. Worshipped Her Royal Scrawniness, Miz Desiccation Herself, the Lady Famine. Scared to death of food. Starved on purpose. All her teeth fell out, bones crumbled. Meanwhile there's this one, same age, starving to death like it or not in one a them starving-to-death countries.

No, it ain't fair. Who said fair? We got our reasons, us goddess types. You don't need to know 'em. You just need to have a little fun. Do some dancin. Eat a little roast pig. Feed a few hungry mouths.

Why do you work so hard to dry up the juices of life? What are you afraid of? That you will eat up the world? Eat and eat until you grow as huge and powerful as I am? Or maybe you fear that the world will eat you? That <u>women</u> will grow as huge and powerful as I am?
WELL, YOU'RE RIGHT. I AM THE FAT LADY. I AM THE GODDESS. I MOTHER YOU, I JUDGE YOU. I DEMAND TO BE FILLED. I DEMAND TO BE SATISFIED. THE WHOLE WORLD IS NOT ENOUGH FOR ME.

Oh, dear, I'm doing it again. This larger than life thing does have its drawbacks. I don't want to resort to The Full Goddess Whammy. Then you'll decide I'm a fever dream and go back to worshipping her royal scrawniness, The Lady Famine. Hell, hell, hell hell.
Look, I don't mean to be a nag. I don't want to be cruel. You are still all my children, boys and men, women who carry their power in their flesh, and my smaller daughters whose power hides beneath flat bellies and tiny breasts. But the <u>world </u>is cruel. People starve. And you were made in my image, with the power to withstand famine and the brains to prevent it. Why do you waste your strength when the world needs it so much?

You need strong legs, big bellies, broad shoulders, and your full attention for the work of the world. <u>That's</u> the way to cheat Death. Use your strength. Feed yourselves. Feed the world. Feed me!

MADAME MEDUSA WOULD PREFER A CHARDONNAY
by Nora Louise Syran

Setting:
A dark, dank cave.
Character:
Medusa

Medusa sits waiting as the last of a long line of heroes attempts to cut off her head. This time she just might let him. But she'd like to sit and talk for a bit first...
A ten minute play inspired by Euripides' Andromeda

A dark, dank cave. The sound of dripping water. A beautiful woman with serpents for curls in her hair sits sipping a glass of amber colored wine with her back turned. Next to her is an alembic still. She is distilling wine. The dripping from the water down the walls of the cave and the dripping of the golden liquid in the still merge. At the sound of the scuttling of a pair of feet, she turns. A final hero has come to cut off her head. She's been there, done that and is tired of turning everyone, including herself, to stone. Once Perseus cuts off her head, her sons with Poseidon, Chrysaor and Pegasus, will be born from her spilled blood.

MEDUSA
Will you just piss off? You're interrupting my sacred hour!

(*Medusa sighs and then speaks gently.*) Come back in the morning, there's a good little hero.(*Footsteps once again.*) I warn you! This wine is highly flammable!

(*Silence.*)

Call me a barbarian but I don't water it down. Moderation, yes, I know, I know… But I prefer it neat. Without the cold metallic taste of the water that drips down these limestone walls. Drip, drip, drip. And I'll not ask you to join me. We'd get chatting, you'd turn to ask me something, our eyes would meet and well, poof. Stone. More stone. More minerals. Men and the metals they carry to cut off my head. And I've no roasted meat to offer you even if you were my guest…

I see you, you know! What I lost in virginity I gained in vision. (*Laughing.*) Thank the snakes. (*In clarification.*) Many pairs of eyes. (*Pause.*) Thank the gods.

(*She waves her glass and lifts her forefinger.*) Well, one, really. (*Sardonically.*) Thanks, Poseidon. I don't know what's worse. The fact that you men are goaded on into going after my head for some vainglorious reason or other or that I turn every one of my heroes into stone with one glassy green glance?

(*Calmly.*) I can hear you, you know. Slinking along the mossy side of the main chamber wall. Thinking I don't see you watching my reflection in your shiny shield. Did Athena give it to you? Or Zeus, himself? (*Mischievously.*) Oh, has no one told you? He likes shiny things. His particular favorite is a shower of gold, light as swan's feathers. Ah, that Zeus! The gods expect us to have restraint but they're just as wicked and wily as we mortals are.

(*She twists her snakes like curls.*) Just as monstrous as the form Athena has cursed me with: my once beautiful ringlets now hissing coils.

Frozen Women Flowing Thoughts

(*Seriously.*) I tried it, once you know. Looking at myself. My own reflection. To put an end to this... (*Exhales.*) life. (*She smiles to herself and sips her wine.*) It didn't work.

(*Pause.*) Oh, it's all so very (*Overemphasis on the first syllable.*) bo-ring. All these years. All these "heroes"... (*To the approaching hero.*) So, just piss off, will you!? Unless...

(*Considering him carefully for a moment.*) You've managed to come quite far without me laying eyes on you. Sorry to give you false hope. I see deep and wide. Especially after a nice noble glass of gold.

(*She contemplates him for a moment, sips her wine.*) Did you bring any wine with you?

(*There is no reply.*) I'll take that as a no. I always ask as my very first hero brought wine. (*Sighs with pleasure.*) Years ago now. Feels like centuries. Probably is.

Some heroes come along with an amphora or two loading down their poor donkeys --who sometimes look my way at the wrong moment. Poor things. Amphorae or leather sacks of wine. But the sheep skins. Ugh! I leave those. I don't much like the taste of a poor ewe's guts with my mezzes...

My first hero came floating along on his current of hubris with wooden buckets full of wine. Wooden buckets. I'd never seen that before. And never since. Floated them here on a raft the virgins had decorated for him strewn with tearful sighs and goodbyes. I found the raft. After. Bobbing gently in the cove where he'd left it. Probably thought he'd have something to celebrate. Pity. For him. He'd have enjoyed it. It was delicious. Earthy. Not mineral in the least. Chilled to perfection in the depths of my cave. I could taste the bark it was stored in. That was something new. And something I've never tasted again...

You're still here, hero!? (*Calling.*) Perseus! Yes, I know all about you. And your mother, Danaë... A woman washed up alone with her

203

precious child. You, Perseus. Son of Zeus. I see you there, leaning against the moss!

Moss! Who am I kidding? It's mold. On the wall you're leaning against. Not moss. If I leave you here long enough you'll be covered in it. Mold. It's worse than the saltpetre caking the walls. God, I've developed such allergies down here... But I'd hardly frighten you heroes off if you met me up in my vineyard, up on the outside. (*Conspiratorially.*) I grow my own grapes. I don't turn everything to stone.

(*She sips her wine.*) You heroes leave a lot behind. Rafts, donkeys, knives, ceramics, even glass. One of the cleverest of you brought along this alembic still which I use to distill my strongest wines. He also left vials of all kinds of things: mercury, sulfur, ash.....and scrolls and wax tablets full of writing and drawings full of symbols and secret messages I'm still working my way through. Well, everyone likes a good puzzle. Even a gorgon. And I've nothing but time to kill.

There are rarely any heroes these days. And you don't tend to bring wine with you anymore. So, I make my own. Experiment to make perfect liquid sunshine. Watch it all gather to a head. (*Has forgotten all threat.*) Now, this wine here--

You know, I almost want you to succeed. Free your mother. It's a noble quest you're on, Perseus. Pity it involves my head.

(*Sighs.*) Maybe it's the wine. But I'm tempted to close my eyes and let you end my life. But only if you promise to make it quick. (*Laughs softly.*) Quick would be a mercy. This alcohol is strong enough to set even the stone of these walls ablaze. But...the agony. I don't deserve that.

No. You will approach and I will turn to face you and you will die.

(*Pause.*) Pity wine-making is not so predictable. Oh, I do wish you could taste this wine with me. It's not bad. I don't pick the grapes until late in the season, you see. Full bodied. Mature. I pick them carefully, one by one. And crush them with my bare feet like the vestal virgin I once was. Daisy-chains on my arms, wrists. I gave up on the wreath for my head. The snakes had a field day with the flowers!

And then I let them sit, macerate. The pools above chill the wine to bring out the taste of the late harvest frost and the sweet concentrated summer of sunshine.

But if I could grow oak trees, I could fashion the bark into buckets, seal them and wait. I think the oak would pair well with my grapes. Much better than those palm-wood buckets my first hero left me. For years I stored my wine in them and for a time after I could just about catch that woody earthiness I first tasted so long ago. But the woods faded, the buckets disintegrated and my mouth filled again with stone. What I would give for an oak grove!

(She sips her wine.) I was frightened at first...of this..."power". Poseidon finished, laughed and then he vanished. Athena's indignation —thundering in my ears-- blended with the hissing of snakes all around me as I fled her temple only to turn to see the guard frozen in place, his arms stretched out as he'd tried to catch me. I ran on and on. Turning men, women and children into statues in my wake. Yes, I was frightened of this— curse. Finally, I came to where my sisters and I spent our holidays, on the coast here below the Pillars of Hercules. With the view of the blue sea outstretched before me. Safe, I thought, from Athens. Not knowing what I carried in my blood. What I carry. What Poseidon gave me.

Worried I might turn myself to stone, I stayed far from the silver mirrors of the sacred pools above this dank cave that became my home and avoided the growing piles of reflecting swords, helmets and other shiny metals which began clogging up the passage once news of the power of my severed head reached the civilized world. Soon heroes came from far and wide to cut off my head.

(There is a sudden sound of feet moving on the stone floor.) Wait! Stop! You're not going to listen are you? And you're going to end up like all the rest. Unless...

(She listens to the sound of the dripping in the cave, observes her glass. Takes a sip.)

I wish I could see my grape vines wrapped around the trunks of oak trees growing tall above this darkness, forever reaching up to the sunlight. This is no place to keep a child of Poseidon to meet my gaze. And children there will be when you sever my head.

(She contemplates her glass and the hero.) I tell you, Perseus. You may have my head and all that comes with it. But take it, please, when I am least expecting it?

(She moves to turn her back.) I'll turn my back.

(Pause as she hears humanity in the distance. Sounds of stone masons, actors, travelers.)

Listen. New cities and towns are spreading like wildfire. More men. More stone. I hear the echoes of people passing on new roads to new places. But there are few heroes on them these days *(Listening)* Listen. There's even a new amphitheatre out there somewhere, across the sea. The voices of the young actors carry. I can hear their pathos strike the rocks. Pity for Atalanta, Arachne, and soon Andromeda. But there's none for me.

(Pause.) When it's done. Before you leave. Carefully bring my head outside one last time, will you, Perseus? And let me gaze on the sun.

CHAPTER FIVE

BIOGRAPICAL

Kim's Story, The Story of Kim Sang Mai
By Renée Baillargeon

Title: Kim's Story
Playwright: Renée Baillargeon

Setting: A park bench
Character: Kim 55 to 65 years old, Southeast Asian, slight accent Gentle with inner strength

I have always lived for my children. I talk to them wherever they are. All of them. Every day. I know they can feel my presence.

When I'm gone, I will miss my family. And my three little grandchildren who live with us. They are so very beautiful and so very happy. There are seven of us, sometimes eight, living in a small semi. Still, it is bigger than where I grew up in Vietnam. And I sleep on a mattress now not on a mat. And there are no longer machine guns ringing through the night sky.

I grew up with bombing and gunshots and screaming. When we heard the planes we would run to the soccer field to save ourselves and my little brother would be in charge of holding tightly onto our pig. The soccer fields were safer because the enemy liked to bomb villages not open spaces. That way they could kill more people. I like the quiet here. Sometimes I get up at night, just to listen to the quiet. It is not the quiet of death. It is the quiet of peace.

Frozen Women Flowing Thoughts

When my father and baby brother fell ill and died, I knew my life would be changed forever. I did not want a prearranged marriage so at sixteen years old, I moved to Cambodia. At first everything was perfect. I fell in love, got married, and we had two children, a son and a daughter. My husband was a 1rst Lieutenant. I was so proud of him. He was handsome and kind. I loved him very much. But during the Cambodian Civil War, there was famine everywhere. Our village was invaded and my husband and son were among the many who were tortured and killed by the Khmer Rouge. The rest of us were rounded up and put into a prisoner of war camp. My job was to collect dead body parts so they could be used for fertilizer. I cried most nights wondering when and if the war would ever be over. Many starved to death in our camp, including my baby daughter. One of the hardest things I have ever had to do was bury my baby.

Somehow I carried on. Slowly and carefully. Vietnam finally invaded Cambodia and the Khmer Rouge fled. I thought the war was over. I returned to my village but discovered it was in ruins and there was no food anywhere. I met and married Sonny there. When I became pregnant again, I wanted to escape to Thailand so our baby could have a better life. The route to Thailand was dangerous. There were many land mines, Khmer Rouge deserters, and Thai soldiers who liked to shoot at Cambodian refugees. Sonny and I became separated. A Thai soldier confronted me. I was caught and imprisoned. The next day, I was released from the Thai prison and told to return to Cambodia. But I didn't. That night with my one-year-old son harnessed to my shoulders and six months pregnant, I set out for the Thai refugee camp. Then, my little son and I travelled for two days straight through the Cambodian jungle and the war zone. We would only stop when I had morning sickness. I hate the woods now.

I hate all bushes and trees and forests. They frighten me. It's much nicer to look at the Niagara River, breathe in the clean air and know there will always be food in the grocery store.

Eventually my son and I crossed the Cambodian border into Thailand. The Thai refugee camp became our home. There were thousands and thousands of us and the time went by very slowly.

There was no school and our tent leaked but my lovely little girl was born there safely. Sonny had found his way to another refugee camp and we were eventually reunited. We had a third child together in the camp. Another beautiful daughter. I wish that I had not contacted a disease in the camp. My little girls were so sickly. We were all given lots of needles. I don't know if they did any good. Maybe.

After three and a half long years in the camp, our family was granted refugee status and immigrated to Québec. In Montreal Sonny and I had our fourth child, another son, Solomon. We were proud to give him a Canadian name. He was a good boy. He was a happy boy. He was so excited to start school. I wish he could've stayed home longer with me.

I found it hard to learn French and English. It was too cold to go outside in Quebec and it was all so confusing. Especially shopping. It was also difficult to find work but at least there were no more gunshots. The happiest day of my life was when we all became Canadian citizens. I will always love Canada. It is my real home now. But Montreal was so cold and many of the other immigrants were a bad influence. They gambled too much. We heard about Cambodians who worked in Niagara at the fruit farms. It was much warmer in Niagara they said. Sonny had a bad back but I was strong enough. So, we moved again. I started working in Niagara eighteen years ago, and I still work every day in the summer packing fruit. The work is very tiring. Our Canadian boss exploits us and cheats us. Last year the Revenue Canada says we owe a lot of tax money because the boss's paperwork is wrong, but the doctor says I must stop working soon because I am so tired. The disease I got in the refugee camp is getting worse.

Last year my youngest son died. My Solomon. My baby. He was 26. He inherited my disease and it turned into an agressive liver cancer. I miss him. I miss my other son, my first husband and my baby daughter too. But they are at peace and I have to go home now. Everyone will be up soon and my living daughter needs me to help her before I go to work. I am thankful that my living son and daughters are so healthy now. There is always food on our table. I am sorry I will not live to see my three little granddaughters grow up but my oldest daughter is a good mother. She is a strong girl. She is the one who I carried inside me through the jungle. My son-in-law is a good man too. He has been offered a better job and wants to move North to a place called the "Soo". A fresh start. He says we can buy a bench in Solomon's memory and look out on the St. Mary's River. The park is called Belle View. I like that name. I will sit on that bench and look at the beautiful view. And it will all be OK. I am at peace wherever I am. Family is forever. Always.

AUTHOR'S NOTE – There is a bench in Belleview Park overlooking the St. Mary's River in memory of Kim Sang Mai and her "Canadian son" Solomon Chau. Unfortunately, Kim passed before she got the opportunity to sit on it. Kim and I share the three grandchildren. Her daughter (whom she carried in utero through the jungle) is married to our son and with her children's help and consent I have been able to share Kim's story.

An Anthology

Mimi Alford
by Molly Breen

Setting: no specific setting - could be at a book signing
Character: Mimi Alford

(from THAT WOMAN - THE MONOLOGUE SHOW - Stories from the perspectives of women involved with JFK)
Mimi Alford was involved with President John F. Kennedy while working as an intern in the White House press office in 1962 and 1963. Her memoir, Once Upon a Secret: My Affair with President John F. Kennedy and Its Aftermath *was published in 2012.*

It begins like this: My senior year of high school, I was editor of the school newspaper. Mrs. Kennedy had also been editor - at the same school. So I wrote to the First Lady to see if I could interview her. Although she was not available, I was invited to the White House to interview her chief of staff. There, at a gathering in the Rose Garden, I first met the President. He asked me a few questions and wished me luck.

One year later, I was hired as a summer intern at the White House. I did not apply for this job, nor do I know the circumstances behind my hiring. I only knew that it was an incredible opportunity. My job duties were collecting news wire cuttings and answering the phone in the press room. I didn't have any skills like shorthand or typing, but I was eager to learn and make a good impression.

On my fourth day of work, I received a phone call from Dave Powers, an aide to the President, inviting me to swim at the White House pool. I was surprised but accepted the invitation. When I arrived, two other staffers, Priscilla Wear, known as Fiddle, and her close friend Jill Cowan, sometimes referred to as Faddle, were there as well. A few minutes later, the President himself entered the pool. We talked for a moment, and then he swam off to join Fiddle and Jill.
I felt thrilled to be there in his presence and confused as to why I had been included. That afternoon, Dave phoned again, this time to invite me to what he called a staff welcome reception at the family residence. When I arrived, Dave, Fiddle, Jill, and another aide were already there. I had one daiquiri, and then another. Then, the President came into the room. He invited me to tour the residence. (His family was away for the weekend). He showed me the dining room, then Mrs. Kennedy's bedroom. There, he began to lead me toward the bed and undress me. I surprised myself by continuing to undress, taking off my blouse. As we were about to have sex, he paused and asked, "Haven't you done this before?" I replied that I hadn't. He asked if I was okay, and I told him I was. When we finished, he offered me something to eat from the kitchen and called for a car to take me home. On the drive back to my apartment, I was a bit stunned but also in awe. Four days prior, I had been a sheltered girl living with my parents in New Jersey. Now I was in DC working at the White House. Four days ago, I was a virgin. Now, I'd just had my first sexual experience - with the President of the United States. Never could I have predicted or even imagined this happening. It was absolutely unbelievable.

When I've talked to others about this night, some insist that I was raped. They are not happy to learn that I feel differently about my experience. That night, it was incredibly exciting for me to feel desired, something I had not felt before, and to be desired by someone so powerful, whom I admired greatly, was all the more exciting for the 19-year-old girl that I was.

The next week, I received another phone call from Dave, again inviting me for a swim. I realize now that had I declined, my life would have been profoundly different. But I was dazzled and compelled by this turn in my path, and I wanted to see what would happen next. So I said yes. This decision marked the beginning of a year-and-a-half long affair. When Mrs. Kennedy was out of town with the children, I would often sleep over at the White House. The President and I liked spending time together. We played records and cooked in the second floor kitchen. That summer I traveled all over the country with him. Dave Powers was aware of our relationship, and he and I became friends. And I loved spending time with Fiddle and Jill.

When I returned to college in the fall, the President said he would call me, and, to my surprise, he did. He used the pseudonym Michael Carter, and I was afraid his voice would be recognized. But no one who answered the phone in my dorm suspected. He would fly me to DC for visits. The night of the Cuban missile crisis, I slept peacefully in the White House, unaware of the danger that had passed.

I loved our time together. Around me, the President was charming and playful, almost like a teenager. But there were boundaries that reflected the incongruities in our relationship— the age gap, the fact that he was married, the fact that he was the President. I never called him Jack, only Mr. President. We never kissed. And although I treasured our relationship, I never believed that it was - or ever would be - more than an affair.

There were a few times, however, that the President pushed the limits of his power over me in a malignant way. Once, at a party at Bing Crosby's home, he offered me capsules of amyl nitrate. When I refused, he exploded them under my nose anyway, and the drug caused me overwhelming anxiety for the next hour. We did not sleep together that evening. Another time, during one of our White House swims, the President asked me to give oral sex to Dave Powers. It was suggested as a playful dare, and I went along with it, an act that immediately afterward, as well as now, I regret with embarrassment. As I left the pool, I heard Dave say disapprovingly: "You shouldn't have made her do that". The President agreed and eventually apologized to us. However, close to the end of our relationship, he suggested something similar in regard to his younger brother, Teddy. This time, I was extremely angry and strongly refused.

Early in 1963, I met the man who would become my first husband. But even as our relationship grew more serious, I continued my involvement with the President. When I became engaged that fall, I knew I could no longer travel with him. We had one last trip scheduled — to Dallas in November — but I was taken off the trip when Mrs. Kennedy decided to attend. Just before he left, I met him at his hotel. It would be the last time I saw him. He told me he wished I were coming with him to Texas and that he would call me when he returned. I reminded him I was getting married. "I know that," he said, "But I'll call you anyway."

The day the President was assassinated, I was with my fiancé. My reaction was far too extreme for someone who had merely worked as an intern, and my fiance noticed. In a moment of grief and shock, I told him about my relationship with the President. He - understandably - was hurt and angry, and the next day, he told me that if we were still going to get married, I must promise to never tell anyone about the affair. I agreed. Many things went wrong in our marriage, which ultimately ended in divorce, but I feel that holding this secret played a strong role in its deterioration.

I realize it seems incredibly naive, but I assumed I was the President's sole mistress. Years later, when other stories emerged, I began to understand the scope of his infidelities. But I had no intention of publicly sharing my story — ever. And oddly enough, I fell under the radar for 40 years. Finally, in 2003, a story ran in The Daily News, with a headline "JFK had a Monica…" I knew it wouldn't be long before I was found. The following day, a reporter tracked me down and asked if I was that woman. I said that I was. My secret was finally revealed.

I wrote my memoir simply because I wanted to tell my own story. I have been criticized by some for telling it. Barbara Walters said: "She'll make a lot of money!" Actually she expressed this four times during our interview. She also asked me: "Did you think at all of Caroline Kennedy, who is alive today, and her children, when you wrote this book, that didn't have to be written?" Even The View facebook page posed the question: "After 40 years of silence, do you think it was right of her to come forward with her story now? How do you think this will affect the Kennedy family?" You, too, may criticize me. But frankly, after keeping this secret most of my life, I'm not afraid of criticism. In fact, I welcome discussion.

On the other hand, I've been supported by many, including my family. As there are purported to be - many, many - women with whom the President was involved, it seems rather... historically inaccurate to simply pretend that we do not exist.

I said this in my memoir, and I will say it to you: "I am Mimi Alford, and I do not regret what I did. I was young and swept away and I can't change that fact....This book represents a private story, but one that happens to have a public face. And I do not want the public face of this story — the one where I will be remembered solely as a presidential plaything - to define me."

ANNA NICOLE SMITH IN COURT
by Grace Cavalieri

Setting: Courtroom, present day.

Character: Anna Nicole Smith

Anna Nicole is fighting for the inheritance left by her deceased ninety-year- old husband.

Anna in court room *sitting on chair on stand*

Anna *(sniffling in hankie)*
I loved him, He was the kindest man I ever knew, the only father I ever knew, and he chose me! *Him,* with all his money and cars, chose me, calling me "Anna his little angel of itching," meaning I made him itch where he couldn't scratch. Isn't that sweet? My lawyer says this should not have to go to trial. He was my husband and he loved me and left me his money. That's it. He was the perfect husband. He wasn't even jealous of the other guys I was with. He even liked to watch. He was a saint that way. He always bought three kinds of liquor in case I didn't like two, but I usually I liked all three. But sometimes I felt like beer. I never asked, "How old are you?" Do you say that to a bird or a bear who is a millionaire? No. They just are who they are. I was his cheerleader and his nurse. I gave him his medications, double doses even to make him feel better. *(Wipes eyes)*, and I was a real wife in every way. Yes, *that* way too. Although once they had to call 911. It was his plastic helper that got stuck. But he

was full of hope. I gave him hope. He was planning to grow a mustache and he had no hair! How many can say that? You can talk all you want about me, but how many of you are married to someone who gives you hope? I earned this inheritance, and if his free will was to marry me; to tell me his secrets, to let me play cheerleader, He chose me, then, isn't that the American way? To have choices? To be a millionaire if you want to be one? Once for my birthday he bought me (sniffles) He bought me (takes out hanky) Money! (Looks at crib sheet in purse) (Sniffling) If there was a villain he would have slain him for me.... (Gavel)

It Was Isadora
by Paddy Gillard-Bently

Setting: New York City, 1924. It's nearly midnight at Jack Kale's Late-Night Cabaret.
Character: Patricia,, 24, is the star of burlesque revue.. She is sultry, sexy, funny and confident.

Patricia at her dressing table is in front of the mirror primping for her next act. She has just been asked what made her want to be a dancer by a young reporter

PATRICIA
Like Shakespeare? *(beat)* I love Shakespeare.

It was Will who led me to the stage. Not by the hand, of course; he was indirectly involved.

It was actually a woman who lured me to the stage. The spring of 1916. I was a very innocent 16. I had the luxury of staying with my beautifully madcap aunt, Lacey. She's the cat's pajamas! She was nearly famous after she had an affair with Harry Houdini that was so scandalous, she was never allowed to…

She laughs.

Anyway, Lacey took me to the Lewisohn Stadium, you know - the place at the edge of Manhattan.

At first I wasn't keen on going, but Aunt Lacey insisted it would broaden my horizons. Who has horizons at 16? It was a Masque called 'Caliban by the Yellow Sands' – put together by Percy MacKaye. You know, the theatre guy.

He collected a cast of distinguished English and American actors along with hundreds of singers, dancers, all kinds of performers, to celebrate 300 years of a world without Shakespeare, who I happened to adore. It was a celebration of the genius of the man whose words pointed us to the stars.

A slew of people turned up, and that was only the first night. I had never seen so many people in one place before. And the music…the music was beautiful. Arranged, no less, by Arthur Farwell. The orchestra hit on all sixes.

And then I saw *her*. She came from the other side of the field – at first walking, as if on a cloud. I knew I was in the presence of something magical – something otherworldly.

I pushed through the crowd to get to the front, my poor aunt trying to keep up. By the time we got there, Isadora was dancing…dancing with a freedom and passion I had never seen before. Every single movement she made was glorious. The point of her toe, each gesture of her hand, every turn was perfect. Effortless. I was captivated. This woman took my breath away. Everyone near me was in the same state of pure rapture.

She was wearing just a shift. No shoes. God, how I envied her - bare feet on the grass, wind blowing her hair.

When she came near, I could see she was not a young woman, but because every movement she made expressed the philosophies of her heart and soul, she seemed twenty-three.

Frozen Women Flowing Thoughts

As she was about to pass by me, I should say us, but in that moment, she and I were in perfect understanding, and no one else existed. As if she heard my thoughts, she turned with the grace of a butterfly, and stopped, just for a hair's breadth she stopped and looked at me. And she smiled.

Isadora Duncan smiled at me, and I knew in that moment, I wanted to use my body, my own body to tell stories, to make people feel, to communicate the love and joy and anguish of life. I wanted to dance just like Isadora Duncan.

Beat.

Of course, burlesque isn't exactly what I had in mind.

An Anthology

Anzia, A Fiction
by Dana Leslie Goldstein

Setting: Outside of time
Character: Anzia Yezierska, any age

Anzia Yezierska was a Jewish American author and screenwriter whose work was published in the 20th century.

ANZIA YEZIERSKA: *(introducing herself)* Anzia Yezierska. Born 1880...ish. (*indicate date is approximate.*) In Plinsk, Poland. Or Plotsk, Russia – who knows, the border kept shifting. Died 1970. (*Proud*) Author. Member of the Federal Writer's Project, New York, 1935. Catalogued the trees in Central Park.

(*Writes in her notebook*) Azalea. Hydrangea. Linden tree.

(*Looks up; addresses audience*) After I died, my daughter, Louise, she wrote a biography about me. In it, she calls **Red Ribbon on a White Horse** – my autobiography – a fiction. It's because I didn't mention her. Louise doesn't figure in the story. I didn't fictionalize her. I just didn't mention her. Or her father. Or my first husband. And I changed a few names. And I invented a few minor characters. To get my point across. *My* point. That's what an autobiography is for.
I was eight - or ten - when I came here, and I was the youngest of seven. The only one in my family who went to an American school. I was also the only one who looked at my father, hunched over his torah scroll, his head bobbing up and down, and – (*looks away,*

ashamed.) In Plinsk, my father was revered. In the lower east side – America – he was good for nothing. My brothers and sisters didn't see it. So I was the only one who left. The only one who rose out of the tenements like a Cinderella of the Sweatshops – that's what they called me – I'm not making that up – it was in the papers.

Rose up to fame, riches, a Hollywood screenwriting contract. My father said I was a deserter, a radical, a hussy. Because I wanted to write.

(*Back to her list*) White Spruce. Empress Tree. False Camellia.

I had written a book, **Hungry Hearts**, about life in the tenements and Sam Goldwyn bought it, and brought me to Hollywood to make it into a movie. I lived at the Miramar Hotel. And I had, for the first time ever, a bathroom of my own. Two faucets. One for hot and one for cold! But it couldn't last. I said the wrong thing. I dressed the wrong way. I was an outcast. On both coasts. My first book had been made into a movie. I published stories and another novel and was offered a 3-movie deal from a major studio. A 3-movie deal for books I hadn't even written yet. Why would anyone offer that? I didn't want the strings. Maybe I didn't want the success either. Maybe I liked being an immigrant. An outcast. So I went back to New York.

The stock crash of 1929 hit everyone: bankers, industrialists, ditch diggers, authors. Publishing houses failed. Magazines folded up. When the Bank of the United States closed, my savings were wiped out. I moved to cheaper and cheaper apartments, until I was finally living near where I grew up, in a room without even a sink, skipping meals and begging acquaintances for work. I had published three novels, but I couldn't support myself. Poverty is a bag with a hole at the bottom. Finally, I hocked my typewriter.

(*Back to list*) Sourwood. Black locust. Siberian crabapple.

Then one morning I was sitting at a bare table with my landlady, who couldn't pay the rent herself, drinking hot water with a tea bag in it that I'd been squeezing the last bits of flavor out of for days, when the radio broadcast a special news report about the WPA. It was 1935. There were already government projects to get fine artists and theater people back to work. Now there was going to be a Writers Project. A new world was being born. A world where artists were no longer outcasts, hangers-on of the rich, but backed by the government, encouraged to produce their best work. The president said so.

They gave the address for the Writers Project right there on the radio. I went immediately. $23.86 a week. That's all I needed to get my typewriter out of the pawnshop.

At first, it was like a dream. For everyone. All these people called themselves writers. One had won a high school essay contest. Another had written a typewriter manual. But some – Richard Wright was one of them – were the next generation of literary masters getting a chance they'd never have without Roosevelt's crazy experiment.

(*Back to list*) Sweet gum. Sugar Maple. Tree of Heaven.

I got paid to work mostly at home, on my own creative projects, because I had a reputation. But then the whole thing started getting criticized for inefficiency. They called it *a boondoggle*. Not a bad word. Boondoogle. Almost sounds like Yiddish. They said we were taking honest taxpayers' money for nothing. Nothing. Suddenly we got a new director. And there were no more individual creative projects. All writing would have a goal – a tangible, government- approved goal. **The American Guides**.

And there was something else: a mandatory daily word count. If you didn't make the count, you were warned. And then if you still didn't make the count, you were let go. Two thousand words each day.

I was assigned to catalog the trees in Central Park for the New York guide. There are over a hundred different types of tree in Central Park. It wasn't a bad assignment. It wasn't fascinating, but it wasn't bad. I did what I was supposed to do. I noted every type of tree. And I logged every word.

Frozen Women Flowing Thoughts

(*Back to list*) European Beech. Japanese Dogwood. Spanish Oak.

Now, looking back, there's a kind of poetry in those guides, a poetry that wouldn't be there if they hadn't been written by us. In a time of great need. When we desperately wanted to be writing our own verse or our novels, but even more desperately, we wanted to eat. That's what binds us all.

Not long after that, I started my autobiography. The one Louise calls a fiction. It's no more or less a fiction than my entire life is, the immigrant who made good, the Cinderella of the Sweatshops, the dreamer who won and lost the American Dream, the radical, the hussy, the storyteller. By Louise's standards, the only true thing I've written is that catalog of trees. And it didn't even have my name on it. It was a paycheck. A life raft. A list.

(*Straight out*) Common Bald Cypress. Weeping Willow. American Elm.

An Anthology

The Dance: A Monologue Based on Real Events
by Paula Hendrickson

Setting: 1916. An upscale ballroom dancing school in Washington DC that caters to wealthy, powerful men — including members of Congress. Mannequins, silhouettes, or non-speaking actors can represent DANCE INSTRUCTORS and their WEALTHY MALE PUPILS. A PEN can stand in for a PEN GUN, or the actor can pantomime holding and pointing a pen gun.

Character: LINNEA LARSON is a tall, nicely-dressed, proper young lady, about 20 years old. She evokes a mixture of confusion and defiance, strength and innocence.

A young ballroom dance instructor pauses class to explain how and why a Midwestern farm girl wound up living an independent life in Washington DC in such a restrictive era.

> *The Dance: A Monologue Based On Real Events*

AT RISE: A WALTZ plays as SPOTLIGHT falls on LINNEA, who towers over her middle-aged PUPIL (or the mannequin/silhouette representing him). As she steps back from the pupil, all motion freezes or fades into the background, except Linnea.

Frozen Women Flowing Thoughts

LINNEA

This is not a charmed life. "Anything but the farm," I thought. Anything had to be better. But this? What is this? It's grand, I'll give you that. But what is it really — if you scratch deep beneath the surface, is anything ever what it seems?

(looks around)

Seven hundred and fifteen miles. You'd think that would be distance enough. It is not. There are some things you can never escape no matter how far you flee.

(approaches dance instructor/facsimile)

You knew it, though, didn't you? You, my lifelong friend, lured me here with promises of a good job, opportunities, and a chance to march alongside our fellow Suffragists. Instead, I stand here teaching the newly-elected Congressman from Iowa — of all places — how to dance so he won't embarrass himself at the Congressional Ball.

(to audience)

He invited me to the Ball, you know. But I turned him down.

(gestures toward his short stature)

For obvious reasons.

(to friend)

You were right, though, friend — if that's what you truly are. Jobs are plentiful in Washington. And because of you I now have three very different professions.

(to audience)

One you may have already guessed. I am a ballroom dance instructor.

(flourishing gesture)

It was entirely my friend's doing. She told me the Capital Ballroom Dancing Studio, where she worked part time, needed another instructor. She said it was a respectable way to earn money while waiting for word about the government jobs for which I had interviewed. Yet even after I was hired as a clerk for the Department of Agriculture — a good, honest job, perfect for a farm girl, don't you think? — she insisted I continue teaching here. Evenings. Weekends. "There's quite a demand for it," she said. Only she failed to explain the type of demand and who was making it. She also neglected to inform me that they were scrutinizing me for a very different type of job, indeed.

                    (discretely pulls small PEN GUN from sleeve)
We had guns on the farm. None so dainty as this. Such delicate engraving here on the side of the...pen.
                    (to friend)
You told me it was for safety, yet it doesn't make me feel very safe. It is much heavier than it appears.
                    (aims pen gun at an unseen object)
Facing this weapon, I fear my enemy would laugh while roughly casting me aside or, Heaven forbid, while slashing my throat. How, precisely, is this tiny thing supposed to keep me safe?
                    (to friend)
And why did you, my friend, decide to foist me into a position where a woman may need to defend herself against violence? Make no mistake. I'm no stranger to self-defense. It was required on the farm every time the old man was drunk or enraged.
                    (waves pen gun toward audience)
I wish I'd had this little toy the time he overworked the plow horse to the point that the poor creature refused to take another step. I had never seen a man punch a horse — not before nor since. I wanted to strike the old man down where he stood. I nearly did, too — my hand was on a pitchfork. I so wanted to ram him through and put an end to his madness, but my brother stopped me. Said the old man wasn't worth it...
                    (beat)
Where was I? Oh, yes...having failed to motivate the horse through physical violence, he had all six of us — his own children — pull the plow. And that was one of his better days. Over the years, how many times did he order us to cut switches? Hundreds? Thousands? The day I told him that if he wanted to beat me so badly, he would have to cut the switch himself, he found a "good" one. You'd think thicker switches would hurt more, but it's the thin and supple ones that inflict the most pain. He knew. The switch he cut ripped into my flesh with every strike, but I never cried, so he whipped me all the harder.
                    (rubs the back of leg)
Yet I didn't shed a tear. I refused to give him that satisfaction.
                    (to friend)
With each whack, I thought about all the letters you'd sent me, filled with stories about your exciting life in Washington. The next day, I

Frozen Women Flowing Thoughts

packed my things, boarded the train and never looked back. Until now. But you knew. You knew all along that they wanted me for this job. Why they wanted me for this job. My real job. You knowingly placed me in danger, certain I could withstand whatever may come. Like when they ordered me to steal a ledger from the Senate office of one of her pupils while she was teaching him the box step right here in this very ballroom. Unfortunately, his assistant — a much larger fellow than my pupil here — returned for a satchel he'd forgotten and caught me red handed. He grabbed my arm and attempted to shake the ledger from my grasp. For a moment I thought I might finally need this gadget.

(waves pen gun)

Instead, I imagined that he was the old man and pummeled him with my gloved fists. Apparently, unlike my father, this man was taught to never strike a woman. Or perhaps my un-ladylike behavior so shocked him that he didn't know how to respond — not even after regaining consciousness. I got the ledger, by the way. I don't know whatever became of the information, but I successfully completed my mission.

Contrary to what you might think — and despite that unfortunate confrontation — this job is far easier than it may appear to an outsider.

(twirls toward pupil)

After all, who would ever think to suspect an innocent girl, so far from home and family, of such duplicity — of spying for our nation's Secret Service?

(bats eyes)

All you see — all you want to see — is an ordinary, dependable, mild-mannered farm girl with a good government job who happens to teach ballroom dancing on the side.

(Linnea slips pen gun under her sleeve. The music resumes. The dance continues.)

That's right, Congressman. One-two-three, one-two-three... .

The stone ship
by Judit Hollos

Setting: an archaeological site along the coastline of Southern Sweden
Character: a female traveler in her early thirties

Two distant generations and fates scattered across time and space become intertwined as old memories bubble to the surface during a long-awaited encounter at an ancient megalithic site. "The stone ship" is a monologue about the impermanence of human relationships and our struggle to accept the reality of vanishing time.

The stone ship
a monologue

Where Österlen's lacy coastline unfurls under the bewitching horizon on the top of Kåseberga ridge, I finally catch sight of Ale's stones—or Ales Stenar as the inhabitants of the Skåne region in Sweden often refer to them. Surrounded by dolmens and graves dating back to the Bronze Age, the monument consists of fifty-nine stone slabs placed in a boat-like pattern, constituting the country's largest remaining ship setting. Nobody really knows whether this peculiar "vessel" perched on a rigid seaside cliff once functioned as a gathering place for casual afternoon chats or an old-school sun calendar, but it has been noted that at the time of summer solstices the sun sets at its northwest point and rises at the opposite point at winter solstices.

Frozen Women Flowing Thoughts

Unfazed by the sharp splinters of sunrays, hoping to be able to spot him aboard, my eyes trail the giant-shaped stones, dreaming different characters into each of them. Scattered across time and space, living in distant corners of the world, we have been planning this meeting for countless months. The tiny boats swinging like multicolored tombs beneath the rocks remind me of how secure I felt on my way here - a country that I would finally be able to call my second home.

Envisioning possible futures, my mind keeps wandering back to the ones who would be left behind on the other side of the sea. There they come, one by, one, fragments of memories unspooling in tainted colors, the dust-laden sunsets with the asylum seeking young man who saved me from sleeping in the subway after I escaped from my abusive boyfriend.

Standing on the ridge, I inhale the petrichor-scented June air. Midsommar is now celebrated with untamed dances all over the country as maypoles, like flowery masts, brighten up the verdant landscape. It should be the very summer solstice of our relationship as well, but the moment I lay eyes on the furrowed brows I sense instinctively that it will prove to be an all-consuming task for me to keep the internal demons he has been fighting for all his life at bay. All of a sudden, as if a heavy weight was lifted between us in the fertile silence, he becomes that twelve-year-old boy again—sitting on a packed train, with a ripening frown, ready to be sent off by his parents to spend the summer vacation with relatives. As the sultry tones of his last lingering white lies fill the evening, there's nothing left for us but to turn away from the ruins and head back to the car.
It appears the ship spills over under the weight of sunbeams and sinks behind my back. I close my eyes to the kaleidoscope of ancient petroglyph sites I have visited so far.

Beneath Ale's stones, there are no kings or brave chieftains sleeping, but layers of several other boat formations hide under the surface of the ground, waiting to be discovered by wannabe time travelers just like myself.

An Anthology

I AIN'T TIRED YET: A play and prayer about Sojourner Truth
by Melissa Milich

Setting: The 19th Century but with a modern feel

Character: Sojourner Truth

During the nineteenth century in America, Sojourner Truth, an African-American woman, was undaunted in her pursuit of justice, equality, and women's rights. Her tireless efforts against slavery and oppression left a lasting legacy in American history.

> **Venus Theatre Dramaturgial Note:** Sojourner Truth's first language was Dutch. Some even say that she spoke no English. The version of her speech in contemporary literature has been an imagining of a character assumed from the South. Enjoy this monologue. Let us know if you've written a Sojourner Truth that speaks a Dutch dialect for our next anthology!

(At Rise: Sojourner Truth with a bundle in her arms that is her small child. She addresses the audience.)

SOJOURNER TRUTH

Frozen Women Flowing Thoughts

Children, I'm going to call you children because we are all children of God. You can call me a children too. But I have other names. We all do. But I'm going to tell you something, children. See, I talks to God and God talks to me. I goes out and talks to God in the field and in the woods. When I wash clothes. Holding the hoe in my blistered hand. When I see another slave beaten. I talks to God. And my God, your God, He listens.

>(Sojourner cocks her head at an angle, and listens.)

SOJOURNER TRUTH

I hear you, God.

>(She faces the audience.)

SOJOURNER TRUTH

Colonel Hardenbergh owned my parents, and he named me Isabella when I was born. I was known as Hardenbergh's Belle. I couldn't read, but you don't have to read to understand God. He communicates with all of us. He does. Good people and bad people. And I was sold when I was ten year old. These were nice people they said. They said wrong. Those nice people beat my back raw with tree branches they heat over a fire. I was just a scared puny girl. Never I understood why I was beat. I didn't do nothing. They just decided to beat me, hot switches on my back. Left ridges where the smooth skin used to be. I cried out to God.

>(beat)

And I kept talking and He kept listening. That's why I am here today. All the fuss. And you know, as serious as God is serious, God has a sense of humor. A mighty sense of humor. He does. One time He said to me, "Ain't you a woman?" Though I reckon, God didn't say ain't. But I knows what He meant. He meant I was strong. He meant I can bear children. I can stand up to the slave owners. Because, my only Master is God. Yes. I can cry for my children when they be wrenched from me. I can tell the hunger in my stomach to wait. I can tell the lashes on my skin from the whip not to hurt. So I could bear the lash as well as a man. I can tell my feet not to pain in the winter when I have no shoes. And I still talks to God. God made women to be strong. To carry the load from the field, and speak. And protect her children. Tell me God, what do you want me to do. And then tell me God, tell me how to do it. And God, I will do it. Here I am Lord, just like Samuel. Yes, Lord, your servant is waiting. And clutching the hoe around the blisters in my hands. They ache like an old woman and I am only twenty five. Only twenty-five.

(The Baby Sophia cries. Sojourner comforts it.)

SOJOURNER TRUTH

And one time, I had to pay hard attention, because God says to me, "Carry your weary feet down the road. Take the small one with you." That's right. Exactly what He said. I did not run off, for I thought that wicked, but I walked off, believing that to be all right. So, I pack up the baby Sophie, and started walking. How far? All day far. Carrying a child. God would tell me when to stop. So I walks.

And God, do you know what? That child wasn't so heavy, and the birds sang, and the trees so green, and the road as hard as it was, felt soft under my feet. And I did not shuffle, there was bouncing to my step. Every foot took me closer to freedom, me and that child in my arms. And you know, my baby didn't fuss nor holler, she just had her little head turned, and she was looking at that freedom road same as me. She knew. The child knew. I suspect she heard me talking to God. Children, they hear God so much better than the grown people. And I got to the first house. Is this the one, God? It was the house of a kind man, a Mr. Levi Rowe was his name. And telling you, that man, Levi Rowe, was on his deathbed, not afraid of death coming, because Levi Rowe had done right by God, and rest his soul, Levi Rowe sent me to the home of Mr. Isaac S. Van Wagener, a Quaker man, and Mr. Van Wagener did not believe in slavery. And he and his Missus, they allowed me and my baby Sophia to stay with them. And that first night, I slept in a bed. I had never slept in a bed before. Hard to describe. But I liked it. Sure did. Yes. Sophia slept good too.

(beat)

But that wasn't all. Mr. Van Wagener read to me from the Bible. Whenever I wanted. He read me Leviticus. He flipped to Chronicles. And ended with Exodus. He read me all these pages. And he kept hitting on this sojourner. The sojourner in the Bible. Sojourner. Sojourner, I thought. That's me. A sojourner on the path to bear witness to the truth. And I listened very hard. I don't think God wanted me to read or write. It might have been a burden too big for my back. I don't know. Only God knows why. I ain't stupid. I ain't a fool. And I could recite that Bible as well as the ones who could read it. And I would take that name. I did. Because I felt God was talking me through the Bible and God wanted me to be his Sojourner for the truth. And children, I am just passing through…

(Sojourner Truth sits down.)

SOJOURNER TRUTH

And then I had to do some more walking. Because the Dumonts sold my boy, Peter, all the way to Alabama. What was going to happen to Peter if I wasn't there? So when I go to the house and find Mrs. Dumont there, she a woman, I thought she would understand. I tell her how I wanted to spare Peter. I know not where he goes. Who has Peter. The law they broke to take him out of New York. God, help me get my child back. I want my child. I don't ask for much. But I am going to ask for my child, Sir.

(beat)

God, you know I knocks at the door. I'm standing there saying, "I'll have my child again." I looked at Mrs. Dumont and she looked at me.

(beat)

Mrs. Dumont, she laughed at me.

(beat)

She laughed.

(beat)

It is me who feel sorry for her. She missing out on most of life if you ask me if she not listening to God. She can read the Bible. How does she <u>not</u> know how to respond when God talks? She acts like she not even hear the Lord. You're supposed to say, just like Samuel, Yes, Lord, your servant is listening. Only, she not listening. I feels sorry for her because she don't know how to listen to the word of God. How I never understand how peoples cannot listen to God. He talks to you. Not just me. He talks to you. And you. And you. Are you listening? Do you know the Psalms? That's God talking. You better listen. You'll be glad you did.

(beat)

When Mrs. Dumont went deaf to God, He told me to go to Kingston and ask the Quakers to help me. For they are doing His work. And so, I had some more walking to do.

(She puts the baby in a basket.)

SOJOURNER TRUTH
I left Sophia with the Van Wageners and I walked. My feet walks for God. Every step. Eleven plus some miles to Kingston. But to me, it was just distance. Just woods. And grasses. And the birds again. One bird more chatty than any of the others, he swooped and dived and chatted at me. The messenger bird. I followed him like a map. And it took some time. I had to call on my friends, the Quakers again, for a place to stay. And food. They say that we are only temporary sojourners on this earth for a small time, and so we better make the best of it.
(Sojourner Truth stands up.)
SOJOURNER TRUTH
(singing)
I ain't tired yet. I ain't tired yet.
SOJOURNER TRUTH
The Dumonts sold Peter to their relative and took him to Alabama. It is illegal to take a slave out of this state. They took Peter, my child, away from New York. Far away. That don't go good with a mother.
(beat)
Rest a little and then time to walk again. I ain't tired. I can walk. I ain't tired. Walk as good as any man. I will walk as long as it takes to get my child back. And I walked into a courtroom. That's why God led me to Kingston. It takes some convincing in that big fancy court of law. It was illegal to send my boy to another state. But you think I know about the law? Well, I can tell you this: God's Holy Spirit is something of a lawyer. He whispered in my ears. Sometimes I just repeated what God's Holy Spirit, another messenger bird, whispered in my ear.
(beat)
First black woman in the United States to win a court case. First black woman <u>and God</u>. But I don't care with that so much as I got my son back. And he was scared and frightened when he came to me, but still my son.
(Sojourner Truth sits down. She rests.)
SOJOURNER TRUTH

Frozen Women Flowing Thoughts

That night when I opened my Bible with all the words I still couldn't read, and I was still named as Isabella. I was a tired Isabella. And the name. I never forgot that name. God's name. "Truth." Can't do any better than that. First, I tried the name out on myself. Would God approve if I took this name? And then, I hear His voice. "Yes, Sojourner. It is now your truth." And so, I became a sojourner for God. I had always been a sojourner, just like the Bible says, but now it was official and nobody could ignore me or God's word.

(Sojourner Truth suddenly weeps in an almost startling way. In a few moments, she gathers herself.)

SOJOURNER TRUTH

Hear my prayer, O LORD, and give ear to my cry; For I am a sojourner with you. Amen. I was beat with a heated branch. Same age as Peter. My owner put it in the fire to make it hurt more. I got Peter back, there were scars on his back. Just like mine. He were quieter too. Not the same boy. Quieter with those scars. I will stop slavery. I will. I will stop slavery. How many miles will it take a sojourner?

(She sings, undaunted.)

SOJOURNER TRUTH
(singing)

I AIN'T TIRED YET. I AIN'T TIRED YET.

An Anthology

BALL AND CHAIN
by D. Lee Miller

Setting: Florida, private place to talk with her granddaughter
Character: Vicki - Woman in her late 60's
It's 2017

        VICKI (holds out a card)

A grandmother can't give a Valentine? - I know Pearl is thrilled about you marrying George but don't get married. Not yet. Listen to me. I spoke with your grandfather after the barbecue.

We're getting a divorce. - Gut punch, huh?. It has nothing to do with your announcement –

Except for what I wish I'd been asked: Why do you want to marry him? - Back in 1969, I was writing poetry endlessly. Grandpa and I were dating: football games, keggers. Everyone was talking politics, the first man on the moon. Woodstock. Oh, I wanted to go so badly but my parents said 'no'. Then your grandfather drove over with tickets and he finally convinced them.

They loved Chris. Clean cut. ROTC. 1969: the draft lottery <u>and</u> the summer of peace and love.. - When we got to Woodstock, we got as close as we could to the stage. But I kept squeezing closer because the music: Santana, Canned Heat - ! We were bathing in it! And suddenly I'm in communion with this crowd and everyone's singing

Frozen Women Flowing Thoughts

and crying! Like no church I ever went to – And then Joplin. – *Me and Bobby McGee*? - God, I've never told anyone this story. – Janis spoke to me – Her music - Her voice so fierce, ripping out of her! Blues poetry! And Chris is screaming, 'Calm down. We have to go.' 'Go'?!!!! Contact high aside, I found my people!! 'Calm down'?! And I broke away and suddenly I'm being body surfed - erupting into the night sky until I landed right at the stage for Janis' last song: *Ball and Chain*. Next minute, I'm standing by the port-o-lets – like two for thousands – oh, it stunk to holy hell - and my sandals are all muddy - and who comes slopping by but Joplin herself. It's me and her, face to face, and I threw my arms around her and she started to cry – a happy cry – and kissed me within an inch of my sorry life – Until her band scooped her up - I turned to watch her go and even though it was dark, I found Chris standing with bouncers a little ways away. - We left. Not talking. He's afraid of my parents because the 'freaks' made us late. We got home near dawn, but they loved him, so I kept my mouth shut… We still dated on and off. Then Joplin was dead. Morrison. No more poetry. We were deeper in the war. We had some fun… He made me feel safe. - Then at the barbecue last night? You and George were by the grill while we were talking rock and roll. I brought out beers and Chris is telling them how he kissed Joplin, at Woodstock, right on the lips – like it was a trophy. He lied about something so private to me we never even spoke about it!

If I'd said it, he'd be explaining me to everyone. Like apologizing for me. That's why I left. – Maybe if I didn't let him silence me back then, I wouldn't be living the same blues. And if I had accepted being a 'freak', I would have discovered my life. ..Shit!! I let him marry the wrong me! ..How many of the wrong women showed up for weddings back then?! No wonder we were called the 'old ball and chain! ..Todays's very scary ..with a lot of lousy music. Until you make sure you're a woman you respect and he respects: don't get married. …I send a valentine to Janis' grave every year. I think the best part of me loved the best part of her. Better to give you a valentine now, y'know?.. Think about it? Please?

An Anthology

THE BEAUTY OF THE DADO. A Monologue for Edith Wharton
by Martha Patterson

Setting: New York City
Character: The author Edith Wharton

Ms. Wharton expounds on her work and reveals that she'd love a statue to be created in her memory.

EDITH's GHOST
(New York City, the present. She is an apparition from the past: a female writer in her 50s, in attire out of the year 1915. She is immaculately dressed in the height of fashion: a gown and fine jewelry. She is speaking to an audience at a museum.)

My friends who support The Mount, a turn-of-the-century home built by me in western Massachusetts, in 1902 -- thanks for coming. And for your philanthropy. Let me speak of history and honoring the dead… I'm Edith Wharton, novelist of the Gilded Age. I am a ghost of my former self. And today, at this museum in New York City, I'll speak of statues, of history, of women. How I'd love to have a statue of myself!

(She steps briefly to the side.)

Oh, dear! I'm tripping over the train of my own dress...forgive me! I've been clumsy -- and really I'm all about taste and morals. Like the idea today of the removals of statues of Civil War heroes who weren't really heroes... For morals are the foundation of the social world. I'm not being superficial. What is it to be truly special? What is a hero, really? And what is true beauty? What is freedom and self-determination? I think about them often, for I wrote on those subjects about women.

I'm just one more high-class socialite who wrote novels. And I had famous friends. But it's only through writing novels that I achieved that questionable status of "special," in my stories of lost women. What is it to turn down the ordinary at every step of the way? Do real heroes do that? I think I tried to, for I wrote of struggling women and I also wrote of the adornment of homes -- how they enliven our existence!

(She smiles.)

The Beaux Arts...the Gilded Age! Such romance. Even though there's been corruption in government, and hypocrisy, and such a loss of the concept of real beauty in the world. But let me speak now of the lovely dado...I first wrote about it in my famous book, The Decoration of Houses...for the decoration and study of how a home ought to be fitted matters. The dado is that lower section of wall above where the baseboard would be, that gives definition to a space, often with moulding at the edges. Charming and delightful and structured, and the foundation of many a beautiful room. These things, these issues of adornment, ought to matter – not admiring the ugly views and achievements of those who supported slavery.

And my novels told stories of beautiful women, women who sought a certain freedom. Do you know Ethan Frome, a country story -- for I adored the country, besides the world of Manhattan -- a sorrowful story of two women who loved the same man. And then again there is my romance, The House of Mirth...it was immensely popular in 1905 -- about a society of irresponsible pleasure-seekers in New York, and a woman whose beauty reduces her to simply a marriage prospect. A woman should have strengths of her own. She ought not to be a slave to love or good looks. It is only through her resources and stubbornness that a woman can survive -- but Lily in my novel does not even survive.

I believe in loveliness and adornment, and ugliness and slavery were like the devil in this country. Even a ghost has opinions about these matters. After all, we do not need statues of failed Civil War "heroes" who fought on the wrong side... Taste is a tribute to beauty, and it reviles servitude and even the idea of slavery, the pseudo-villains of the Civil War. Let's remember beauty, generosity, and values. Let's not forget the dado, that memorial to taste -- and let's not forget freedom, truth, and grace!

    (Lights go down.)

The Family Zoom
by Faye Sholiton

Setting: At a desk, with an open laptop
Character: Dorothy, a Jewish grandmother This monologue was written for Dorothy Silver, Cleveland's beloved leading lady for more than five decades. Dorothy performed the piece - virtually, as the times dictated - just months before her death in 2021, at age 91.

DOROTHY, early 80s, squints at her open laptop.

DOROTHY

(Reads) "The "Host" will let you in shortly?" Who do they think called the meeting?!
> (Faces we can't see pop into view. They're waving silen-greetings, judging from her response.)

Oh! Hello! Hi. Hi. Hi, sweetheart!
> (Blows a kiss, followed by several more. Her smile broadens.)

Looking at all your beautiful faces, I'm reminded of our chaotic attempt at a Seder that first spring. We had our own "four questions": "Are we on?" "Can you hear me?" "Can you see me?" and, of course, "Is this working?" ...Well, is it?

(Signaling a hopeful thumbs up)

Good!

So, why the "emergency" meeting? And why the mute button? No, you don't have to dial Nine-One-One. ...You've all been asking what I *need,* right? Well, I've prepared a short list.

(She reveals a scribbled stack of index cards that contain her outline. It's a Power Point presentation for the ages (80-90): First card reads:

"GOOD SOUP."

GOOD SOUP, for openers.

Not from the deli. All they know is salt, which not only lacks imagination, it makes my ankles blow up. No. Something from *your kitchen.* I can make a quart last for three days. ...But, please, not all of you at once! Call ahead to be sure I have room in the freezer. As you know, storage is an issue in this apartment.

A JIGSAW PUZZLE.

No more cats, please. Also, no more than 350 pieces because I don't want to start what I can't finish. It should also last for three days.

A LIST OF ITEMS YOU WANT FROM HERE, things you've had your eye on but thought it indelicate to ask.

I recently read a list of heirlooms that kids don't want anymore. Number one item: photographs. Honestly, *photos?!* ...Then came jewelry and *chotchkes.* You know, the treasures Pop and I would have rescued, as flood waters overtook the house.

...My grandmother's cut-crystal vase (on the credenza) comes to mind. She hand-carried it through Ellis Island, something I can't imagine, now that I've seen the place. How ridiculous was it she didn't just pitch it into the ocean, in sheer exasperation! ...Do I have any takers?
          (scans the group)
Fine. You may ask me privately.

TIME.

It weighs heavily these days.

You've all heard about Evelyn. To those who have sent me a note, message, text, smoke signal – thank you. I'd certainly talked about her enough, from the moment she knocked on my door to introduce herself. ...Evelyn, so full of life and brilliance, is now another star in the heavens. And the vocabulary on that woman! You may not know that Webster's College Dictionary was produced right here in Cleveland. Evelyn was among the editors. Always knew the right words to say – and when she corrected you, she did it with such tact, you were more grateful than mortified. Alas, she lived long enough to see language replaced by emojis. One could legitimately surmise that's what killed her.

As much as I grieve her loss, I'm positively dumbfounded at how the world has ignored her passing. This pandemic has reduced deaths to 150-word obituaries. Two hundred, for the more celebrated. A simple death notice now costs a week's salary.

Hoping the era of the Zoom *shiva* is nearing an end. You'll find a well-ventilated space for mine. Just stipulate masks.

What else.

A CHALLENGE.

I need something to DO during this dreadful pandemic. Somebody dare me to write my memoir. Or, better yet, make a quilt.

(She checks the screen.)

Good. You're laughing. Never did figure out which end of the needle to thread..

A CLEAR CONSCIENCE/...

Michael! ! Are you *TEXTING?*! ...Put that away right now, or I'll leave all my china and stemware to YOU.

Where were we... Ah, "Clear Conscience."

Which leads to Being Forgiven. Evelyn used to say "forgiveness" should come *after* "guilt" in the dictionary, not before. She said how much time we waste judging people instead of understanding them – yet another alphabetical mix-up. Only she said it more eloquently, because that was her way.

What I didn't tell you – because I couldn't, at the time – was that Evelyn was in trouble well before the stroke that killed her. She'd been losing her words, which made her furious. In particular, it made her short with her children, who by the way, never failed her for one minute. She would rage on about what they did - or didn't -say or do. If I didn't know better, I might have even believed her.

But then the virus hit with such gale force, it stripped away her rage. And here's the odd thing: It *calmed* her. She didn't complain, like the rest of us, about her life. Her care. Her confinement. Because let's face it, a studio apartment can get positively stifling.

And therein lies the miracle, my darlings. In this new state of hers, she forgave everyone – her family, God – the whole universe – for everything.

This morning, it dawned on me that "forgive and forget" should always happen in just that way: in the wrong alphabetical order. ...In the end, forgiveness is all about love, isn't it.

I didn't want to wait another lucid minute to share that.

Are we on?

Can you hear me?

Can you see me?

Is this working?

An Anthology

Fania
by Nina Solomita

Setting: Russia (No setting needed)
Character: Fania

The monologue consists of excerpts from my full-length play, Fania, which is about a Jewish woman in the Ukraine (then Russia) whose vocation it was to be an actress, but she lived in tumultuous political times (1889-1954), and in the process of following her dream and saving her son, she made the painful choice of sending him away to live with relatives when Jews were in danger in Moscow. Her husband was away in the army for years.

Part 1 of the monologue begins the play. Part 2 is a memory of bringing her son to the train to live with relatives where he would be safer. Part 3, a short memory of her time at the Moscow Art Theater. Part 4 describes the night she is taken away from her home and exiled to another place because she is Jewish, and Part 5 takes place in a factory setting occurs after she is released from exile and lives a life as a storyteller for the USSR going to factories and other places the government sent her to perform. There is no need for a set.

Frozen Women Flowing Thoughts

Fania

(This is a monologue in sections. The actor will indicate a short break between sections. The actor playing Fania will play different ages throughout, beginning and ending at about the age of 55.)

Part 1

Good evening. I am a storyteller. My name: Fania Verkhotseva. Born in 1889 in a small village in the Ukraine. I've been resurrected, dragged out of my grave by one of your curious contemporaries. Actually it's not so bad—the peace of the grave is overrated. It's really—well, you'll see!

In any case, it's not so bad now that I'm here. These solid floorboards beneath my feet feel like home. Your faces—upturned, hopeful, attentive—are familiar. I've seen them before. And this quiet. . . different from the grave. I haven't heard this hush in a long time, since long before I became a storyteller when I was an actress—the silence of a holy place. *(Listens)* Yes, being on stage is something to savor.

But what is a stage, after all? Wood and nails. Shakespeare calls it an "unworthy scaffold." "Pardon, gentles all . . ."—gentles all, what a lovely way to address you.

"Pardon gentles all, the flat unraised spirits
that have dared on this unworthy scaffold
to bring forth so great an object."

The 'object' being, in a broad sense, life. I've often thought of these words, having stood on this scaffold for most of my life and at great cost to myself and pain to others.

Shakespeare continues. You, he says, must make allowances for the humble players:

"Piece out our imperfections with your thoughts:
Into a thousand parts divide one man,
And make imaginary puissance." And
"Tis your thoughts that now must deck our kings,
Carry them here and there, jumping o'er times,
Turning the accomplishment of many years
Into an hour glass . . ."

Puissance means strength or power. It was Konstantin Stanislavski who introduced me to this prologue and it was he who made me aware of the power of an actor, *when* an actor knows her craft.

That power, of course, is limited to the stage. As an ordinary person walking about on the earth, I had very little power. I found myself, along with everyone else, confined and imprisoned by the warring time I happened to be born into. Pushed and pulled and nearly killed simply because . . . because something about me was not to someone else's liking. Yes, I was stuck. On earth and in my time.

But here on stage, one can 'jump o'er times.' Time can be compressed. Expanded. All inclusive. Thus the flashback, the flashforward, the simultaneous execution of events. Your physicists tell us that it's all happening at once anyway, but because it's too much for our little psyches to handle, we must separate past from present from future. So the stage is really the answer to a physics problem; it can bring all time together.

Well, we're together, aren't we? And Shakespeare is here as well. When an actor stands and gives breath to words written 400 years ago, those words live again within the body of the actor and those with whom the words are shared. It's a miracle!

I'm remembering myself when I was young. My whole body and soul burned with the desire to be on stage. If ever there was someone whose destiny it was to be an actress, it was me. Yes, I made a decision very early in life. I would be an actress no matter what it took.

Part 2

I don't remember how we got the train. I do remember an old woman's face; she said something to me. I don't remember what it was. I don't remember the last words I said to my son. He did not cry or think anything was amiss. I remember his smile when I handed him a small notebook so he could write about his journey. He asked if he could draw in it too. He wanted to draw the train and the conductor with his whistle. He said he would show me his drawings and read to me too when I joined him for New Year's Day. I remember in that moment it was difficult to breathe.

Frozen Women Flowing Thoughts

I remember my mother's voice. I don't remember my father's voice. I don't remember when I first wanted to act; it was in my heart and soul, it seems, forever; there was never any question. I don't remember ever thinking I'd made a mistake.

Part 3

Mr. Stanislavski was a hard taskmaster but never asking more of others than he did of himself. Rehearsals for *The Blue Bird* were long and tough. My role was important. My character, Light, assured the little children that they would be safe.

"Do not cry, my dear little ones.
Never forget that I am speaking to you in
in every spreading moonbeam . . .
in every twinkling star,
in every dawn that rises,
in every lamp that is lit,
 in every good and bright thought of your soul."

Olga Knipper, known then as Chekhov's widow, the Moscow Art Theater's star actress, guided me gently but firmly through the most trying stretches.

Such a joyful time.

Part 4

I remember the night I was driven from my home. The pounding noise made by the footsteps of the police. The banging on my door. I felt my legs shake and my breath get short. The sharp cold air slapping me in the face as they pushed themselves into my apartment. What would happen to me? Where would they take me? My fear was sucking me in and I thought I'd deflate and fall onto the floor like an empty balloon. They were inside.

"You must come with us. Get a coat and pack some overnight things. Hurry, we have no time to wait."

I remember the younger one, his smooth face, his voice. It sounded loud and pushed. He was afraid. I felt it, smelled it in his breath. He moved to the window, pushed the curtain back. Now I think he was looking at nothing in particular. It was a pose, a stance, nothing more. The older one was wearing a wedding ring.

I wondered about his wife, what she was like, yes it's true, it flashed through my mind. What was his wife like? Did she know where he was? What he was doing? Did he think of her when he gripped me by the arm and shoved me out the door?

I remember thinking it might be better to be dead, but I don't remember truly wanting to be dead. I don't remember the names of the other actresses I worked with during my exile in Krasnoyarsk. I remember their faces, the plays we performed. I remember that the only time I could be away from my fear was on stage. Even if it was in the fear of another character, it kept me away from mine. I don't remember ever feeling as whole on the earth as I felt on the stage.

Part 5

(Back from exile, Fania is performing as a traveling storyteller at factories, etc. She is having an internal dialogue as she performs.)

I want his attention. The wise guy with the beard and the loud laugh. I want him to stop nudging his comrade and shifting in his seat and competing with my performance. I want to quiet him, hold him under my spell. I want his eyes on me, his mouth still—a sensual mouth, like my first husband's. He has the same twinkle Sasha had as a young man. I want to pull Sasha from my past and hold him here in this moment.

A younger actress, less experienced, less worldly, would prance about, display her wares, gesticulate broadly, but that is not the way to hook an audience. True, I have to speak loudly to be heard by the two hundred or so workers in the hall, but the trick is in the modulation, the tone, the story I'm telling, the characters I'm becoming. This is an old fable: a father, a mother, a child, several wishes, a journey, separation and loss, grief and bewilderment, a return, rejoicing. Another loss.

This story has become my own—the sacrifice, the choice, the loss of a son and a husband. I must make him see the depth of my story. He is settling a bit now, but he still defies me. I slow my movements down and lower my voice; some of the workers try to shush him. He feels the pressure. He is embarrassed. His bravado has lost its punch and sits on his face like a fading smile.

Frozen Women Flowing Thoughts

    I lower my voice, making it quieter still. The mother is returning to her once-full home—alone. The mother has made a choice; she has chosen herself first. She returns to her home but is captured and taken away by a hostile army. She is alone and in bondage. She dreams of her son, her husband, her old life. She sees her son's face, a seven-year-old, as he looks out the train window to go away for what he thinks will be weeks but she knows will be forever. In her dreams, the train never leaves the station, is only about to.

    The man is silent now. I've got him. My eyes and his reflect our tears. His sorrow and mine are one. He is my husband, my son, all I've lost. I can only have them in these moments. The choice I made haunts me, but God knows I truly had no other. This was my destiny, is my destiny. This is why I tell this story.

CHAPTER SIX

REPRODUCTIVE

Figure Out How to Live
by Victoria Z. Daly

Setting: A hospital room (an empty space)
Character: Sharon, in her 30's

Any actions are meant to be mimed -- i.e., no actual pulling up of shirts, etc.

SHARON is holding something in her arms, or possibly talking to it as it lies beside her.

SHARON

Oh fuck. Oh fuck! I better not fuck this up. I can -- touch you! And you're breathing! And -- you exist! I mean, I really BETTER not FUCK THIS UP. Oh, Jesus! A hour or so ago you were nothing but a curled-up -- idea. Don't get me wrong -- solid, inside me -- and you could kick -- which means you had to be IN there, right? But still, INSIDE me. A concept, in my abdomen. And now -- Holy shit! You've come out with fingers! And skin! And oh -- You're looking at me! .... Hello!

Hello!!

Your eyes. Crystal blue. Not like mine at all. How can you look at me so intently when you're only a few hours old? Is that even normal, that you'd look at me that way? Is it? And, and Oh! You also have a name now. Grace Margaret. Grace for -- well -- Grace, because you can never have too much of that, and Margaret, for MY Mom, which ...

... frankly, that's a mixed blessing. But -- she's really going to appreciate that we gave you her name as your middle name. I mean, I really HOPE she appreciates it. She can be such a black hole of upset and need ....

No. You didn't hear me say that. Your grandma will be THRILLED! And -- Oh my God! Your lips! .... Your lips!!

(She breathes hard.)

Excuse me for a moment. I think I need to breathe. I can breathe as deeply as I want right now. Thank God for the pain killers.

(Her breaths calm.)

See, Grace ... Gracie? ... Gracela? Yeah, anyway -- I've never done this before. I have NO fucking MODEL for how to be a good parent -- Aggghh! God! I mean, I have no model! From now on I'm gonna clean up my mouth. Let's start on the right foot. My Mom and Dad were ....

(beat)

They did their best. They did! But their best wasn't exactly what a child, with needs -- what I think of as normal needs -- would call ... you know ... enough. My childhood wasn't filled with ... what? .... Light. It had ... yelling. Slammed doors, name calling. Them, not me. So I spent most of my time in my room, hiding. You can't meet your grandpa, 'cause he's dead now -- finally! But my Mom, your grandma? Right now she's outside in the hallway. Waiting for me to let her in so she can meet you. And I just want to warn you first -- Actually, no! NOOO! I won't prejudice you. What they did was FINE.

Frozen Women Flowing Thoughts

Sort of. The point is, I'm going to be different from them. I'm going to give you what you need. A great Mom! A good Mom? What is that, even?

    (Coos to her.)

Hi.

Holy shit. Everything has changed. Suddenly, big time.

    (Gasps.)

You made a sound! Did you understand me? When I look in your eyes I feel like I'm falling down this endless well. It hurts. I don't think it's the Cesarian. It feels wonderful, and so awful, and …. Don't ever tell Daddy. But I've never felt this way about ANYONE. It makes me feel lost, and desperate. If you don't love me back, what'll I do?

You're making that sound again.

Oh God, we love each other already, don't we? We will love each other -- deep into the heart of books -- I'll read to you, curled up together, love each other up to the stars and back, and -- we'll speak French, and no one will understand, and -- I'll ache, and I won't know why, and -- what is that sound you're making? Oh! Oh, you're hungry? …. You want these? I haven't learned how to use them yet. I know they're part of my body, but -- Hey, I read a book. To prepare! It's called BESTfeeding -- yeah, isn't that funny? Ok, I'll try, hold on -- shh! Please! Hold on!

    (She pulls up her shirt.)

Here they are, go for it.

    (Tries to get baby to latch on.)

Just, just -- Ow! ... Ow! No, wait! Let go. I said, Let. Go! .... Good. First, you gotta open your mouth .... like this, see? Real wide, and ... and then take a big mouthful. All around the --

 (She indicates her aureola.)

This. Weird, right? But that's what the book says.

Oh! .... Oh! There you go. There you GO! That's it. That's .... Wow. Oh wow. I don't have that much milk right now, but give me a day or two, and, and, I will be, so .... So good at this. Wow.

We'll be best friends! And speak French! And LAUGH and laugh and love each other up to the stars. Crazy in love and just, just ... figure out how to live. You and I. Just ...

 (unsure)

figure out how to live.

Synchronized Swimming
by Alli Hartley-Kong

Setting: A stage at an open mic night.
Character: Present-day

Infertility—a topic that goes over like a lead balloon at the open mic night! Or does it...?

An empty mic at the center of the stage. KATERINE takes a deep breath, then walks out and holds onto the center stand microphone for dear life.

KATHERINE
Hi. Wow. There's a lot of people of here.
That light is really bright too.
I guess it's better, I can't see any of your faces.
Because the subject of this comedy routine—it's gonna go down like lead balloon. But stick with me. It gets better I promise.
Hi, I'm Katherine. This is my first time performing like this...
But what I say is important. I mean, everyone thinks that don't they?
All I mean is—I'm not standing up here telling dick jokes—quite the opposite, in fact! I will be telling ovary jokes.
Because what I'm here today to talk about is.... Drumroll please....
Did you guess it...? going down like a brick I swear.... Fertility treatments!
Yup. Like I guessed. No laughs there.
Like for instance, the first thing that I think is funny—I'm geriatric.

Thirty-seven and here we are! Can I tell you how much I hate that word… geriatric pregnancy? How is that allowed in a medical chart. It's fucking rude!
And what the hell is it supposed to mean? Is there a nursing home for Aged Out Ovaries? Do they get to do stretches every Thursday? Chair exercises?
But if you ask me… the exercise that aged-out ovaries really do is synchronized swimming.
Because if you've ever had an ultrasound, you know that sometimes, they make you chug a gallon of water beforehand, and then you have to hold it, because water makes the image clearer.
But you know what else having a belly fully of water makes you do… It makes you fucking comfortable that's for sure!
I had this tech once, and when she was pressing on my stomach with the wand, I heard her say "huh, that's weird", and then she said… "I can't find it."
Now bear in mind…this is the external scan so I know she hasn't left anything in me. I calmly ask her "what can't you find?" and she says "your left ovary."
Now isn't the first time my ovary hasn't been visible….
Once when I was going in for a PCOS scan, I had a cloud of gas, and the tech had to press on my stomach and bicycle maneuver my legs like I was a constipated newborn….
But still when you hear they can't visualize your organ, and you can't help but panic a little.
So then I'm laying there with this ginormous dildo-like contraption between my legs and trying not to push it out as I panic, and then the tech says "well it has to be in there, we probably would've noticed if it exploded".
I'm sitting there thinking, lady, I have endo and PCOS, would I have noticed?
Or would I feel an exploding ovary and think…well, that's just Tuesday for me.
But she follows up with, "there's too much water, why'd you drink so much water?"
Surely—surely, I didn't decide on my own, oh I'm going chug 8 glasses of water in five minutes, then drive here without driving off

the side of the road while holding my pee for an hour, then let you press this cold wand on my stomach while I try not to pee on you. Why'd I drink so much water indeed?
And then she told me to go pee a little, but not pee it all, as if she somehow the floodgate to the Nile isn't gonna burst open the minute I see a toilet....!
If I had to do some analogy word test game and had to associate a sport with infertility, the first thing that comes to mind would not be synchronized swimming.
If infertility was a sport, it's a long distance obstacle run where someone's beating with you a stick every couple of meters.
The end line keeps getting further away, and everyone in the stands is seven months pregnant.
But if there was a sport that should happen in the Nursing Home for Aged Out Ovaries, it's synchronized swimming.
Ladies and gentlemen, thanks for laughing.
My name is Katherine, and as I'm about to start my third round of IVF, I believe comedy should talk about everything that's real.
There is joy in the sadness. There's shit that happens in my appointments that is so fucking funny, and even when there's not, I have to find the funny otherwise I'll drive myself insane.
Thank you for letting me share the funny tonight.
This was my first comedy routine.
This was my first time talking about what's going on to anyone.
I hope we can all one day talk about what's real.

An Anthology

Sugar and Spice
by Caytha Jentis

Setting: An apartment
Character: Cassidy

A confident, fashionable Gen Z college junior

Cassidy (20) is home from college for the weekend. She has just returned from dinner with an older man whom she met on a sugar daddy app. Her mother does not approve. Cassidy addresses the audience.

CASSIDY (with a wry laugh): My mom thinks I'm a sex worker. Maybe you do too. So, what if I am. Isn't all dating transactional? Swipe Left, Swipe Right. One Click Shopping. For her generation it's take me out to dinner three times and then I'll fuck you. Whatever.
(She points to her crotch.)
This will always be a commodity.
There's always rules. Benchmarks to the booty. In Sugar Dating there are too, right? Explicit ones. Wants and needs are all on the table. But I'm no 'escort' even though my mother calls me a whore. Whatever. It's different. Because it's not always about sex... Seriously.
My Mom's just jealous. *"Hope I die, before I get old"* Right?
Anyway, I'm demi-sexual, so I'm not going to fuck someone unless I have feelings for them, but I also want money. I need money. And I don't play games. The mating ritual. It's all a game. If you withhold responding to a text for three days, you advance to the next round.

Frozen Women Flowing Thoughts

Whatever. I plan to go to Med school. It's expensive. So, it may not happen. My parents are divorced, and grad school wasn't carved out in their settlement. I mean I've got loans, scholarships, savings, and a job job doing research for one of my professors to help pay for my overpriced entitled Ivy League degree. I don't take any of it for granted. Nobody owes me. I have agency.
Besides I have no time for a boyfriend and love. Love... Love is a distraction. Love is boughie. And I don't want to just have sex... for sex sake. Been there, done that.
Situationships. Been there. Looks like a boyfriend, acts like a boyfriend, fucks like a boyfriend... but... not a boyfriend. Done that too. I'm young, smart, and pretty. And I have a personality. That has value.
Guys my age are... well... Don't see the value. They don't make an effort to treat respectable girls right. Yeah. Respectable. Too many girls my age don't value themselves.
Even the rich guys with their fancy cars, trust funds and big swinging dicks just think about themselves. Like they're entitled because they are entitled because girls fall for it.
They buy us drinks or shots and when we're good and drunk, they shame us into anal or something kinky because we're 'sex positive' feminists, aren't we?
(She holds up her hand in a raised feminist fist and turns it into around and gives a middle finger.)
I'm a brag-worthy conquest. A hot girl head to scalp and proudly show off to the brotherhood. Been there done that too. I mean I like sex... when done right. I'm no prude.
A Daddy makes you feel special. Like a princess, so you act like one. I mean Cinderella and all the other princesses weren't fully canceled when I was growing up. They were our girl power preteen porn fantasies.
Even choice feminists want the option to feel like a princess, right? It's nice. Fucking nice. I'll be your little sub for a night.
I loved when my real Dad called me his little princess. I miss my dad. He moved to LA to take care of rock and roll princesses in the music business. It's all transactional.
###

Orbit
by Rebecca Kane

Setting: Any possible room – big or small – where group therapy could take place. Modern day, with some flexibility.
Character: Cynthia
A mother, any race, age is flexible.

[*CYNTHIA is seated in a chair. She's obviously physically uncomfortable, no matter what kind of chair she's in. She looks put together, almost a little too much, and fixes her hair throughout the monologue.*]

CYNTHIA:

Hi, I'm Cynthia, thank you for welcoming me today. Not really used to the whole group therapy atmosphere, do we—do we thank—well, too late, I did. And I meant it! Thank you, all. For being so welcoming. As welcoming as we can be.

When I was thinking of—of her, today—it was when I went out to look at the sun. And no, I wasn't staring at the sun. I'm not self-harming. Well, not like that. Not anymore. I haven't for years. Right after she—right after she went away—I mean, left us—I mean, died, I am able to say it, it was five years ago—but right about then, there was a brief period of time where I felt like I didn't want to live anymore. Not like killing myself, per se, but not like living anymore either. No plan or anything, just, I'd look at the sun and I'd wish to be absorbed into it. You know, lighthearted wishing like that. Haha. A little joke.

Frozen Women Flowing Thoughts

For those of us who had lighthearted wishes. I'm sure you all can relate. Anyway.

Now I realized when I look at the sun, just for a minute, I don't think of it as the sun. I look at it and I realize I still think of it as "Hoo-wee." I know. Ridiculous, right? I look at the sun and I actively think of it as "Hoo-wee." "Hoo-wee sure is burning bright today. Better go put on some sunscreen or Hoo-wee will get me today."

You see, the reason is, my dad – he would come to baby sit a lot – he loved her – I mean, who didn't, she was, you know, that age is so cute – only three when – well, anyway, he's one of those guys who speaks like, every morning in the summer, he'd let out this noise like, "Hooo-weee the sun is SHINING today, folks!" And he figured out pretty quick that when he made that noise, she'd laugh. And when she laughed, I laughed, and everyone was laughing. So he would get up, creep out of the guest room to surprise her, and he'd go, no warning—"HOOOO-WEEEEEEE" and he would make it bigger and bigger every time. And wow, how she'd just cackle with delight, every time, without fail. Soon he forgot to even keep mentioning the sun. It was just their little morning ritual. Even when my dad wasn't visiting, she would look at the sun outside and say that. "Hoo-wee! It's the hoo-wee! Grandpa hoo-wee!" And half the time she'd crack herself up. But even as she began to get older and get other words – like moon, and stars, all that she'd get – doesn't hurt that Goodnight, Moon is her favori—was her favorite book. So the moon, she knew well. But she just had this one word— She'd point at her picture books. [(miming pointing at pictures in her lap)] "Moon. Star. Cloud. Rain. Hoo-wee. Snow. Tornado." Isn't that funny? Tornado, she knew. Not the sun.

Yeah, um. So. The sun. The hoo-wee, as we call it in my house. Not sure where I'm going with that. It's sunny a lot here. Florida, you know – I mean, sure, you all know, you all live here too – but yeah, I mean, when you're driving, it's sure—it's a bitch, huh? Really. Haha. Going down I-95 some days, I can barely see, and I wonder – how are we not all just crashing into each other non-stop? Why are we going so fast? Why are we going so fast down the freeway like that?

Why does everyone here drive so fast? When we can't see anything at all? Like we can't even see anything behind us when we're backing out – but still people just—they just zip down their driveway like— Like there's nothing behind them—

When there IS, when there IS SOMEONE BEHIND THEM—

I mean it's been five years so that particular thing, it doesn't get me so angry anymore, but it does—does get me a little angry. Still.

What really gets me is that I'll see something, a word that's long and complicated, and what I'll think is, "She never got to learn that name." And it just comes out of nowhere! The other day I was in my garden, trying to plant some romaine for the first time, and I took a look at the little seed packet. It says on it, lactiva satica. And out of nowhere, it comes to me. She will never hear that phrase. She will never hear lactiva satica, never know it means romaine lettuce, never know the word antioxidant or that it's found in romaine lettuce or – did she even ever get to try romaine lettuce? She already hated salad. Hated her vegetables. Only three and already giving me lip about vegetables. But she'll never know how good some of them can be. How good some roasted vegetables are, how to plant something in the yard, what the scientific names of other plants and animals are, how we find them. What the sun is called. What it means to us and the plants. How we orbit around it. She orbited around it and never knew what it was called. Or maybe she did, and she chose not to. I don't know. I'll never know.

Yeah. It's that. It's what she didn't get to know. That gets to me. It's been getting to me a lot lately. I can't look at things without thinking of her not knowing it.

… I'm sorry, what's that? Her name? Oh it was—
Well.
I think maybe—sometimes I just have trouble—
Maybe next time. I think it's someone else's turn now. Just, yeah, I'll name her then—um—yeah.
For now it's just, uh, you know. "Hoo-wee."

Uterus-less
by Stacey Lane

Setting: A therapist's office. May be a bare stage.
Character: Alison: a woman of child-bearing age who cannot bear children
Time: The present.

ALISON

I have no uterus. I had a hysterectomy at twenty-two. I pretty much went into adult life knowing I was never going to have a baby but decided I would not let that define me.

I was ballsy about it. Almost acted like I was proud. I started first dates with "This body can't make babies. You've got a problem with that, well, there's the door." Needless to say I didn't have a lot of second dates, except from the sleazy guys, who were cool with it. No chance of getting this one knocked up.

Then Jordan came along. Perfect, perfect Jordan. Perfectly understanding Jordan. Two and a half years later, we got married. Jordan came from a large family. Fertile, as large families tend to be. Jordan's sperm were strong. Strong, proud sperm, ready to procreate. I mean I assume… based on his continually multiplying nieces and nephews. But Jordan never said a word about kids after that first time I told him my deep dark secret that I didn't usually keep a secret. Never. Not once. When we were in public, he'd go so far as to act like he didn't even see all the cute children and happy families surrounding us. He feigned disinterest, if not mild disgust, in the loads of toddlers scampering about his family reunions. We skipped every baby shower we were ever invited to, until we stopped getting invited. We were happy.

Then one Saturday night, we went on our usual every other weekend double date with Marcus and Olivia—Jordan's brother and Jordan's brother's wife of four years and three babies. Olivia—who always wears yoga pants and mascara, regardless of the occasion, and who always manages to get on my last nerve—Olivia—out of nowhere, with half a mozzarella stick dangling from her hand— Olivia says, "Marcus and I have been talking and I want to offer my services." Her services? What could she possibly have that I'd want? "I want to be your surrogate." I was floored. We hadn't asked her. We hadn't hinted. We hadn't considered it. "And you can even use my eggs," she threw in, as casually as if she was lending a cup of sugar to a neighbor in need. And the icing on the cake—our unasked-for-angel would do it all for free.

I was surprised, confused, outraged. I felt like my brother-in-law's wife had just offered to screw my husband in our Applebee's booth and then hand me their baby nine months later. You know because she's so generous. Which is exactly what Jordan said. Not the first part. The second part. "That is so generous of you, Olivia." I waited for the "but we'll have to talk it over." Jordan is the picture of perfect politeness, remember. Which would be followed by the car ride home when we'd "talk it over" about what a crazy presumptuous bitch she was.

But then I looked over at Jordan. He looked like a kid on Christmas. Smiling more brightly than he had on our wedding day. And I knew at that moment that my happy life was over. My dead uterus had come back to haunt me.

Later, Jordan would swear up and down that this was a complete surprise to him too and that the three of them had not planned a surprise attack. I still have my doubts. My unwavering trust in the man I married just the slightest bit cracked from then on out.

The car ride home was silent. Each of us afraid to hear out loud what we knew the other was thinking. We got home. He got on the computer and did research. That's what he does.

Just look at all the money Olivia's generous womb would be saving us. Upwards of a hundred grand. Hate to break it to you, Jordan, but having a baby is not the way to save money. It's not a good financial investment. Ever. I countered his research with an article that says that it costs $245,000 to raise a child. And that's for a healthy child. A healthy child who doesn't go to college. And doesn't ask you for another penny the day he turns eighteen. For that price tag, you can buy a thirty-foot yacht or a chateau in Paris. Okay, a small chateau, but still. I don't even know what year they were basing those stats on, so I'm sure it's even more expensive now.

But Jordan wouldn't stop trying to sell me on this bargain baby. I mean all we'd have to do was pay for the in vitro fertilization. Where else are you going to find a deal like that? I pointed out that since being cheapskates was such a high priority, my husband and his brother's wife might as well just go ahead and make a baby the good old-fashioned way. Completely free. He calmly told me to "grow up."

When all his math and logic failed to sway me, he switched tactics. He read me sad, sad posts of couples begging for surrogates, stats on surrogate waiting lists, horrifically heartbreaking blotched plans of untrustworthy stranger surrogates backing out of the deal, absconding in the night with infant in arms. Message after message, blog after blog, support group after support group of wounded women, hoping, praying, begging, bartering, for exactly what had been offered to us, without us even having to ask. I volunteered to personally send every single one of them Olivia's number.

I did some research of my own and concluded that Olivia was addicted to being pregnant. Look it up. It's a real thing. When three puking babies and not-yet-potty-trained toddlers were all that she and Marcus could manage, she decided to start giving babies away. Jordan said that it was really sad that I thought it more likely that Olivia had a mental illness than that she was just being nice.

At some point, Jordan decided that the real problem I had with this scenario was that the biological mother of our child would be a woman that for the rest of our lives I would be stuck seeing hang out with my child and my child's half-siblings, slash cousins. He understood that that might be "a little bit awkward" for me. He was certain that I'd feel much better if we used an anonymous egg donor. I mean, sure, my puffed-up pride would cost us an extra $15,000, but we could swing that. With a loan. From his dad.

When I didn't immediately lovingly latch onto somebody else's eggs, Jordan formed a new theory about me. Since I could never have a baby that was flesh and blood mine, then I didn't think Jordan should get to either. Our baby would always be truly his and never truly mine. I don't know. Maybe deep down in the recesses of my psyche, I am that selfish. But I'm afraid it might be something far worse. Maybe, just maybe, I don't want a baby at all—any baby. That somehow I lacked this fundamental evolutionary trait was too terrible for either of us to ever say out loud. So we didn't.

Now we've been on an adoption waiting list for two years, been through untold forms of bureaucratic and emotional torture, and spent $13,000. Olivia had another baby of her own. And then another for her neighbor's cousin. And I am pretty sure now Jordan hates me, although he's too polite to admit it.

The Girl Who Survived The Highway Hunter
by Ali MacLean

Setting: Outside of a Frosty Treat ice cream store
Character: Arkansas Woman

A slight wisp of a young woman, unremarkable except for a wine birthmark that covers the right side of her face. Upon closer inspection, you see that her arms and legs are covered with scars.

> *Lights up on ARKANSAS WOMAN, she sits making a chain out of chewing gum wrappers and speaks in a Southern twang.*

ARKANSAS

I didn't report it. I do wonder about what it would be like if I did. And I still wonder 'why me'? Cause he coulda picked anybody. Lots of pretty girls in Arkansas. And out here all the girls hitch hike so he coulda found one. My Mama always told me that with this face no man was ever gonna want to be near me. But he picked me. So, that's gotta mean somethin', right? (Pause.) I tell people I don't remember a lot of it, but that's a lie. I still remember the car slowing down behind me and him calling for help. And me getting off my bike and going up to his window. He had his map all twisted and didn't know which way was up. So I was looking at it and was trying to help him find the right roads, when he asked if I wanted some chewing gum. "Hell yeah, I do!" I said, and he laughed. It sounded like a tin can rattling down the street.

> She gets up and turns her chair to the side, leaning over the top of the chair as if through a car window. She reaches her arm out.

ARKANSAS

He reached over to hand me a stick of Juicy Fruit. That's what he smelled like. Old Spice, sweat, and Juicy Fruit. And I tried to take the piece of gum, but he grabbed my arm.

> She plays tug of war with an invisible opponent for a moment.

ARKANSAS

At first I though he was being all playful like, but then I saw his eyes. They were the same eyes I see right before I get walloped. But his were different. More intense, like a General in command. Before I could do anything, he pulled me all the way through the window. I bit his arm and tried to open the door, but he clobbered me with something so hard that I was sick on myself. Then it went all dark.

> She pulls out another pack of gum. She unwraps all of the sticks, shoves them in her mouth and chews. When wet enough, she sticks them under the chair.

ARKANSAS

When I came to, I was in a field. I coulda been anywhere. There was a tree. And grass. The sky was still there. I know cause I laid there checking to make sure it didn't fall in on me. At first when he was pullin' my jeans down, I said no. I didn't want to do it, cause I was bleeding, you know, from the curse. So I told him that I didn't feel like it, doing sex. And he laughed at me. Real hard.

> A beat, as she remembers this vividly.

ARKANSAS

He d "You don't feel like it, princess? Did I say you had a fucking choice?" I started to cry. I knew that this was a big life moment, and I didn't want it to be with me bleedin'. He took em off me and saw the red between my legs. He asked me if I was embarrassed and I nodded. And he stopped. I was in the middle of thanking Jesus, when I saw a flash of bright light in the sky. I thought maybe it was God, but it was his knife. He sliced deep into both my thighs so the blood all mixed together. Then he said I didn't have to be embarrassed about it no more.

> She stands and unfurls two of the chains which roll down her legs like liquid.

ARKANSAS
(matter of fact)
He had his way with me, and the bleeding felt like tears running down my legs. He was real intense...the way he was all over me, it was like he wanted to swallow me whole. When he was done, he leaned back and smiled like he'd a really good time. I tried to sit up a bit, and asked if we were going home. Then he punched me in the face a bunch till I blacked out. When I came to, I was all alone, tied to a huge white oak tree. Like this.

> She takes two wrapper chains and loops them around her wrist, binding herself.

ARKANSAS
I watched ants crawling around in the blood on my legs for what seemed like hours till I fell asleep. When I woke he was sitting there. The moment he saw my eyes open, it all happened again. And again. And then I stopped counting.

> She slides off her chair onto the floor and hugs it, as if tied to it — or seeking protection.

ARKANSAS
I don't know how many days I was there. People ask why I didn't try to get away. I was tied to a tree. You don't ask Jesus why he didn't try to get off the cross do you? Now, I'm not saying I'm Jesus or nothing! I'm just saying that we both know that you can't get away when they tie your hands tight. (Pause.) Every time the man left me there, I thought I'd never see him again, but he kept coming back. I know it sounds weird, but I never had that from a man before, so I was glad to see him even if he did hurt me. (Pause.) But then he stayed away

for several days. I could tell by the sun. When he did finally come back, he cut me so deep that we both knew I didn't have long. So, he drove away and I whispered goodbye.

> She pauses and places the chains around her and sits in the circle.

ARKANSAS

When they found me, doctors said there's no way I shoulda survived. People in town bet their good earned money that I was dead. My Mom even went in with eighty bucks and that's more money than she makes in a week. Well, I'm disfigured for life, but I'm still here. At first, the Pastor thought that me still breathin' was the Devil's work, but he decided it was a great renewal of life, like Jesus in the tomb. Which is flattering and all, but now all anyone thinks of when they see me is HIM! I'm just 'the girl who survived the HIGHWAY HUNTER'. My Mama said, " At least they think something. No one thought of you much at all before this happened." (A slight smile.) Isn't she sweet?

> She rips the chains apart.

ARKANSAS

A few people donated their winnings to me for my doctor bills. I don't know what's nicer. The money, or that they bet I was alive. I gotta admit it's a real kick in the 'you know what' knowing that something bad had to happen for people to be nice to me. But I guess that's how people are. They feel bad once you're hurt and they want to fix you like a little bird with a broken wing. Guess they feel good about themselves when they help you to fly again. But once you do manage to fly? It's open season. They'll shoot you right out of the sky.

> ARKANSAS mimes skeet shooting birds that she sees flying across the horizon. She hits one and watches it fall.

Frozen Women Flowing Thoughts

ARKANSAS

I guess some people felt sorry for me cause I'm even uglier now. I got deep scars like worms running all over my body. The register guy at the Kwik Stop calls me Frankenstupid and the cone guy at the Frosty Treat said that I have the 'stink of rapist' on me. I said back "You mean Juicy Fruit?" And I just started laughing and laughing.

> She starts with a giggle, which builds to a full manic laugh.

ARKANSAS

He didn't get it. (Pause.) At first I didn't even mind 'the stink'...or being cut up so bad, because people were a lot kinder. Is that messed up? (Pause.) I just wanted someone to care about me so bad. And like I said, for a short while a lot of people were real nice. But you know what? I don't think that's enough to make me happy anymore. (Pause.) He hasn't come back. He just left me there to die. Maybe that's what he does with the other women, but there was more to him and me then that. I know there was. Why else would he have kept me alive for so long? He needed me. I made him feel better. But why hasn't he come back? That makes me feel worse than any time he cut me. Every day that he wakes up and doesn't come get me, I get more and more mad. I feel like I wanna go down to the station and tell them about what he looks like so they can draw up his picture... But I won't do that. Cause the time between him and me? That's mine. They can't have it.

> ARKANSAS gathers the chain bits. She pauses, not sure if she should say the rest. She continues.

ARKANSAS

He did it to another girl and I coulda stopped it. All I had to do was tell people. But I didn't say nothing and he went and killed some co-ed from UArk. The pictures in the paper made her seem real pretty. Do you think that's why he killed her, and not me? I wonder if he tied her to a tree? I wonder if he cut her thighs on her Moon Days. I don't think he did. But why did he kill her and not me? Why did he leave me here like this, alive and worse off than before? I don't understand. Why didn't he pick me?

An Anthology

The Nearest Far Away Place
by Aleks Merilo

(A young woman is looking out the passenger side window of a car. She is 17. She has a backpack and a high school yearbook in her lap.)

YOUNG WOMAN
3 miles.

(She flips through the pages of a the yearbook.)

Were you voted anything in high school?

(Pause.)

Is it weird that my high school mascot is "The fighting orphans"? How do you think they thought of that? You ever see that funny billboard when you drive south from Lost Springs? Its got this old picture of two boys fist-fightin', but they're both wearing school uniforms and smiling with missing teeth. And it says "Home of the fighting orphans"? Drivers don't notice they drove though our town. But they usually remember that billboard. You ever seen it? There's not even an orphanage in town, I checked.

(She looks out the window.)

Frozen Women Flowing Thoughts

You got a really nice car. My friends make fun of anythin' that isn't a Ford F-Series or a Silverado, but you've got a really nice car. My boyfriend says when he's rich, he's gonna get me any truck I want, but now I'm gonna ask him for a...

(Reading.)

Ford Fiesta.

(Pause.)

2 miles to go. I've never been this far from home.

(Pause.)

You're my third driver since Elk Mountain. The first one was a classmate on their way to Rock River to see her dad. Not a friend, just a classmate going the same direction on the highway. She asked where I was going. I said it was a college visit. She asked what college, and the only one I could think of was "Wossamotta University". Then she said, "ain't that the school from that funny cartoon with the moose?" It was the only name I could think of. The second driver looked like a bible-salesman. Really neatly combed hair, but it looked like plastic. His wife - tellin' the truth - I wouldn't have been surprised if she kept a fuckin' apple pie in the glove compartment. She glared at me the whole time. She's sittin' right in front of me, but she thinks I can't hear what she's whisperin' to her husband.

Sorry, didn't mean to swear. My English teacher, she says people cuss to sound tougher than they are. But Bible-boy ditched me when I was in the bathroom at Carl's Junior! I actually saw the wife glare at me when they drove away. That's why I was so upset when you saw me. You know, they didn't even get food?

But it's okay. My boyfriend gave me more money than I needed. I'm tellin' you this because... I can pay you. I wanna pay you. For gas. For the Carl's Junior.

277

An Anthology

(Pause.)

1 mile left.

(Looking at a yearbook.)

Wanna know something funny? I wasn't even gonna buy a yearbook. I knew I wasn't gonna be voted anythin'. I had to work at Checkers to help my mom out, so there were no sports or clubs or nothin'. But I showed up for picture day. So this shot of me in no make-up and my work t-shirt stained in oil from a deep fryer kinda saved me, huh?

(Turning pages.)

I didn't even know we had a bowling team. "Most likely to be Miss Wyoming." "Most likely to be a billionaire" Ain't millionaire enough?

(Laughs.)

"Most likely to eat something off the ground?" That's just mean!

(Pause.)

"Most likely to go to jail."

(Long silence. She is focused on something they are driving towards. She squints.)

Quarter mile to go. Wait. Pull over here. Stop. Is that it?

"Welcome to Colorado. Drive sober."

(She looks around.)

That's it? You don't need to check-in? Or sign something? But it's a new state? I thought at least there'd be someone to wave to? There's not even a line on the ground!

Frozen Women Flowing Thoughts

(Pause.)

Guess I thought a different state would look different. But they got different rules for us there just 'cause of that sign?

(Pause)

Before you drive any more I gotta say... If I had told you I was on a college visit, would that have worked?

I thought of a funny response - You would ask what I was going to study, and I was goin' to say that I got a scholarship to major in "undeclared." And we'd laugh. Or how about that I was on a mission for church? Or that I missed the bus to a dance competition, and I need to catch up with my team? Could you believe that, if I asked you to? I'm not a good liar. But I think you know why I had to lie. Why I needed to hitchhike. Why we said no bus. You know they can follow cellphones on a map? I had to lie because we were scared we'd leave a trail. Anyone could find it if they just opened our search history. I need you to know, he wanted to come with me. He begged to. But people would notice if both of us were gone. And they'd ask why. We even use code words. Know what we called today? My trip to "the nearest faraway place." He's a nice boy. I don't want you to think he's anything but a really nice boy. He's a good person. And he even bought me extra underwear and a hoodie, so I could hide my face from any cameras on the way. How many teenage boys would do that? He's gentle. He's kind. But he'd probably put Gatorade in a baby bottle.

Wanna know somethin' funny? I wasn't going to get a yearbook. But my boyfriend worked extra shifts at K-mart to buy me one. He said since I don't have a drivers license, I could use a high school yearbook as an ID at the clinic. And can you believe it? The girl on the phone, that one I made the appointment with? She said he was right!

(Silence.)

If you don't want to be part of this you should drop me off here. It's still a way to the clinic. But I could find another ride. I wasn't honest with you. But I would never tell anyone you gave me this ride. And if anyone found out, I'd tell them you didn't know why I needed one. I'd tell them you really thought I was a Colorado State student who needed to get back to campus to accept another scholarship. I could be, someday. You know? Do you think I could be? If you're gonna drive me past that sign... It's gotta be your choice, not mine. But even if you don't... I want you to know how much... "Kindest". I would have voted you "kindest."

(Pause.)

Colorado. My English teacher says its name means "The color of sandstone." I guess that makes sense.

(She looks out the side window.)

A Trick Baby's Tale
by Amy Judith Reuben

Setting: A sickhouse room circa 1908, New Orleans, La.

Character: SADIE, 22 years old. She is a naturally pretty light skinned black girl. She has long flowing dark hair, and an average build. She is in a modest full length skirt, simple white blouse, hat, gloves, lace up boots and has a shawl wrapped around her shoulders. Underneath she wears a white chemise, opaque black stockings and white pantaloons. She is uneducated and speaks in a New Orleans dialect.

At Rise: SADIE is seemingly chipper and in an in-and-out-of hallucinatory way that can be misconstrued as intoxication at times, then perfectly lucid other times. While she's delivering the monologue she is undressing, and dressing confusingly.

SADIE

Where's everyone? Clara? Adele? Where's everyone?
(Pause) You know where I just been? Celebrating! Over by Miss Emma Johnson's studio. Yes, Momma still works for Miss Emma, old as they both is.
I axe Momma, "how old you is?"
(Laughingly) She say to me, "old 'nough ta be ya Momma."

I know that's right, though I may not know how old you is, I know how old I is. Twenty. Today. Lotsa trick babies born'd up in them attics, but I's the only leap year baby borned by Miss Emma's. When the house was on Gasquet before the District came legal. Wednesday, February 29, 18 hundred and 88. Was Dago Annie who delivered me. Midwife to the whores. I see her even now with her little black satchel, hurrying to a house to deliver a trick baby, old as she is.

"Who's my Daddy, Momma?" It's my birthday! Tell me, as my gift.

"Just one of them tricks who paid for a screw."

I don't blame you, and I ain't ashamed of what you is, or what I am, cause I ain't had no choice in it. Don't know if that's a good thing or a bad one. Don't know if my life is a good one or a bad one, but I do know it's a better one than yours. Miss Lulu treats me better than Miss Emma ever treated you and better than you ever treated me.

I know you was the girl who screwed the pony in Miss Emma's circus. What was that pony's name?
(Laughingly) Did it even have a name? Or was it just *the trick pony*?

Daytime it be out in the yard for all us children to ride. Evenings you rode. You was screwing that pony more than any men.

(Laughingly) Well, almost more cause you got caught by a trick and here I am.

Them other children called me a centaur. I told 'em like you told me, "Sadie, you ain't no centaur cause they's half horse and half man, and you ain't no man." I told 'em. Didn't matter, especially to them little urchin boys. They teased me somethin' fierce.
Truth is, Momma, no matter how sweet you made the bath water with fragrance you always smelled of that pony.

I don't remember a time I didn't know what you was doing or what a man's prick looked like. Tricks never bothered me much back then, cause I didn't have nothing to feel, but they sure liked to have me around in the room when they screwed you. Some even give me a dollar to keep me there. Soon as I found out what tricks would pay for I started all kinds of stunts with them, except screwing cause I was too young for that.

I didn't never screw no trick ponies, neither.

There was that one birthday, Saturday evening, February 29, 18 hundred and 96. Miss Emma dressed me up in a white party dress to look even younger than I was. She told you, "bring Sadie downstairs." So you did. There was these four customers. Half-juiced. Miss Emma told me, "suck 'em all." So I did, and one of 'em was feelin' up inside my drawers while I sucked him.
He axe me to go upstairs with him. So I did. Don't know where you was when I went up. We get into a room and he axe me if I ever been sucked and I said "no," cause I never was. I be honest Momma, he did it to me. It felt alright, but nothing happened cause I was too young. I made me fifty dollars all by myself, which is pretty good for an eight year old. Happy birthday to me! No, Momma I never told you cause it was my money, and I didn't wanna give it up to you. You ain't my Madam, Momma. Miss Emma let me keep half.

Was right after that you gone to the sickhouse, again. I never knew what you went through all those times you was afflicted with the great pretender. I always thought it was the life made you crazy, but now I know it was the illness. I know what's in front of me, too.

Men come to me with the clap not knowin' what they got. Penis bent down instead of up and thick yellow and green discharge comin' out the tip. Us whores is supposed to tell better than any doctors. I milked 'em. I promise you, Momma I washed 'em off good with a clean cloth and some permanganate of potash like you taught me. I know you didn't know nothin' 'cept whorin'. You taught me nothin' 'cept whorin'. I done all I could every time with every man shy of clapping both sides of his penis between books in an attempt to push the pus and discharge out. How do they not know, or do they just not care?

Clara? Adele? Where are you? Will you go see Momma for me? Miss Emma won't let Momma leave the house, let alone the District. Tell her it's my birthday. Tell her where I am. Tell her if she ain't gone to the sickhouse, that I's here. Tell her how I am. Will you do that for me?

On your way back will you run one errand? Go to Toro's for a roast beef po-boy? Dressed, no onions. My customers don't like the smell of onions.

Why is it people think whores can't have children?

Regrettable
by Bara Swain

Setting: Milly's home
Character: Rhoda, widowed; Milly's mother

Rhoda is determined, quirky, sensitive, unrestrained, and remorseful. The birth of her first grandchild complicates Rhoda's relationship with her daughter.

AT RISE: RHODA calls out to her daughter, MILLY, who is departing from the room. RHODA implores.

RHODA
STAY!
    (*pause*)
Please don't leave, Milly. I can talk to your back. I know the stories on your hindside by heart, from the contracture scar over your right hip – a chicken coop fence. Barbed wire, I'll never forget it – to the tattoo of a house finch on your lower back. (*SHE whistles a finch call*) A Tramp Stamp, that's what they were called back then. You were dating that shy senior on the field hockey team. An infatuation, I thought. "My first love" … that's what you called him. Your father called him "Nora." I can't remember why – (*SHE frowns*) – but I recall your boyfriend's doughy arms and pasty face … and such sweet eyes. (*snaps her fingers*) EFRON, EFRON! Your chubby goalie with eyes like an angel was named Efron! (*SHE spells*)

E.F.R.O.N. That's Hebrew for "bird." (*affectionately*) And your father loved birds. Songbirds, waterfowl, herons – Big Bird and chick flicks! Oh, he was smitten by chick flicks and your grandmother's Chicken Fricassee. God, I miss him. Miss my mom, too. I don't miss her legendary braised chicken, and that's an understatement. (*calling heavenward*) MY MOTHER'S FRICASSEE GAVE ME FLATULENCE, LOUIS, DO YOU REMEMBER?! (*to MILLY*) Your father had a stomach of steel. The rendered chicken fat gave me terrible heartburn. (*happily*) And that was Dad's favorite Nora Ephron movie. "Heartburn!" (*after a moment*) Nod if you're listening, Milly.

(*Pause. RHODA makes eye contact with MILLY. SHE squirms under her daughter's gaze.*)

(*calling hearvenwards*) OUR DAUGHTER'S GIVING ME A DISAPPROVING LOOK, LOUIS … LIKE TALKING TO A DEAD PERSON IS A CRIME! (*RHODA's voice quivers*) A MISDEMEANER. (*After a moment, solemnly*) A mistake.

It was a mistake, Milly. What else can I say? Another regrettable … accident! – like the chicken coop fiasco at Tim's Lodge – that working farm outside Quebec. (*shaking her head*) A contracture scar. Improbable, right? (*RHODA shrugs*) Your father insisted it would build character – gathering eggs and shoveling cow pies over summer vacation. I said, "Building our daughter's resume with farm chores isn't going to get her into an Ivy League school," that's what I told him.

(*Silence. RHODA chooses her words carefully*)

And I'm telling you now that … that the kind of – profound loss you're experiencing? … It will also build character –

(*MILLY starts to exit. RHODA calls after her*)

– WAIT! COME BACK! (*urgently*) CRYPTO! CRYPTO-SOMETHING! PLEASE, MILLY, STOP!

(*Relieved, RHODA nods. SHE gathers her thoughts and continues, earnestly*)

Cryptococcosis. It's a fungus. From inhaling pigeon droppings. Remember the pigeon poop on our terrace? Before we installed the balcony enclosure. Like little marbles, all over the terrace. I told your father. A hundred times, I told him, "The terrace is off limits

Frozen Women Flowing Thoughts

to our daughter. You want to birdwatch together? (*pointing*) Look out the window! Go to Prospect Park! She could get sick!" And your father waved me away with his binoculars that I got him for his 40th birthday. Two hundred eighty-nine dollars at L.L. Bean. Like a fifth of what I lost in salary when I took Family Leave ... without pay, Milly, to take care of you, to care for you. (*shaking her head*) Cryptococcosis. What are the chances, right!? The rash on your hands? We thought it was an allergy. (*SHE shrugs*) Like mother, like daughter. I spent half my childhood soaking in baking powder baths and Epson salt. Milk, strawberries, marshmallows. My adulthood, too! Your father used to say that I had more food allergies than bird species in New York City! Okay, that's an exaggeration. (*calling heavenward*) YOU EXAGGERATED, LOUIS. (*SHE adds*) AND I KNOW THAT YOU HID MALLOMARS BEHIND THE CASSEROLE DISH IN THE BOTTOM CLOSET! (*to MILLY*) Gelatin. Marshmallows have gelatin, another trigger for hives and itchiness. And the worst? The eczema! – those crusty patches on my hands, neck, elbows, chest. I'd scratch them so hard that they'd leak ... (*calling heavenward*) ... LIKE THE FAUCET IN OUR FIRST APARTMENT, LOUIS! IT TOOK YOU TWO YEARS TO CALL A HANDYMAN!

(*RHODA feigns anger, shaking her fist. SHE laughs, then gathers her thoughts*)

Anyway, the day you broke out in a rash, your grandmother brought over a box of marzipan and my favorite book when I was a little girl. <u>Now We Are Six</u>. A.A. Milne. I wasn't a Winnie the Pooh fan, but I loved Christopher Robin. Idolized him, I did! And your father? He used it against me when we were choosing baby names. It was one of our first quarrels, too. (*after a moment*) He wanted to name you 'Robin.' Wasn't going to happen. I never liked gender-neutral names. 'Loathed' is a better word choice. (*smirking*) Robin, Kim, Drew, Jordan. (*calling out*) I KNEW WHAT YOU WERE UP TO, LOUIS!" (*to MILLY*) See, your father's favorite bird was the Robin Redbreast. And every day of my third tri-mester, he tried to convince me that it was an ideal name for our daughter. Even when I was seven centimeters dilated, he's still making his pitch. "The bird is a symbol of good luck and happiness and rebirth," he said. "And sometimes a messenger for lost loved ones." (*SHE smiles*) Your fa-

287

ther – what a character he was – he'd see a Robin Redbreast and call out, "Hello, Grand Daddy!" Every time, remember? "How 'ya doing, Aunt Bertha? Want a peanut?" Dad crushed peanuts for them, too. Peanuts and raisins. I'm highly allergic to them both.
    (*RHODA encircles her neck with her hand, as if she can't breathe. Then SHE shrugs, then sighs*)
And … and so when the bumps appeared on your hands, we thought it was the almond paste. Marzipan. That's what we … assumed. (*SHE repeats*) Assumed.

So last month … when I went to the nursery to visit my first grandchild? – six pounds, nine ounces. Your bundle of joy, Milly – I didn't know! My hands? I thought the rashes were from the take-out Thai food that I ordered when your contractions were still twenty minutes apart. Fish sauce in the Chicken Stir Fry, that's what I assumed. And so I took an antihistamine – Benadryl. The liquid gels – and packed my EpiPen, just in case. Do you think I would have visited if I knew I had shingles? Do you think that I would have held my beautiful grandson if I had an inkling, an ounce of knowledge that he could get chicken pox and sepsis, and… (*in a whisper*) … die? Never! (*shaking her head*) Never, never, never, never, never, never, never, never.
    (*RHODA looks up. SHE sees that her daughter is leaving.*)
WHERE'RE YOU GOING!? I KNOW WHAT YOU CALL ME, MILLY! AND YOU'RE RIGHT! I'M A MURDERER.

    (*RHODA watches MILLY exit. Silence. Then RHODA turns and gazes out the window. A faint sound of a bird call is heard. RHODA closes her eyes and listens intently. The song gets louder. RHODA opens her eyes and tilts her head. SHE steps closer to the window. It is a Robin Redbreast. SHE gasps, then calls out in baby talk.*)

Hello, Baby Boy! How'ya doing? It's your mommy's mommy, how 'bout that? (*after a moment*) Your mommy calls me 'the murderer.' But you can call me 'Grandma.'

Frozen Women Flowing Thoughts

(*RHODA smiles. Beat. SHE inhales deeply, then slowly exhales as the lights dim. At the end of her breath, the lights go to black. The Robin Redbreast song is heard for several more beats, then silence.*)

babybreath
by Octavia Washington

Setting: The Bed
Character: Angel, a black woman in her 20s (& The Husband, older than her)

Angel is lying horizontal on the bed in her pink robe and bonnet, one leg exposed. She keeps rubbing at her temples. Her sheets are undone, unmade, fraying; every second away from her temple goes to its exposed strings. Her husband is sitting in a chair across from her, monitoring for any worrying signs — well, more worrisome than her usual. She's surrounded by dial-up telephones, receivers as far as the eye can see. Another ring — and no answer. The phones get bigger and smaller all around her; they shrink and balloon, and she follows their lead with her movements. Angel hears a click after each name. No telling if the husband can hear them too.

Angel
Kolin. Kerolle. Kerstein. Khafif. Khan. These are the first instruments of the baby machine. I have to take a nap but I can't stop thinking and I need you to help me carry my thoughts. Okay, can you do that? I need you to carry my names and then we'll all find some peace in dreams. Okay, can you promise that? Alright. I have - pass me that. *(He passes her the crumbled piece of paper on the floor; she unravels it.)* These are my physicians but I don't think they went to school for medicine. I think they're fake. Don't look at me like that. Forget the degrees painting the walls and the pillows that devour and the games

in the waiting room and the snotty receptionist at the desk and the fancy Ivy Leagues of it all. They majored and degreed in Baby Killer MD. And now I have something to say. I stand and shout *(Angel tries to stand up but falls back down)*, I sit and shout: I have something to say. I have -- what was I -- I'm sorry, I'm not -- oh, Kolin.

That was the first stop. All aboard the abortion express. Sorry. That's not funny, I know you don't like when I make, when I make light of things like — dark things. I just meant that he was my pediatrician and that's why I saw him first. Kolin's hair went like *(she gestures)* whoosh; he had the quaff, baby, the quaff, okay, it was the 90s. He found me in the waiting room playing with the piano rug, the long one with all the keys, you ever seen those shits? No? Well, I was brushing my foot over *c* and humming something so loud that I didn't hear him and he had to tap me twice with his ghost hands because he's known me since I was small enough to have to put my whole body on *c* to get it to play.

And when I took off my pretty dress from Puerto Rico and sucked my butt into a paper gown, he waved some blurry black photos of my insides and said, do you know what this means, my Angel? And I said, please don't tell Daddy, because I already had three hot messages from him in my voicemail that I hadn't listened to but they went something like, I'll pay for it, blah, just like your mother, blah, hardheaded, blah. And he said *we* have to tell Daddy. And I said, nuh-uh. And he said, uh-huh. And we went like that back and forth and I guess the stress got to be so much that something in my stomach suckered in, *(hold breath)* spun, *(exhale)* and whirled into a vacuum. *(Spit)*

And that's one down. You can find them at siete-uno-ocho cuatro-tres-cuatro y dos-nueve-nueve-dos. See, I don't even need the paper. I'm smart. Your baby is smart. I memorize all their names because time freed me. And now I have space for lullaby.

Here are the - I - can I talk? Can I talk? Thank you.

An Anthology

Angel lies flat on the bed, spreading her arms and legs so that she's in a snow angel position.

Here are the weapons they used to destroy me: Kolin. Kerolle. Kerstein. Khafif. Khan. Khasidy. Kamin. Kamal. Kassof. Kaminski. Kaiser. Joseph. Julien. Jofe. Jack. I remember Joseph best! I remember that bitch. I remember Joseph with the green Jordans. I remember because I went, damn, you got it like that? Not mister uptighty bitey tidey-whitey whitey who won't make eye contact when he puts his instruments in me got some Jays? I asked about them when he was putting his cold stethoscope on my teta, just because I got his number from this white lady in my building, the one with that badass kid — oh, you know her, Jacqueline! How is she? Oh, yeah, yeah, he didn't say nothing. He shrugged then parted my knees with the gloves. I was trying to get to know him, you know, because I had never met him, and I like to know people before they look in my hoo-ha and put rubber on my panties because I am a classy lady, alright, I was raised alright. But he didn't want to be known I guess. I guess in his program they tell him the patient is just a chart and a number and a birthday and a history of smoking and cancer in the family. He didn't talk to me one bit, except to tell me that he noticed some bleeding when he parted me, and that he was very sorry, but he didn't hear a heartbeat.

You can find him at siete-uno-ocho seis-tres-tres y uno-uno-cuatro-dos. Afterward, I went around to everyone I could find. I grabbed people's jackets on the train. I yelled on the bus. I yelled so much the bus driver said can someone shut that miss up? But no, no one can stop me when I start hurricaning.

I said, do you need a doctor? Preferably better than him? This is where you can find them: Kolin. Kerolle. Kerstein. Khafif. Khan. Khasidy. Kamin. Kamal. Kassof. Kaminski. Kaiser. Joseph. Julien. Jofe. Jordan. Jefferson. James. Jerome. Jayasundera. Jean-Pascal. Jean-Brice. Jean-Noel. Jean-Pierre. Jean-whatever. So many men and they all rot of babybreath. *(Getting up)* I am thirsty. I want water. Your baby wants water!

Frozen Women Flowing Thoughts

Husband runs out of the room. We can hear water being poured off-stage. He comes back, helping Angel sip her water.

I'm sorry for yelling. I just get upset when I think about Joseph. The way he was looking at me, you know? Like I was procedure, not person. But if he knew me, if he really opened his ears and consumed me, I'd have her. I'd have a baby. We'd - I'm sorry. I know you like me to speak for myself. From now on we'll say Jo-shush. Can you repeat after me, Jo-shush? You good? Good.

Listen, will you listen? *(sung mostly to herself)* Kolin. Kerolle. Kerstein. Khafif. Khan. Khasidy. Kamin. Kamal. Kassof. Kaminski. Kaiser. Jo-shush. Julien. Jofe. Jordan. Jefferson. James. Jerome. Jayasundera. Jean-Pascal. Jean-Brice. Jean-Noel. Jean-Pierre. Jean-whatever. Issac. Ibsen. Inna. Now this one's gonna get you mad. Issac. I only know his name because I looked for him in the thing that's online? Yes, you can -- yes, you can! You can look people up by their inmate number and that's what I did. After. Not before. I know you don't like it when I get all feelings first. When -- what was it you said? When I move with my anxiety, not my logic. And this was one of those times where I was holding my anxiety but I was desperate. You'd get desperate too, okay, if every path kept taking you to the grave instead of to heaven.

So what had happened was I traveled down the yellow brick road and down a gray alley where there was a woman sitting with her dog in her lap and she was looking at me and I was looking at her because she kinda looked like Tia Flores, a little if I squinted and tilted, just like her with a little more dirt under her nails. And I asked her if she knew which way Gravesend was and she said, why the hell do you wanna go over there, that's where people get ganged and banged and I said, I'm a hero, I'm saving my new baby, and there's a man there who will protect her and me from demons and doubters who are forged in the fire of exacting supremacy. Yeah, I see you shaking your head but that's what I said, okay, I said that shit, because that's what I thought and I say what I think, always, because I don't believe in doublespeech like you men of gun, I believe in the truth, the truth is what brings you closer to God, the truth is what keeps the devil at bay, the truth is free. But anyway, I said that and she pointed down to the left, to the left so I followed the yellow brick road and found a gray apartment door on the corner of Avenue D. I knocked. He answered. He had one gold tooth and I thought, man, this really is a private, private, private practice. He said I should leave on my shoes and I immediately got a bad feeling because what type of home doesn't have you take off your shoes? A bad one, that's what. He gestured that I should sit in the makeshift living room turned lab turned armchair turned stir-ups and under the flickering lights he put his scalpel on my thigh and said, so you need to get rid of this one? And I said NO. The opposite. He asked me if I was sure. I said YES. He kept shaking his heads and I mean heads because at this point the chlorine -- he had just cleaned before I got there, right -- was getting up in my nose and into my brain. He said I was too pretty and too young to be ruining my life. I didn't respond because I was getting bothered. The gold, the light, the gray. Instead, I snapped my knees together and stood. And he was like, you still have to pay! And I said MY CURRENCY IS MY FOOT and kicked him in the balls like Tio Rod told me to do when people started looking at me funny. And he screamed YOU BITCH and I ran and ran and ran and I started flying and dropped the latest baby on the way down the street, past the lady, past the trash, past the construction guys who said why you running ma, past the cops who gave me the good ole red and blue and said SLOW DOWN, but then they took pity on me because I was crying so hard that it turned into burps and I looked like the black one's little sister. Snot and all.

(Beat)

See, I knew you wouldn't like that story. But that's what happened. Deadass, that's what happened.

Can you call my mom? You don't have your mother-in-law programmed into your fancy little gadget? It's siete-uno-ocho tres-ocho-dos y cero-cinco-cero-cero. I know we're not talking right now but I would really like to listen to her breathe. Can you --? Gimme me. Thank you.

Frozen Women Flowing Thoughts

Husband hands over his cell phone. As the phone rings, the receivers around her stop breathing — or stop moving so much, whatever's easier. Angel makes a call. No answer.

(To the voicemail)
Hi, Mommy. It's your Angel. I have a secret: *(quiet)* Kolin. Kerolle. Kerstein. Khafif. Khan. Khasidy. Kamin. Kamal. Kassof. Kaminski. Kaiser. Jo-shush. Julien. Jofe. Jordan. Jefferson. James. Jerome. Jayasundera. Jean-pascal. Jean-Brice. Jean-Noel. Jean-Pierre. Jean-whatever. Issac. Ibsen. Inna. Irwin. Iwanicki. Ingber. Ingberman. Igor. IIina-Yelena.

Wait, stop talking. I hear something.

Pause as they look around. Then comes swelling, sweet music. It sounds a little like an aria but of many rhythmic, popping voices. It's clear to Angel that it's her babies singing.

My parasites came to visit. They sound so good! You can't hear them? Stop this bullshit: you hear them!

Angel gets up and spins herself. A lovely, if clumsy, pivot.

They're getting hungry. They need something to eat. Do you have anything? Give me something! No, not that! Watch me: *(Angel does a fast step routine)* Kolin. Kerolle. Kerstein. Khafif. Khan. Khasidy. Kamin. Kamal. Kassof. Kaminski. Kaiser. Jo-shush. Julien. Jofe. Jordan. Jefferson. James. Jerome. Jayasundera. Jean-pascal. Jean-Brice. Jean-Noel. Jean-Pierre. Jean-whatever. Issac. Ibsen. Inna. Irwin. Iwanicki. Ingber. Ingberman. Igor. IIina-Yelena. Henry. Hollander. Horne. Hope. Are you full yet?

(Abruptly stops dancing)
Maybe she changed her number. She moves around a lot, you know, I was just trying the kitchen phone. Do this one: Siete-uno-ocho siete-cuatro-tres y cero-cuatro-seis-cuatro.

No? Nothing?

That's okay. I have one last story for you. Although you were there for this one. So it's not a story, I guess, for you, it's a memory. You like Henry. I like Henry. He's not a whoosh, or a Jay, or a gold tooth. He's a cackle. Literally. He's more laugh than person. What! It's not an insult! He goes *(she does his laugh)*. It's trustworthy. A man who cackles is not a man who lies. And he's brown and he's pink inside and he's purple on the outside. That's a person you can trust. You can trust a cackle. It's not his fault his attendant -- okay, you're getting upset. I thought the song would cheer you up. No, don't cry. You don't see me crying. This one was almost full-term. I should cry. I stink. I smell like babybreath.

I was getting a bagel that day when I felt it. This quick suck. Quicksand in my belly. I begged the guy at the bodega to call the Mr, tell him to meet me at Bellevue, okay, tell him I'm going to Bellevue. And I closed my eyes and willed myself down 1st Ave. When I transported to the receptionist desk, I said, I'm hurt. And the attendant was passing by on his lunch, yes, the old white one, and he said, no, he whispered because I wasn't supposed to hear, he whispered, can it hold for my cholecystectomy? And the nurse nodded and then put her needle nails in my arm and said hurt how? But she wasn't looking at me, you know, her eyes were around and about. And I said I'm hurt*ing* now, right now, it's hurt*ing*, because that's the only way to get them to take you seriously. She said sit down, the doctor will be with you soon, and I said, I need Dr. Henry now! Give him to me, give me to him, whatever, but it needs to happen now, right fucking now or I'm gonna explode, there's a bomb in my chest. And she said, ma'am, that's a serious accusation, if that's true we will need to call the police and I said, call the fucking police call the governor call the SWAT team call the FBI call motherfucking Batman you dumb bitch if you don't get me Kolin Kerolle Kerstein Khafif Khan Khasidy Kamin Kamal Kassof Kaminski Kaiser Jo-shush Julien Jofe Jordan Jefferson James Jerome Jayasundera Jean-pascal Jean-Brice Jean-Noel Jean-Pierre Jean-whatever Issac Isben Inna Irwin Iwanicki Ingber Ingberman Igor Ilina-Yelena Henry Hollander Horne Hope Hassan Hausknecht Halper Handler George Gary or Goldstein I will kill you. And then you arrived, wrenching yourself out of a cab.

Frozen Women Flowing Thoughts

And when I saw you I knew. My insides broke in the lobby and I just knew. It wasn't Henry's fault. It's not your fault.

That's why I'm telling you right now that I'm not seeing another doctor. Not even if it's a woman. Not even if it's light itself. I'm not leaving my bed. You can call them right now. Go ahead. I don't care if it's Fred or Fong or Feurman or Flores or Fuchs or Friedman or Ferzli or Fazio or Feldman or Fairwa or Frenkel or Francois or Epstein or Erber or Empire. And when you call Siete-uno-ocho seis-tres-tres y ocho-uno-ocho-tres, tell them my wife and my kids said, I banish you!

No one believes me. No one ever believes me. No, you don't. No, YOU DON'T! I don't like to be told who I am and what I am and what compels me and what magic makes me! I'm not a liar! I had all those babies and they ate each other up in my womb and they ate me up, and now I'm not going outside anymore. I'm going to lay here for the next forty-eight hours, or days, or months, or years. No, I want to get up. No, I want to sit. Fuck you! I don't know!

Angel stands but she bumps into too many things. She trips over one of the phones and ends up on the ground. She vomits into the waste bin. Not real vomit, of course. She's puking out all of the names; it's a strange, glittery occurrence. Her husband stands behind her and holds her head. When she's done he smoothes her edges and holds her.

Sorry for yelling. I believe in the sun, you know? I salute the sun. I cast a hex on all those naughty men. I reach into the void and pull out a wand and I curse them for financial ruin, for emotional instability, for a toilet that never flushes, for a washer that always stains, for a drain that always clogs, for shoelaces inevitably untied, for sickness do we part, for hell and beyond.

Thank you for understanding. Sorry for yelling. And these are the names of all my babies: Daisy, Dagney, Daphne, Diana, Dorothy, Destiny, Desi, Dali, Dayo. Chantel, Charmaine, Candy, Catherine, Catalina, Carolina, Caprice, Camila, Cristina. Bella, Belcalse, Bethany, Bianca, Blanca, Brianna, Belinda, Brandy, Birdie. And I'm their only angel.

Angel sighs then stops talking. The Husband shakes her but she doesn't stir. It seems she's fallen asleep in his arms.

CHAPTER SEVEN

SENSATIONS

Crinoidea
by Ella Baldwin

Setting: Deep Sea/Bushwick Comedy Club
Character: Peocilometra Baumilleri

20-60, a member of the crinoid family, stalked species variety
>We are in the deep sea, we are in a comedy club somewhere in Bushwick. Both. A stool, with a glass of water perched on top. There's a stronger drink somewhere nearby. Blue light drapes the space, and velvet curtains fall on either side. There's a speaker, a mic stand, a spotlight. Things feel slightly tipsy, very shimmery. PEOCILOMETRA BAUMILLERI enters, looking nothing like what they are.

                POECILOMETRA BAUMILLERI
Hey guys
Thank you so much for being here tonight
It means a lot
I mean. It doesn't mean that much
It's kind of like a blip in time really, to me
But like for you it's a big deal
and I appreciate that for sureee
Like you could be anywhere
and you're not, you're here with me
I'm just testing stuff out
I've been thinking this is maybe the most effective
way to communicate with you Unless you'd like to

see me dance, people say dance is a universal language. Pina Bausch fucking wisheeess
    Worse than Elaine-dancing
I guess I should probably introduce myself
Hi! My name's Star. Obviously, it's fitting. I am a star. I'm not famous, or mythical like, I don't know, the kraken..
But I am full of thoughts, and dreams
Like him
Do you want to hear my dreams? I could dance them for you? no, I'll just tell you Here's the thing about me, okay, I really didn't plan it, I promise I didn't I swear I didn't ohmygod. I'm a little clairvoyant.
No seriously! I can predict that you will never grow a tail
Pretty amazing, right?
ANYWAY
I'd been having this problem, kind of a crisis, if you will
I felt really out of touch with everything around me
I felt like I wasn't keeping up with the times
I felt lost
But then the solution just came to me recently, kind of in a dream, kind of on the current
The current
    Snapping into it
Sorry, um.
Like what if
What if
I could create my own autonomy
A foreign concept in this climate
What if I had within me the power to change
To eat new foods, meet new people, access experiences that I can't reach. It's all about reframing. If something isn't working I try to reframe it and try again. And then one day I just kind of did it. Mhm. Straight off the vision board. People say that's super hard to do but for me it really wasn't. I mean it took a while to get to that point, the point where I could really achieve those things.
But you'd never have known that for an obscenely long amount of time I was very much anchored to the floor, very stuck in my ways, very Taurus-energy
Any Tauruses here tonight?

What's it like? Tell me about it, tell me about yourself
> *Someone responds, begins in earnest. The lights shift towards them. She cuts them off, lights pull back to her.*

I'm a Pisces!
We're super dreamy, super drifty, the creative types that every other person really envies. I cry a lot.
I'm crying right now. The world is on fire, death is imminent
I'm so upset. Can you tell?
You can't tell?
Great, that's comedy. See? Reframing.
I should tell you about my brush with death, probably.
That seems like something you would be interested in
You morbid sickos
Actually wait let me set the mood.
> *Lights shift. Ocean noises, oscillating between calming and terrifying, a therapist's couch and a submarine.*

This just like, helps me focus and calm down.
It's very healing, right? Are you feeling healed already?
Breatheeee
> *Guides breathing exercise. It's possible, no, plausible she lights a cigarette.*

Okay now stop!
Just kidding!
So it was a few years ago, truly no idea what time it was.
It was after a bender, which sometimes I do
because I need a *release* dammit. No idea if it
was day or night, no clue
I'd been eating nonstop but everything was just kind of
Passing through me
That's my, um, IBS
Just kidding, I don't have IBS
That's a you problem
But all of a sudden there was this guy
You know the way that men sometimes have claws and by claws
I mean
Their aggression just makes them seem so crablike
And he just like came up to me and was like
Hey I feel like I've seen you on Hinge and I was like
oh I don't think so

Frozen Women Flowing Thoughts

If you're here and you see me on one of those, no you didn't, you imagined it. And he didn't say if he matched with me or not, which I thought was weird because my profile is very cute. And then very much out of the blue
He snapped my arms off
Men, right?
But then I must have fallen asleep, or, I dreamed, and they grew right back   Sorry
I'm like, wow, overheating.
Do you feel that?
> *Pours water glass, we see a strange formation on PEO BAUM's back, it's all tentacles and fronds and petals. Grotesque and beautiful.*

You're shocked
It's a shocking incredible story
It's like a murder story but I LIVED and that's insane
It's like the best true crime podcast that's ever existed
> *Drinks entire glass of water, begins pouring another.*

Do you like true crime?
I love it
I love how crime is so subjective
> *Drinks. She pours another and it spills. Keeps spilling.*

For example, I did not press charges against this man
I probably should have, but my arms grew
back so I wasn't even that upset   Ladies,
we've all been there.
> *Pours. Drinks. The water begins to spill over the stool, and keeps spilling. The water refills itself and spills itself over and over.*

The arm thing? I think maybe that's something you might have a hard time letting go of. But me? No.
I was focusing, manifesting, dreaming.
So I wasn't even thinking about his crime or not crime
I didn't think *I've been* crimed
I thought *I am going to* (see that **reframing** thinking?)
regrow this limb. Fresh, anew, even better than before, why not?
Sorry I'm like, wow, overheating.
Do you feel that?
Maybe not, maybe it's just me.

303

Ohmygod.
I really did forget to introduce myself.
Um
Do you get it now?
Yeah, I know, this must have been so unsettling
...
I'm not a sexy human woman
I'm a sexy ancient sea lily
I'm an ancient sea lily
> *The slow flood intensifies*

Sea Star, colloquially.
Peocilometra Baumilleri for those who know.
I guess it's been a while, definitely I'm not the most popular deep sea creature. I may not have the glamor that you're used to, but I have the longevity. I swear.
Let me show you, actually, let me just show you my profile
> *She reaches for her phone. Pulls up photos, x-ray style, and fossils, but Hinge format.* I feel like I look really cute here! This one was at my cousin's wedding. *Images of crinoids*

Have you ever heard of me? Probably not.
I feel like the creatures that have really seen things
Are the ones that choose not to be seen
But that's just, so not me. At all.
I think I have a lot to give, a lot of knowledge to impart
And I really just want to feel included, I want to feel like I can give something helpful back. Because I've been around!

Seriously!
> *Peo Baum is splashing around now onstage, skeletons (fossils) begin to collect nearby. It would be biblical if not for the martini glass in her hand.*

I mean, you guys have obviously been up on (what remains of Earth) doing things How long have you all been alive? Anyone, anyone?
Your species, the current one at least, has been here for, what, 300,000 years? If you want to be technical, when you split from chimpanzees and gorillas, maybe 6 or 7 million? Cute, so cute. Adorable, even.

Frozen Women Flowing Thoughts

ME? I've been here, my fam-il-y, for four fucking hundred and eighty-five million years. I've seen the way that things can go
I've seen everything
I've seen the way that creatures can die, the beauty in temporality
And what it takes to sustain
    Is she getting taller?
I saw the first fish walk
I saw the first crackle of electricity
I saw the first Happy Meal
I know that things move in cycles, change is the only constant within existence and death has the capacity to encourage
You probably think I'm talking out of my ass with all this..
But that's a common misconception actually, my anus is just close to my mouth. I have a U-shaped gut, so it's really like I said: in one end and out the other. It's all just flowing through, consistently, moving through. When I said IBS it really wasn't that far off. ANYWAY
I've been on the
Bottom of the sea, surviving, becoming my best self. Some people just need to get up off their asses and work. That's what I've been doing. Cultivating myself. Evolving. Literal evolution. Paleozoic, bitch
Sorry
    She sees something above, an offstage "time's up!" signal.
    The flood stops abruptly. Everything drips.
Wow, overtime?
This is very much a work in progress
It's been like several hundred million years but
Still working on that tight five
Thank you folks so much for coming
Have a great rest of your night!

Dopamine Deficiency
by Ana Sorina Corneanu

Setting: An empty space, sounds are more important
Character: Joy

Dopamine Deficiency tells the story of unveiled depression, of struggle of a woman who's voice isn't properly heard

Characters: Joy, a young, thin, brunette girl, looking lost and sad
The voice (can be performed by an actor/actress, but can also be a very good idea to use a voiceover, like a voice coming out of nowhere.

I felt like it was a funeral in my mind. With howling mourners, against the backdrop of a service covered in pounding drum beats, like a monotonous sheath. I felt my mind numb, my insides empty, and I was just a big ear with a hard pain that sends you to the doctor.

I was confused by the thought. The cement broke under my feet and then I started to fall lower and lower - and lower, and lower in the dark, until I stopped thinking.

You have the feeling that you are afraid all the time, without knowing why you are afraid. That's when I started thinking that it was too painful to be alive.

Frozen Women Flowing Thoughts

This snake coiled me.

A moving creature with cold and insidious skin. It entered, bit my core and then I started dripping underneath. I'm afraid, I'm always afraid of drowning in myself. If I fill up, because of those drops, I'd flood and drown. The snake left, but it covered my core with the cold skin. And that bite still flows. It flows.

My mind is a box where you can find everything you want. A tiring rattle - left there by an ignored child, a monotonously dripping and mesmerizing pipe, a pair of headphones - which I wear when I can no longer stand the noise, a videotape with the scariest scenes recorded in my life so far, an inhaler, to cover my mouth when I run out of air, so that the snake won't slip through my throat again. And the snake skin. It's left there.

On the battlefield I struggle to reach the haven. Even if they are not bloody, these fights inside myself are just as bloody. And the wounds cannot be bandaged.

These are everyone's beatings. Everyone knocks on one door, but no one knocks on the door that matters. Some we beat with our hands, others with our feet. Or we beat the plains. And the battlefields with paper flowers.

I'm going to shut myself in for a while. Until a door opens. I'll drink vodka, break the bottle and leave the tomato juice at the door. To think it's blood. Only when the pain bleeds… it matters.

things my mother told me while standing in front of a mirror, getting dressed
by Layli Rohani

Setting: A small bedroom with a twin bed and a standing mirror

Character: Greta

Greta, 28, stands in front of her bedroom mirror, dressed for a fancy night out. As she speaks, she slowly takes off her jewelry, her make-up, and undresses. Then she dons a pair of sweats and puts her hair up in a bun.

Occasionally, when I'm standing in front of my bedroom mirror, getting dressed, my mother will pop into my head. And she's there, as always, under the guise of, "I'm helping you get ready!" but she's just intruding on my space. I don't want her advice. Not because she's a horrible mom who gives bad advice! That's not what I said—though she'd take it that way. She reminds me of helpful things like, "Suck in your tummy, it's unflattering letting it hang like that." Sometimes it feels like she wishes I looked more like my skinny-ass sister. Which is fine, I guess, who wouldn't want to look like my sister? But it never stops there.

She has to ask, "When was the last time you weighed yourself? When did you last work out?" Then she tells me, "Stop slouching. Remember, if the doctor says you're overweight you probably are." So, I tell her to leave. I try to remember she's just a voice in my head, she's not actually there in the room with me, but sometimes I think all that does is make her more powerful.

"Don't wear that, it shows off too much of your arms. Well, now that one shows off too much of your legs and your cellulite is showing; put that away, no one wants to see it. That top shows off how saggy your boobs are, and you're only 20 they shouldn't look like that." I'm almost 30 now but the sentiment stays since I have no kids, and only then are your nipples allowed to droop below your shoulders.

I try on other things, but it's never good enough. "Your hips are much too wide for those leggings, put on something that wouldn't show how much your thighs touch. You'd think with legs like that you could jump higher. You know, if you actually went to the gym you wouldn't jiggle so much when you did jump. Or run. Or sneeze."

Her voice takes over the entirety of getting ready for what should be a fun night out. And it doesn't stop. She refuses to stop until I am a heaping pile of sobbing, wet goo curled up on my bed, shame-eating a granola bar in my sweatpants.

Yet somehow...I hear her still. She tells me I'm pasty, that I should get a tan. But not a suntan or I'll get cancer. Don't spray tan either or I'll get cancer. Why am I wearing *these* pants now, my butt doesn't look good in them, my hips aren't wide enough. My toenails aren't painted either, so don't even think about the sandals. Always keep a pedicure otherwise my feet look weird. I have to make sure my top isn't patterned if my pants are. Take off my gold jewelry, it clashes with the silver and gold is a whorish color and I wouldn't want to look like a hooker, especially with all this make up. She tells me foundation is bad for me, it'll clog up my pores and I'll end up with zits everywhere. I took off the sweater, as she reminded me turtlenecks bring out my double chin and it make my tits look small, and no boy is going to want to have a baby with me if I look like that, and—

I know...I know I sound crazy because I haven't lived with her for, like, a decade, and still every time I get dressed, I hear everything she's ever told me. What to wear, what not to wear, how I look, everything that's wrong with my body—with me. My therapist tells me it's her own doubts and fears about herself projected onto me, but I can't help internalizing them. I don't think I'll ever not hear her voice...I'll never be good enough for her.

So, on a night out like this, I guess...this is what I'm wearing. And I'll go out and be happy and try to feel good and enjoy the time with everyone. But she'll still be scratching at the back of my mind, reminding me of everything that's wrong.

Excerpt From Shadows and Regrets - Jozi
by Madison Sedlor

Setting: The old Stewart Garage.
Character: Jozi Meyer

Late 20s / Early 30s. Stewie's girlfriend who ODed a week ago in his garage.

JOZI

Take a deep breath through your mouth
That's the way it goes
Then when you're ready to calm yourself
It goes back out the nose.
Involuntary motion
An unbroken chain of breaths
The only level playing field before imminent deaths.

Somehow things get complicated
Social structure appears
Suddenly you're judged for what?
Too tall? Too fat? Too weird?
You're pushed toward people like you
They don't like you
Insecure
Trivial reasons you end up with heroine at your door.

An Anthology

Years later you're alone
On your garage floor.
Boyfriend couldn't be there
Has to make sure we had more
Alone with your thoughts now
Traintrack arms now

Scared to death-
Trying to remember now, the pattern of your breath.

Take a deep breath through your mouth
That's the way it goes
Then when you're ready to calm yourself
It goes back out the nose.
Take out a new needle
Plunge it you
Feel the warmth
It feels like I've stopped running for a moment I've transformed

You now look to see your boyfriend
His eyes so far away
You wish that you can do something,
Something to make him stay
Crop tops, skirts and fishnets
We have high sex, fabric torn
Forgetting that it's January and you're on the garage floor.

In the moment being nervous feels so silly to me
His eyes not far away anymore
His focus is on me,
I whisper how I love him
I adore him, I am his
The silence lingers over us, and that is all there is.

Take a deep breath through your mouth
That's the way it goes
And I can't seem to calm myself
Nothing out the nose.

Frozen Women Flowing Thoughts

Harder to remember
Lost my center, where am I?
The warmth is gone all cold now, am I already done with the high?

You've lost track of your breathing
Now the panic sets in
Until another wave of warmth washes over your skin
Panic now is over
You've never felt like this before
This new sensations crashes in like waves upon the shore

I tried reaching out for you but you weren't there
Left me on our garage floor
Dying, freezing, scared.
Eyes closed for a second
My life plays before my eyes
They say that's what happens to you before you up and-

CHAPTER EIGHT

TRANSGENDER

DANIELLE
by William Robert Carey

Setting: A bare stage or sitting in a chair or on a bed
Character: DANIELLE, a late 20s transgender woman

She is speaking to her father. The monologue is from a 2-act expressionistic play, DANIEL-DANIELLE, about the relationship between a parent and transgender child and the conflicting values in their family.

Why did I leave home? After you sent me to Pray Gay Away, I didn't feel safe, Dad. I didn't trust you.
Do you even know what went on there?
(Sniffs and shakes her head.)

I knew it. You didn't ask because Father Hayes recommended it, right? And it had *"pray"* in the title. How bad could it be? Well, it was bad, Dad. Right from the get-go. There were about 25 of us at the orientation – mostly men, but a few teenagers like me. Pastor Shandman – a Pentecostal, I think – lectured us on the evils of homosexuality. He said God created everyone heterosexual, but demons planted wicked thoughts in people's minds to make them gay, creating disease, depravity, and misery. As he spoke, they projected gay lifestyle pictures on a giant screen beside him. It was kind of Orwellian. Most of the people in the scenes looked like drug addicts, but a few shots were kind of erotic, which confused me. At the end of his rant, he told us to work on our masculinity and buddied us up with hyper-heteros. Mine was tall, blond, and athletic – pretty hot actually, which confused me even more. His name was Josh Armstrong. *Josh Armstrong.* I always wondered if that was his real name. He often had a toothpick in his mouth and, when he coached me, he liked to put a foot up on a chair and lean on his leg, like he was doing a Harley Davidson commercial. He called me Dan the Man all the time, as if saying it over and over made it so. On the second day, he took me to a Target to buy Levi jeans and Henley shirts. He made me throw away my penny-loafers and buy western boots. I thought he was going to make me buy a gun. After that, we worked on man spreading. I had to sit like this all the time. If I crossed my legs, he'd slap my knee and glare at me. It was good conditioning. I didn't stop sitting like this until I started wearing dresses. On the fourth day, I was taken to electroconvulsive therapy. I think they got the idea from "A Clockwork Orange." Original thinking wasn't their métier. They strapped me to a chair, attached electrodes, and made me watch gay movies. During sex scenes, they zapped me. I begged them to stop, but Pastor Shandman said, "the sufferings of this present time are not worth comparing with the glory that is to be revealed." That's Romans, 8:18, if you're wondering. The next day they gave me nausea-inducing drugs and showed me more gay movies. That got pretty nasty. I made a mess of my new clothes - not that I liked them much. The rest of the time I took cold showers, read holy-roller books, and prayed the gay away. It was supposed to convert me from homo to hetero but all it did was make me feel bad about myself. I thought I was ugly and evil and considered killing myself. It's true. I did. But I couldn't figure out how to do it. I'm afraid of heights, so jumping off a bridge was out. I don't like the sight of blood, so cutting my wrists was a no-go. And I didn't have any pills. But I think what really prevented me from doing it – and this will shock you – what really stopped me was my fear of eternal damnation. Just enough religion survived in me to keep me from offing myself. And thank God it did because a few months later I had an amazing experience. A friend took me to a party at his brother's apartment. When we walked in, there was a woman standing in the center of the living room surrounded by a bunch of guys. She was tall and slim and had long blond hair and wore a low-cut lavender blouse. She looked amazing. I couldn't take my eyes off her. She seemed to glow. My friend saw me staring at her and said, "You like that, don't you?" I didn't know what to say. I mean, I was fascinated, but not attracted, you know? So, I said, "She's very pretty." And my friend said, "Yeah. Except she's not a she. She's a he." She was pre-op transgender. I was stunned. I had never known anyone like her. My friend said her name was Aurora and she performed at gay clubs. Later, when I was standing alone, she spotted me staring at her and walked toward me. I nearly had a heart attack. I thought she was angry at me for staring. But she introduced herself and said, "You're intrigued, aren't you? But you don't know why. And that's okay. You're young. You'll figure it out. And when you do, never be ashamed of who you are. Never be afraid to be your full self. And in the meantime, remember, chaos gives birth to shimmering stars." Then she kissed me and walked away. I was so overwhelmed I almost cried. It was like she released something inside me. I realized people were trying to change me into something I wasn't. *From* something I wasn't. How crazy is that? I couldn't let that go on anymore. I was who I was. I needed to be that. To love that. And people needed to accept it. Including you. But you weren't ready. You'd get in the way. That's why I left. But you're my father. My flesh and blood. How do I change that? How do I forget it? I can't. I had to come back. I had to try. But it isn't easy, is it? Because you are who you are. And I am who I am. And I think it's easier for me to change than you.

Let The Winds Of Mystery Take Us
by Carol Lee Campbell

Setting: Washington, DC
Character: Ellie

Ellie, now fifty-something, recounts her trans journey (Warning: Suicidal Ideation Content)

The first time I wore women's clothes I was on my way to a trans support group. It was broad daylight and I was scared to death. I thought, everyone in all of traffic-dom is looking at me out of the corner of his or her eye. But they weren't. Everyone was just trying to get home.

It took a long time to stop seeing myself as a woman imitating a man imitating a woman. By coming out I was taking an impossible step, an insane turn, a path I'd been told all of my life did not exist.

I was just shy of four years old when I learned I was different. I had gotten into my mom's make-up. I know, I looked garish. I trotted myself down to show my mom, I was so proud. She grabbed my wrist and dragged me over to see a neighbor. Shaming me. A public hanging.

The problem wasn't the make-up. The problem was I was sentenced to being a boy for life. Mom was the nice one. Dad was violent. I

Frozen Women Flowing Thoughts

was a perfect target for his anger until I was sixteen. From his rants of wanting to kill me or send me to reform school and the barrage of countless name calling, I learned to hate the real me. I played the part, because the most dangerous thing in the world was to be myself.

There were moments I couldn't resist. Like when everyone was out of the house I would sneak into the laundry and put on mom's dress. And the time I finally found a book at the library I could relate to; it was the hardback copy of Conundrum, by Jan Morris. Told the librarian, I'm writing a report, you know. Of course she knew.

The book cracked open a doorway and gave me a sense of the possible although I was light years away from that truth being a part of my truth. Like many trans women, I machoed myself up to the other end of the spectrum. It's no coincidence that Caitlyn Jenner strove for hardcore athletics to prove her maleness.

Ultimately, to prove my machismo, I joined the military and it turned out to be a really good experience for me. It gave me positive reinforcement that I'd never had before. I worked at the Pentagon and I was good at it. They kept giving me things, like graduate degrees.

The real me hadn't gone anywhere, of course. I began to focus on suicidal ideation. I knew I couldn't actually commit the act so I deliberately signed up to be stationed in places where death might show up. Like Somalia. I was marking time.

I got married, had a couple of kids. Tried the traditional lifestyle. My wife was brilliant, and I truly loved her. And, she had demons of her own.

Finally, in the year, 2000, I decided, I'm going to come out. I owed the military one more year and ... did I mention I worked at the Pentagon?

On the morning of September eleventh, 2001, I was at a meeting in Roslyn when we heard the news. When I showed up for work the

next day the building was still burning, there were firemen everywhere.
I figured it wasn't the best time to leave.

Around the same time my wife, who had battled depression for years, finally lost the fight. I became the sole caretaker of my children. I loved parenting. My girls and I took day-long road trips, small adventures that beat back the sad moments. I'd make a game out of it. *Everybody in the car, time for a mystery ride. Let the winds of mystery takes us away!* Which was code for... let's go look – life must be waiting for us.

I still had a death wish. And death hadn't found me so it was time to go and meet death.

I had a plan. I was going to drive to the marine base and buy a gun. Find a quiet spot to put a bullet in my brain. But the night before my suicide I had an epiphany. I realized I had to risk telling the truth rather than let my kids lose another parent.

I went to the Whitman Walker Clinic and they helped me find an incredible therapist who I call Yoda. Yoda said, you don't need help transing, you need help healing. I became an emotional Jedi.

When I came out to my girls, young adults by this point, they were shocked, but within a day or so, one said, "I'm so proud of you." My cheerleader. The older one is the shaman. She nods wisely. "This is good, I can see this." They brought me a big pink box with flowers on it– inside was my woman starter kit. Make-up and nail polish and all that good stuff.

Simone de Beauvoir said, "Women aren't born, they're made." My life is awakening to a future full of possibility. I know it's waiting for me.

Dinner
by Joan Lipkin

Setting: *Caro's front door, somewhere in urban or even suburban America.*

Character: *CARO, a transgender woman aged early thirties to fifties*

CARO, a transgender woman aged early thirties to fifties who lives somewhere in urban or even suburban America, answers a knock on her door late at night. She is speaking to her unexpected visitor, a younger cis/het man whom she met on Grindr and hooked up with a few times enjoyably. He has startled her by showing up outside her door.

CARO

(CARO *opens door)* You do know what time it is, don't you? Oh, oh, you were just in the neighborhood and you wanted to see me? Uh huh, so what were you doing before this. Before you showed up at my doorstep at midnight? I said, What. Were. You. Doing. Before. This?

Dinner. You were having dinner? Well, I like dinner. What did you have? Greek? I like Greek. Those little pies with the spinach in them. What do they call them? Spana what? Spanakopita? That sounds good. Oh! Oh, and that lemon soup. I love that lemon soup. Uh huh, so how about taking me out to dinner before showing up for a booty call at midnight? Come on. You know that's what it is. Ok, yes,

yes, I liked it. But that doesn't mean I'm going to do it again. Well, not without dinner.

Are you kidding? No, that doesn't make me a prostitute. It makes me a lady. I can buy my own fucking dinner. But I want to go out with you. Not just stay in. Go out. I fucked you once, ok twice. And you liked it. Obviously. And I liked it. Obviously. So now, how about something more.

It doesn't have to be dinner. It could be coffee. Or, I don't know, a movie. Yeah. You like the movies, don't you? I mean, everyone likes the movies. You know, something. A conversation. So we get to know each other. Like, where are you from. Do you have any brothers and sisters? I'm an only child.

Yes, yes baby, I think you're fine. We wouldn't be having this conversation if I didn't. But I want to know why it's ok to fuck me and not be seen with me. No, really. I want to know. Oh, so it's not an issue to be seen with me? You've just been busy? Uh huh. Ok. Ok. I get that. So maybe slow down. I don't know. See what's possible. Like, where did you go to high school, anyway? What does your family call you? Are you in touch with your family? You know, it's hard being trans. A girl gets lonely. So . . . how about dinner?

Frozen Women Flowing Thoughts

Please refer to the Dramatists Guild of America for a contract template to produce playwrights.

An Anthology

FWFT Bio's and Contact Info

Renee Baillargeon, Sault Ste. Marie Ontario, Canada.
renee_baillargeon@hotmail.com
(underscore between names)

Ella Baldwin, Brooklyn, NY
luminatheatre.com

Claudia Barnett, Tennessee by way of the Bronx
www.claudiabarnett.net

Ben Beck, Omaha, NE
pwcenter.org/profile/ben-beck

Christine Benvenuto, Western Massachusetts
https://newplayexchange.org/users/77023/christine-benvenuto

Doc Andersen-Bloomfield, Oxford, England
docinengland@hotmail.com
New Play Exchange

Molly Breen, Nashville, TN
tnplaywrights.org

Carol Campbell, MA - Oakton, VA
www.carolleecampbell.com

Frozen Women Flowing Thoughts

Grace Cavaleire, DMV
www.gracecavalieri.com

Maureen Chadwick, London, UK
www.macfarlane-chard.co.uk/maureen-chadwick

Liz Coley, Cincinnati, OH
Lizcoley.com
newplayexchange.org

Cindy Cooper, New York City
www.cyncooperwriter.net

Cecilia Copeland, A Latina from the Midwest and Middle East.
https://www.nymadproductions.com/

Sorina Corneanu, Romania
https://www.facebook.com/anasorina.corneanu/
https://theatrum.ro/persoana/ana-sorina-corneanu/
https://www.ziarulmetropolis.ro/spectacolul-frici-de-ana-sorina-corneanu-marele-castigator-al-celei-de-a-treia-editii-a-proiectului-lecturi%C2%B3/
https://www.agerpres.ro/cultura/2020/05/21/uniter-hai-sa-vorbim-despre-viata-desemnata-cea-mai-buna-piesa-romaneasca-a-anului-2019--509699

Allie Costa, Los Angeles, CA
http://www.alliecosta.com   http://www.imdb.me/alliecosta
https://newplayexchange.org/users/995/allie-costa

William Robert Carey, Chicago
williamrobertcarey.com

Migdalia Cruz, Bronx
www.migdaliacruz.com
Agent: Peregrine Whittlesey, pwwagy@aol.com

An Anthology

Victoria Z. Daly, Connecticut
victoriazdaly.com

Allison Fradkin, Chicago
newplayexchange.org/users/16309/allison-fradkin

Fengar Gael, Irvine, California
www.fengar.com

Carolyn Gage, Southwest Harbor, Maine
www.carolyngage.com

Paddy Gillard-Bently, Kitchener, Ontario, Canada.
http://www.skyedragon.com/plays.html

Vivienne Glance, Perth, Western Australia
www.vivienneglance.com

Dana Leslie Goldstein, Brooklyn, NY
https://www.danalesliegoldstein.com
or contact the Michael Moore Agency, Agent: Michael Moore, Michael@MichaelMooreAgency.com

Melinda Gros, New York City
newplayexchange.org/users/22529/melinda-gros

Fran Handman, New York City by way of Canada (a couple of times)
Fran Handman is on YouTube

Alli Hartley-Kong, Washington DC
https://newplayexchange.org/users/47640/alli-hartley-kong/

Paula Hendrikson, Illinois
HendricksonWrites.com

Judit Hollos, Hungary

Allston James, Carmel, California
Full-credits found on LinkedIN

Caytha Jentis, New York City
www.caytha.com

Moriah Joy, Richmond, Virginia
https://newplayexchange.org/users/80435/moriah-joy

M. Kamara, Illinois- a first-generation Sierra Leonean American
kamarawrites.weebly.com

Paula Kamen, Evanston, IL
Paulakamen.com

Rebecca Kane, Queens, NY.
https://newplayexchange.org/users/16500/rebecca-kane

Jayme Kilburn, Santa Cruz, CA.
www.jayme-kilburn.com

Judy Klass, Nashville, Tennessee by way of New York City
https://www.concordtheatricals.com/p/836/cell-klass
https://www.nextstagepress.com/after-tartuffe/

JM Lahr, Sacramento, CA by way of St. Louis, MO

Stacey Lane, San Diego, California
www.StaceyLaneInk.com

Joan Lipkin, Saint Louis, MO
https://newplayexchange.org/users/63172/joan-lipkin

Kristen Lowman, New York City

Sherry MacDonald, Vancouver, Canada

An Anthology

Ali MacLean, Los Angeles by way of Boston, and can often be found populating London.
www.alimaclean.com

Helen Cheng Mao, Olney, Maryland by way of Lawrenceville, NJ
https://youtube.com/playlist?list=PLOBWRX6h1_Qm8VQZqP-WymVGFIkfruadkU&si=eA1l6qSldG77ebuU
https://www.linkedin.com/in/helencmao/

Daria Mayeko Marinelli, Los Angeles, CA
www.DariaMiyekoMarinelli.com
https://newplayexchange.org/users/2948/daria-miyeko-marinelli

Aleks Merilo, Pacific Northwest
Aleksmeriloplaywright.com

Karissa Murrell Meyers, Chicago by way of Boise, ID
www.kmurrellmyers.com

Melissa Milich, Watsonville, California
melissa.r.milich@gmail.com

D. Lee Miller, New York City by way of Poughkeepsie, New York

Elena Naskova, Seattle, WA by way of Macedonia

Jennifer O'Grady, Pelham, NY
https://newplayexchange.org/users/799/jennifer-ogrady / www.jenniferogrady.net

Marj O'Neil-Butler, Miami Beach, FL
https://newplayexchange.org/users/2803/marj-oneill-butler
dramamarj@yahoo.com

Dorian Palumbo, Central New Jersey
Dorianpalumbo.com

Martha Patterson, Boston, Massachusetts

https://mpatterson125933.wixsite.com/martha-patterson-

Judith Pratt, Ithaca, NY
www.judithpratt.com

Amy Judith Reuben, Toronto-born New Orleanian, who has spent half my life in NOLA.
Amy Judith Reuben | New Play Exchange
http://newplayexchange.org/users/22700/amy-judith-reuben

Robin Rice, New Englander transplanted to New York City.
www.RobinRicePlaywright.com

Jass Richards, Canada
https://www.jassrichards.com

Layli Rohani, Eugene, Oregon
https://newplayexchange.org/users/66727/layli-rohani

Kathryn Rossetter, Peekskill, NY
www.kathrynrossetter.com and also registered on NPX

Madison Sedlor, Buffalo, New York.
https://newplayexchange.org/users/15543/madison-sedlor.

Joyce Newman Scott, Miami, Florida

Chloe Selavka, New York City by way of Worcester, MA.
20chloe24@gmail.com

Germaine Shames, Tucson, AZ
https//germainewrites.wixsite.com/buzz

Faye Sholiton, Cleveland, Ohio
www.fayesplays.com

Samara Siskind, South Florida
Samara Siskind | New Play Exchange

An Anthology

Nina Solomita, Boston, MA/Carmel, CA
ninasolomita.com

Bara Swain, New York City
www.BaraSwain.com

Nora Louise Syran, Chicago/Nice, France
www.noralouisesyran.com
https://newplayexchange.org/users/34709/nora-louise-syran

Kanika Asavari Vaish, New York City/Mumbai
kanikavaish.com

Alana Valentine, Australia
www.alanavalentine.com

Kathleen Warnock, New York City
www.kathleenwarnock.com

Octavia Washington, New York City

Julia Weinberg, New York City
JulieWeinbergplaywright.com

Chloë Whitehorn, born in Berkeley California, now living in Canada
www.chloewhitehorn.com

Chris Wind, Canada
https://www.chriswind.net